CW01475549

HENRY VIII
AND THE
PLANTAGENET
POLES

For Henry, Oliver and Margot

HENRY VIII
AND THE
PLANTAGENET POLES

THE RISE AND FALL OF A DYNASTY

ADAM PENNINGTON

PEN & SWORD
HISTORY

AN IMPRINT OF PEN & SWORD BOOKS LTD.
YORKSHIRE - PHILADELPHIA

First published in Great Britain in 2024 by
PEN AND SWORD HISTORY
An imprint of
Pen & Sword Books Ltd
Yorkshire – Philadelphia

Copyright © Adam Pennington, 2024

ISBN 978 1 39907 171 0

The right of Adam Pennington to be identified as Author of
this work has been asserted by him in accordance with the Copyright,
Designs and Patents Act 1988.

A CIP catalogue record for this book is available from the British Library.

All rights reserved. No part of this book may be reproduced or transmitted
in any form or by any means, electronic or mechanical including
photocopying, recording or by any information storage and retrieval
system, without permission from the Publisher in writing.

Typeset in Times New Roman 11.5/14 by
SJmagic DESIGN SERVICES, India.
Printed and bound in the UK by CPI Group (UK) Ltd.

Pen & Sword Books Limited incorporates the imprints of Atlas,
Archaeology, Aviation, Discovery, Family History, Fiction, History,
Maritime, Military, Military Classics, Politics, Select, Transport, True
Crime, Air World, Frontline Publishing, Leo Cooper, Remember When,
Seaforth Publishing, The Praetorian Press, Wharncliffe Local History,
Wharncliffe Transport, Wharncliffe True Crime and White Owl.

For a complete list of Pen & Sword titles please contact
PEN & SWORD BOOKS LIMITED
George House, Units 12 & 13, Beevor Street, Off Pontefract Road,
Barnsley, South Yorkshire, S71 1HN, England
E-mail: enquiries@pen-and-sword.co.uk
Website: www.pen-and-sword.co.uk

or
PEN AND SWORD BOOKS
1950 Lawrence Rd, Havertown, PA 19083, USA
E-mail: uspen-and-sword@casematepublishers.com
Website: www.penandswordbooks.com

MIX
Paper | Supporting
responsible forestry
FSC
www.fsc.org
FSC® C013604

Contents

Family Tree

Houses of Tudor and Pole and their descent from King Edward III

The Tudor & White Rose Family Tree

Note: This illustration is intended to give an overview of the descendants of Edward III. Not all marriages/children are represented and births may not appear in date order

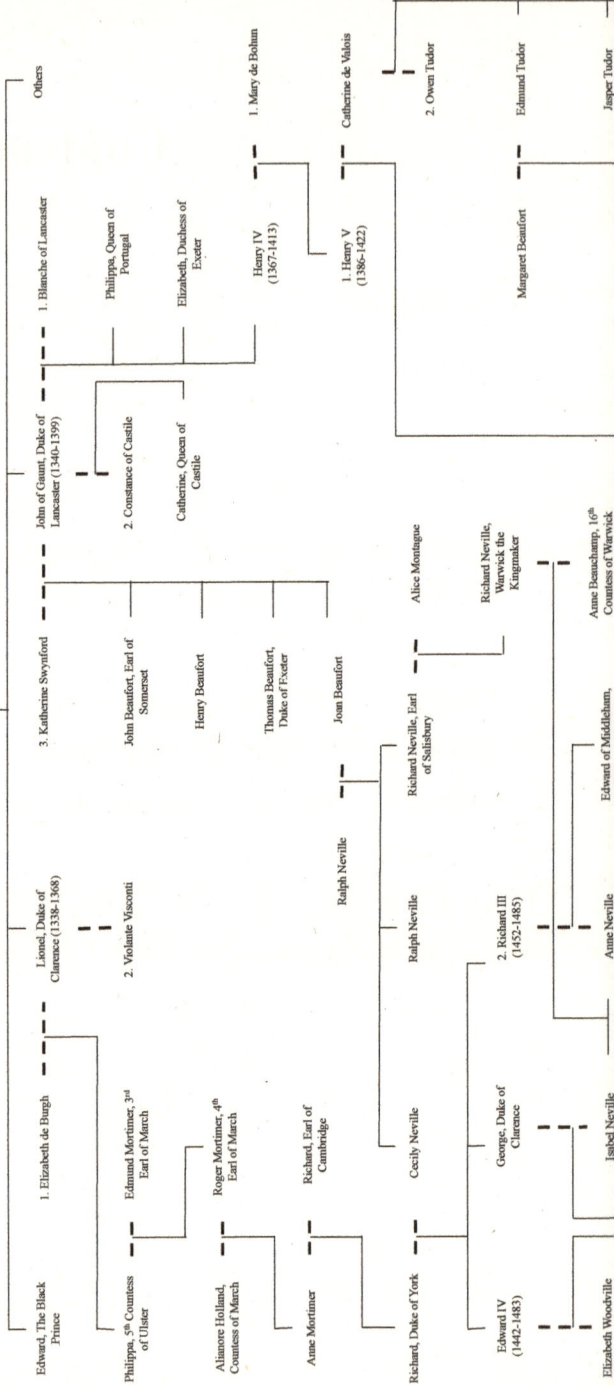

Edward III
1312-1377

Philippa of Hainault

Edward, The Black Prince

1. Elizabeth de Burgh

Lionel, Duke of Clarence (1338-1368)

Philippa, 5th Countess of Ulster

Edmund Mortimer, 3rd Earl of March

2. Violante Visconti

Alianore Holland, Countess of March

Roger Mortimer, 4th Earl of March

Anne Mortimer

Richard, Earl of Cambridge

Richard, Duke of York

Cecily Neville

Ralph Neville

Ralph Neville

Edward IV (1442-1483)

George, Duke of Clarence

2. Richard III (1452-1485)

Elizabeth Woodville

Isabel Neville

Anne Neville

Edward of Middleham

Anne Beauchamp, 16th Countess of Warwick

Richard Neville, Warwick the Kingmaker

Richard Neville, Earl of Salisbury

Alice Montague

Joan Beaufort

John of Gaunt, Duke of Lancaster (1340-1399)

3. Katherine Swynford

2. Constance of Castile

Catherine, Queen of Castile

John Beaufort, Earl of Somerset

Henry Beaufort

Thomas Beaufort, Duke of Exeter

1. Blanche of Lancaster

Philippa, Queen of Portugal

Elizabeth, Duchess of Exeter

Henry IV (1367-1413)

1. Mary de Bohun

1. Henry V (1386-1422)

Catherine de Valois

2. Owen Tudor

Margaret Beaufort

Edmund Tudor

Jasper Tudor

Others

Owen Tudor

Margaret of Anjou

Henry VI (1421-1471)

I. Edward of Westminster

Mary, Queen of France
1. Louis XII of France
2. Charles Brandon, Duke of Suffolk

Henry VIII (1491-1547)
1. Katherine of Aragon
2. Anne Boleyn
3. Jane Seymour
4. Anne of Cleves
5. Katheryn Howard
6. Catherine Parr

Henry VII (1457-1509)

Elizabeth of York

Margaret, Queen of Scotland
1. James IV of Scotland
2. Archibald Douglas
3. Henry Stewart

Mary I (1516-1558)

Elizabeth I (1533-1603)

Edward VI (1537-1553)

Six daughters, Mary, Cecily, Margaret, Anne, Catherine and Bridget

Arthur, Prince of Wales

Katherine of Aragon

Princes in the Tower: Edward V, Richard, Duke of York

Edward Plantagenet, Earl of Warwick

Sir Edward Stafford

William Stafford

Sir John Stafford

Elizabeth Stafford

Ursula Stafford

Dorothy Stafford

Dorothy Stafford, Lady Stafford

Sir William Stafford

Margaret Plantagenet, Countess of Salisbury

Sir Richard Pole

2 daughters – Catherine & Winifred

Henry Pole, 1st Baron Montagu

Jane Neville

Henry

Thomas (Disputed)

Arthur Pole

Jane Lewknor

1 son - Henry

3 daughters – Mary, Jane & Margaret

Ursula Pole, Baroness Stafford

Henry Stafford, 1st Baron Stafford

7 sons – Henry x2, Thomas, Edward, Richard, Walter & William

6 daughters – Elizabeth, Anne, Susan, Jane, (2 names not known)

Reginald Pole, Archbishop of Canterbury

Geoffrey Pole

Constance Pakenham

5 sons – Sir Arthur, Thomas, Edmund, Geoffrey & Henry

6 daughters – Catherine x2, Elizabeth, Mary, Margaret & Ann

Acknowledgements

Having grown up in the leafy London/Surrey borders, history was quite literally always around me. Hampton Court Palace was ten minutes down the road, central London with all its tourist attractions just twenty minutes on the nearby tube. My childhood home as good as looked over Nonsuch Park, home of the sadly lost palace of the same name. I couldn't have grown up in a more historically significant corner of England, something that I never take for granted. This, and my mother's insistence that my sister and I knew our history ignited a lifelong passion for all things Plantagenet and Tudor. Around the age of 10, I started to learn about the Tudors in school. I can recall with piercing clarity that it was also at this time that I first saw *Anne of the Thousand Days*, the 1969 masterpiece starring Richard Burton and Geneviève Bujold as King Henry VIII and Anne Boleyn. From there, I was hooked. Like many during the early stages of the COVID-19 pandemic, I had a moment of contemplation, a chance to reset. I decided to channel my knowledge and passion for history into a blog and social media accounts – The Tudor Chest. With no expectation for what would happen off the back of it, I have developed a wide network of friends and acquaintances who help feed, nurture and challenge my own knowledge and understanding of our past. I feel it prudent to state that I am not a qualified historian. Any knowledge I have is broadly self-taught, and so I implore anyone reading this, who is also passionate about history, to not be afraid to make the leap. There is no room for imposter syndrome, we all have a right to share our passion with the world.

Acknowledgements are typically a moment for a writer to commend those who have helped them on their journey to publication, and as with the expected format of speeches delivered from the condemned on the scaffold in Tudor England, I shall not deviate from tradition. I would like to start by thanking my parents, Elaine and Christopher – two people who never put a single foot wrong. They have given me, and my sister Lucy, quite simply, the happiest lives anyone could ever wish for. I speak for us both when I say **thank you, thank you, thank you**. In my nephews Henry and Oliver, and my niece Margot, Lucy and my brother-in-law Scott have given our family its next generation; they are, without question, the loves of my life. I am blessed to have a wide circle of friends, who engage with, and tolerate in equal measure, my passion for our past. These include, but are not limited to, Sam, Carly, Ryan, Sophie, Kate, Natalie, Laurily and Gemma. I would like to make a special mention to Carla, Dale, Emma and Lee, my oldest friends, who continue to make me smile no matter the occasion, and to Jonny, my best friend; I love you like a brother, without you in my life I honestly don't know where I'd be. I would also like to thank the Tudor community who have been so incredibly supportive and generous with their time and insight. To my research assistant Susan, thank you for all of your help in making this book a reality. Finally to you, the reader, I hope you find this book both informative and enjoyable in equal measure. I wanted to shine a light on a family who remain on the fringes of history, but hopefully, in time, may take on a more starring role. Until such a time, I will simply say, happy reading.

Preface

On 27 May 1541, a 67-year-old woman was awoken in the Tower of London and told that she was to die within the hour. In an age of fervent religious belief, the notion of making a 'good death' in which one prepared the soul for eternal life and made peace with the world, pervaded the thoughts of many. As Gareth Russell asserts 'A benefit of being executed was that one avoided any chance of the dreaded mors improvisa'[1], a sudden death, and this is broadly true. Those awaiting execution had time to set their spiritual affairs in order. As the minutes ticked by the condemned would pray and distribute remaining worldly goods, perhaps to still-loyal servants. The important thing was that they had time to prepare, although this sometimes had the opposite desired effect. A major factor in some of Anne Boleyn's own distress prior to her execution were the delays that preceded it – an example of the prisoner having almost too much time to be at ease in body and soul. The 67-year-old who was surprised with the news that she was to die that very day, was, in fact, Lady Margaret Pole, former Countess of Salisbury. Margaret Pole had languished in the Tower of London for over two years, and had seen her eldest son, Henry, Baron Montagu, beheaded on charges of high treason, along with several other members of her extended kin. No longer the high and mighty Countess of Salisbury, but simply Margaret Pole, she rejected the sentence laid at her feet, stating that no crime had been presented to her nor had any been committed. To be told that she was to shortly die was therefore not only an almighty shock, but robbed her of the chance to make a good Christian end, something Margaret, a deeply devout woman, would have regretted bitterly. Her protests would come to nothing, and shortly thereafter she was led to a low wooden block in the shadow of the White Tower to be beheaded. As a woman of exalted birth, she would not face a public beheading before the baying crowds of London on Tower Hill, but be given the dubious honour of a private execution. This aside, such was the speed of her sentencing that it is believed even the customary scaffold was omitted. Margaret would instead be required to prostrate herself directly on the ground. The execution, famously botched, marked the final dreadful act in what had been the near total eradication of an entire family, and by extension one of England's greatest dynasties. A family whose possible only crime had been the lineage of the blood that ran in their veins. This family were the Poles.

The Poles are relative unknowns in mainstream British history. Against the backdrop of their infinitely more famous cousins the Tudors, the Poles have slipped under the radar and their story is seldom touched on or explored at any great length. Were it not for defeat on the field of Bosworth, it's entirely plausible that a member of the Pole family might one day have become king, or maybe even queen. I say Pole family, but at this point it is more accurate to call them the Plantagenets, because it is the Plantagenet side of the Poles which makes them so extraordinary and provides the dynastic ties that go back into legend. The aforementioned Lady Margaret is undoubtedly the most famous member of the family because shocking execution aside, she was by birth one of the most ennobled members of the Tudor court. As the daughter of George, Duke of Clarence, she was the niece of two of England's kings, Edward IV and Richard III, and therefore the first cousin of Elizabeth of York, wife of King Henry VII, and thus a first cousin once removed of King Henry VIII. This meant that Margaret was also the direct descendant of six earlier English kings, beginning way back with Henry II. In other words, Lady Margaret Pole and her family mattered; they had royal blood, and this was arguably their biggest problem in a life played out at the court of King Henry VIII.

Lady Margaret and her children endured periods of great uncertainty and political irrelevance, to be replaced with prestige and significant riches. Such was the assiduous nature with which Margaret ran her vast estates that she was soon one of the richest landowners in England. Unfortunately, Margaret's bloodline was ever present and placed a burden on the lives of her five children who grew into adulthood – Henry, Arthur, Ursula, Reginald and Geoffrey. Each would play their own role in helping to establish the Pole family as a great Tudor force of power, but would in turn suffer from, at best, broken marriage alliances, to worst, in paying the ultimate price. This book will tell the story of this oft forgotten family, exploring the lives of its key players but also their households, their friends and their enemies. Just how did the Pole family go from being at the zenith of Tudor society as blood relations to the king, to social pariahs and convicted traitors?

Introduction

The House of Plantagenet

Although this book explores the downfall of a family who lived during the reign of King Henry VIII, I feel it prudent to provide a brief backstory of the Pole family's ancestry, for it is in this ancestry that we can understand why they were so consequential. The Pole family, like practically all families, gained their name through marriage, but it was the ancestry of Lady Margaret Pole that provided their significance, for her family name was far grander – Plantagenet.

The House of Plantagenet ruled England for longer than any dynasty before or since. Their lineage can be traced back into legend, but it was King Henry II of England who is widely regarded as the first of the true Plantagenet kings. His marriage to the infamous Eleanor of Aquitaine, one of the great European heiresses of her time, began a centuries long bloodline that provided England, Wales, at times Scotland and Ireland, and not to mention large swathes of France and the rest of Europe with some of the most colourful, dramatic and temperamental monarchs in history. Although highly noble, the house did not initially start out as royal, but would gain this status through advantageous marriage, chance, and a thirst for power. Geoffrey Plantagenet, Count of Anjou, is credited as being the dynasty's founder, and it is also to Geoffrey that the family name can be attributed. It is believed that 'Plantagenet' actually developed from a nickname. The young count of Anjou was prone to displaying a sprig of the broom plant, planta-genista in his hats, becoming famous for this touch of millinery flair. This would develop from the Latin name of the shrub into Plantagenet, and from there the family name of his descendants.

The centuries-long rule of this great house saw some of the most turbulent periods of European history unfold. From Joan of Arc to the Battle of Agincourt, to the Wars of the Roses and birth of the Tudor dynasty, the impact of the house of Plantagenet can still be felt today. The identity of England and the relationship between monarch and people would also undergo a huge shift, laying the foundations for much of what we still recognise when assessing the role of both the monarchy and nobility in the modern age. It was, for example, under Plantagenet rule that the noble title of Duke was first introduced to England, that the printing press came into use, and perhaps most significantly of all, that the English language truly developed in its own right. It was not until King Henry IV, the ninth Plantagenet king who reigned from 1399 to 1413, that the English sovereign even spoke the English language as their native tongue, which by extension dictated the language spoken at court. After the Norman conquest of 1066, French had been the officially recognised language of the royal house, but this, like so much more, would change under Plantagenet watch. This was an age of high intrigue, of battles both in the field and in the marriage bed, of Geoffrey Chaucer, warrior kings and battle-hardened queens. It was, in short, the time in which the notion of English identity truly developed. One that was independent, unique and self-made.

It was during the reign of King Henry VII nearly 350 years later, that the Plantagenet dynasty was finally made extinct in the legitimate male line. During that time there would be an unbroken line of fourteen kings; for context, that is more rulers than the houses of Tudor and Stuart combined, highlighting both the strength of, and natural suspicion around, those carrying this dangerous royal name. The line of rulers may have been unbroken, but it was famously fractious. Although the crown would be passed from father to son, grandson or brother for the first half of Plantagenet rule, by the time of King Henry IV, usurpation had triumphed over primogeniture. If the monarch was deemed unsuccessful or incompetent then why not snatch the crown away, place it in another's hands and let them try their luck? This may sound trite, and is certainly simplifying things, but when Henry IV made his bid for the throne and removed the psychotic and ineffectual King Richard II, the latter half of the Plantagenet rule became undoubtedly tainted by seizure. Unbeknown to those at the time, this would create a dangerous precedent that would have long reaching consequences for nearly everyone bearing the Plantagenet name. This was further compounded by the enormously complex bloodlines of King Edward III, whose descendants would eventually break into two cadet branches, Lancaster and York. It is in the Yorkist line that Lady Margaret Pole, Countess of Salisbury and her family traced their descent, and although not nearly as monumentally significant as the marriage of Henry VII and Elizabeth of York, Margaret's own marriage to Sir Richard Pole also united these two branches into one. Margaret was a Princess of York with unquestionably noble blood, and Richard Pole was a minor member of the landed gentry, whose sole claim to grandeur was his maternal grandfather's relationship as a half-brother to Lady Margaret Beaufort, mother to King Henry VII. That such a husband could be considered suitable for a girl of impeccable breeding, a princess of royal blood, is a mark of just how desperate the status of the Tudor cause was during the early stages of their reign. Those of strong Plantagenet blood were in abundance at the court of both Henry VII and his son, Henry VIII. There was the Pole family of course, but also their kin, the De La Poles. Then there were the Exeters who would famously fall alongside the Pole family, the Lisles, the Nevilles and the Staffords. Where the number of people of significance carrying the name of Tudor could be counted on one hand, the Plantagenets, like their family sigil, had many offshoots, which intermingled into a network of connections across the country, an ever growing spider's web of cousins and half-siblings, of marriages and increasingly minimised authority. Abundant in numbers they may have been, but like all changes in establishment, opportunities arise, whilst elsewhere heads will roll.

Chapter 1

A Niece of Kings

'God forbid that I retreat one step. I will either win the
battle as a king, or die as one'

King Richard III

Legend has it that these were the words spoken by King Richard III as
he prepared himself for the biggest fight of his life. It was a fight he
would lose, and so on 22 August 1485 the expected future of England
was irrevocably altered. At the top of Crown Hill, near the village of
Stoke Golding in Leicestershire, a circlet which had until very recently
sat atop the head of the king, was placed into the hands of an obscure
Welshman, Henry Tudor. At this moment, the 331-year rule of the House
of Plantagenet came to an end and a new ruling dynasty, the Tudors,
was established. This would spark an immediate and seismic shift in the
political powers within the English royal court and sow doubt on the
future prospects for those who shared a close blood bond to the fallen
king, these being, of course, the remaining members of the Yorkist
dynasty, including as she was then known, Lady Margaret of Clarence.
That the newly crowned King Henry VII was even able to claim the
throne is nothing short of miraculous. As the great-great-grandson of
John of Gaunt, fourth son of King Edward III by his mistress and later
wife Katherine Swynford, Henry Tudor did have a tincture of royal
blood running in his veins. His problem was that this blood was damned
twice over, for being both via an illegitimate relationship (Henry's great-
grandfather had been born out of wedlock) and that it passed through
the female line, a technicality which made his bloodline all the more
undesirable. Moreover, although Henry's ancestors, the Beauforts, were
legitimised by King Richard II, at the same time it was made clear that
they could not inherit the throne. That several members of the York
dynasty remained very much alive, and boasted supremely greater
claims to the throne, was thus problematic from the outset of the reign.

We now know, thanks to the discovery of his remains in 2012, that there was ample truth in King Richard III's own physical shortcomings. Whilst to his modern day supporters this had been nothing more than mere Tudor propaganda, the skeleton of this most infamous of monarchs proved beyond doubt that he suffered severe scoliosis of the spine, and so put greater stock in what had been told through the annals of time about the king's apparent deformity. By contrast, his direct predecessor and elder brother, King Edward IV, was everything the ideal fifteenth-century king should be – lusty, strong and affable, boasting the quintessential Yorkist good looks and an endearing personality. Indeed his grandson, the man who would become King Henry VIII, greatly revered his maternal grandfather, being favourably compared to him throughout his youth. King Richard III may have cut a less impressive figure than his brother, but there were at least strong familial ties, unquestionably noble blood and true English identity. Henry Tudor, by contrast, could claim none of these attributes; he was, in effect, Edward IV's direct opposite. He was slight of frame and described as cool and aloof, with a notable squint, and in the early days of his reign preferred to converse in French as opposed to English. This and his own highly questionable right to the throne adds up to Henry Tudor being a less than conducive choice to be England's king. As Tracy Borman wryly observes 'The Tudors had no business being on the throne of England at all'.[1]

Due to its own enormous capacity for self-destruction, the downfall of the house of Plantagenet had been brewing for a number of years. 'The Wars of the Roses' as they have become popularly known were called The Cousins War by those who were at the very centre of the many years of conflict, for the ongoing battle was between the two primary branches of the Plantagenet family – the Lancastrians and the Yorks. In the last twenty-five years of Plantagenet reign, each side would claim the right to rule and for a time the crown would be passed back and forth between the two men who sat at the top of their respective branches, King Henry VI and the aforementioned King Edward IV. Although Henry VII's eventual victory at the field of Bosworth would bring the rule of the York dynasty to a close, this branch of the Plantagenets had been the considerable victors over the past quarter of a century. Due to their efficacy in child bearing, the York network was vast and unquestionably noble. It was crucial therefore for the Tudor dynasty to align with the Yorks; to try and rule without them and the support they felt from the common people would be folly. Marriage was the most obvious course of action, and so Henry Tudor took for his wife the York dynasty's greatest asset, Elizabeth of York, cousin of Margaret Pole. Their union finally brought the warring houses together and the decades long conflict came to an end.

The rise of the York dynasty as England's rulers was born out of mental illness, a thirst for power and as referenced earlier, the extraordinarily complex bloodlines of the late Plantagenets. It began, in the context of this book, with Richard Plantagenet, 3rd Duke of York. The duke was one of, if not the, premier noble in England, and benefitted from royal blood in his own right, twice over in fact, being the great-grandson of King Edward III on his father's side and the great-great-great-grandson of that same king via his mother. He therefore possessed a very strong claim to the throne, and to those who accepted that this could be passed through the female line, would argue that it gave him a greater claim than that of the king. Indeed until Henry VI had his own legitimate heir by his notorious wife, Margaret of Anjou, Richard was recognised as the king's natural successor. The duke's marriage to Cecily Neville, a daughter of the Earl of Westmorland, produced no less than twelve children, eight of whom were boys – the stuff of dreams for their future great-grandson, King Henry VIII. The three most well-known of these children, the 'brothers of York', were Edward, later King Edward IV, George, later known as the Duke of Clarence, and father to Lady Margaret Pole, and most famously of all, Richard – the man who would later become the Duke of Gloucester, before seizing the throne and becoming the very last of the Plantagenet kings. The strength of York's ancestry and his large brood of children provided a stark contrast to the ineffectual man occupying the throne. Where the duke had his many sons and daughters, all from a well-made and legitimate marriage, the king's nearest descendants were his half-siblings, the children of his mother's scandalous second marriage to a lowly Welsh courtier, Owen Tudor. The king himself had been born to perhaps England's most celebrated and militarily successful monarch, King Henry V. Famous as the hero of Agincourt, the fifth king Henry had conquered large swathes of France, returning them to English rule, and by extension established a cult of English chivalry, made all the more famous by Shakespeare in the following century and the performances of Lord Laurence Olivier and Sir Kenneth Branagh in the twentieth century. Henry V's sudden death at the age of just 35 in 1422 threw England and its many territories into years of the ever dreaded prospect of minority rule, for the new king would ascend to the throne aged just nine months, giving Henry VI the distinction of being the youngest monarch in English history to rise to the throne. By the time Henry VI reached maturity, the royal court was barely functioning. It became clear that the old adage of the 'apple not falling far from the tree' could not have been more inaccurate when comparing the king with the achievements of his heroic father. King Henry VI was inept, militarily naive, and staggeringly slow to action. Were it not for his dogmatic wife, it's reasonable to conclude that he would have been overthrown earlier than he was. Nearly all of his father's hard won overseas lands had been lost, and in the summer of 1453 the king suffered a complete mental breakdown. From here, what we would now characterise as the Wars of the Roses would begin. The Duke of York would make an attempt on the throne himself, and would almost win, but that was to reckon against the swift actions taken by Henry's formidable queen. Mustering the royal army, Queen Margaret would face down York and his allies at the Battle of Wakefield, delivering a crushing victory which resulted in the duke's own death. The queen's actions would see her immortalised by Shakespeare as the 'She Wolf of France', a sobriquet still closely associated with Margaret of Anjou to this day.

Alas, the Lancastrian victory would not hold, for within six weeks a more dangerous opponent made his own bid for the throne. With his father dead, the mantle of displacing the house of Lancaster to be replaced by that of York fell on the shoulders of the duke's eldest son, the aforementioned Edward, then titled Earl of March. At 18, tall, handsome and swaggering, the young earl was cut from exactly the sort of mould that the people of England looked for in their monarch. He was certainly a more imposing and authoritative figure than Henry VI, who aside from ineptitude and continued bouts of mental illness, had sired only one, albeit male, child. With charisma in abundance and popular support in London, as well as the enormous military backing achieved through a close relationship with his cousin Richard Neville, 16th Earl of Warwick, known to history as the 'kingmaker', Edward soon accomplished what his father had failed to do and removed King Henry VI from the seat of power. The rule of the House of York as England's royal family had begun. The new king soon married, and chose for his bride the beautiful and alluring, but wholly unsuitable Elizabeth Woodville, who aside from already having two sons and a dead husband who had fought on the side of the Lancastrians, was by no means of high aristocratic blood. Elizabeth's mother, Jacquetta, had a great deal of noble blood in her veins, and through her first marriage to John, Duke of Bedford, an uncle of King Henry VI, developed a great friendship with Margaret of Anjou. Her children, however, had come via her second marriage to a mere member of the gentry class, Sir Richard Woodville, and that is what mattered to Elizabeth's contemporaries. Jacquetta's marriage was viewed with outrage at the time, firstly because the union had taken place in secret, without the approval of the king, but more importantly because Richard was so inferior to Jacquetta in status. This clearly had little impact on the success of their marriage, for Jacquetta would give her second husband fourteen children. Like her parents, Elizabeth Woodville's marriage to King Edward IV appears to have been a rare thing for the fifteenth century – a true love match – and they were as equally prolific in the marriage bed as both their sets of parents had been, with several children arriving in quick succession. But it wasn't all smooth sailing, and would take some time before the all-important princes were born to the new king and queen, which when they did, shored up the dynasty's future.

Unfortunately, the king's middle brother, George, now known as the Duke of Clarence, was not enamoured by the influx of Woodvilles pervading his brother's court, nor was the Earl of Warwick any happier, for he had negotiated what would have been a highly advantageous marriage for England between the king and Bona of Savoy, a sister-in-law of King Louis XI of France. When news reached Warwick of Edward's secret marriage, he was not only affronted that it had been done behind his back, but more importantly incensed that it caused such embarrassment in his negotiations with the zenith of European nobility. Unsurprisingly, Warwick soon began to act with belligerence towards Edward, and found a willing accomplice in the Duke of Clarence. With no living sons, the Earl of Warwick had long coveted George and also his younger brother, Richard, now the Duke of Gloucester, as suitable husbands for his two daughters, Isabel and Anne. As two of the wealthiest heiresses in England the matches were, at least on the face of it, entirely suitable, for Isabel and Anne were of the right age and rank. However, King Edward IV was not content to further strengthen the ties between the houses of York and Warwick. For the king, these matches could prove problematic in years to come, and so he looked to his two younger brothers to do for England what his own marriage had not – build greater overseas allies, which would in turn strengthen Yorkist rule. Warwick and Clarence, despite knowing that acting against the king's express wishes was nothing short of treason, chose to act anyway. Conveniently for Warwick, his younger brother, another George, was the Archbishop of York, and once the necessary approvals had been received from Rome, he gave his daughter Isabel in marriage to the king's troublesome brother. For Warwick, there must have been a (arguably understandable) sense that despite playing such a momentous role in enabling King Edward IV's path to the throne, that in recent times he had been treated poorly. Warwick was undoubtedly the key power behind the throne and had expected greater treatment from the man he'd help make king. Warwick was used to getting exactly what he wanted, when he wanted it, but his major mistake had been to overlook the evident love between the king and his new queen, which appeared to override all other business in the kingdom. In going behind the king's back and allowing the marriage of Isabel and George to go ahead, I rather suspect Warwick was thinking 'measure for measure'.

George and Isabel were wed in secret on 11 July 1469 in Calais, Warwick's family and George having fled the centre of the English court to cross the channel. It was from here that they launched a campaign to displace Edward. The rebellion did not hold and after just a few months of wrangling on either side it simply melted away to insignificance. The short-lived revolt had far reaching consequences though, for under its direction Warwick had authorised the execution of members of Queen Elizabeth Woodville's immediate family, most notably her father and brother. Unsurprisingly, for the queen this would cast an enormous shadow over any future relationship she held with her husband's wayward brother. Almost a year later, the young Isabel, now Duchess of Clarence, went into labour whilst aboard a ship held in Calais, but disaster struck when her child was delivered prematurely, not living long enough for even the sex to have been committed to posterity. Getting increasingly desperate, Warwick's own loyalty to the wider notion of Yorkist rule was put under enormous scrutiny when he allied himself with none other than Margaret of Anjou – possibly the most hated figure in Europe for hardline Yorkists. The wife of King Henry VI had travelled to her native land of France where she had been eking out a pitiable existence as a poor relation of the French king. Fortune's wheel, a saying popular in the middle ages for the ever present ebb and flow of power, turned back towards Margaret, and she agreed to a suggested marriage alliance between her one and only child, Edward of Lancaster, to Warwick's other daughter, Anne. Margaret accepted this, I believe, as purely a means to an end, namely the removal of King Edward IV from her husband's throne, which would then go to her son in time. She was open in her dislike and distrust of Warwick and upon meeting him to discuss the negotiations made him remain on his knees for twenty minutes before allowing him to so much as to speak.[2] She was, however, ultimately backed into a corner, and knew without the support of Warwick that there was little hope of her and her son ever returning safely to England. The marriage went ahead and also achieved its key ambition – King Edward IV fled the country, opening up the throne for the return of its predecessor, King Henry VI.

The marriage between Edward of Lancaster and Anne Neville may have secured one alliance, but it arguably broke another. For George, getting into bed (figuratively speaking) with the woman who had authorised his father's execution was intolerable. The ousted Edward IV soon began to fight back, steadily building a considerable army, hell bent on restoring their leader to the throne. Upon landing back in England in the spring of 1471, Edward faced Warwick at the Battle of Barnet, north of London, with the latter killed in the melee. George had jettisoned his former ally and instead returned to the side of his brother, cap in hand and tail very much between his legs. The king appears to have welcomed him back with open arms, although one suspects Edward's queen had a very different take on the matter. Just a few weeks later the Yorkists delivered another resounding defeat against the Lancastrians, the key casualty of the fighting being none other than the 17-year-old Edward of Lancaster, the last great hope for the beleaguered Lancastrians. It had been his first, and last, experience of battle. Margaret of Anjou was arrested and her husband, who had been incarcerated in the Tower of London, was soon proclaimed dead. Although it was said to be of natural causes, few doubt that he was put to death on the orders of the now re-established King Edward IV. With Warwick also dead and an attained traitor to boot, his extraordinarily vast estate was soon being sliced up between the king's brothers. With George and Isabel settling into married life, Richard, with his brother's blessing, married the newly widowed Anne Neville, something her father had long hoped for his younger daughter. Clearly, with Warwick out of the equation, the king was more relaxed in allying his immediate family in marriage to the Neville women. The financial end goal of the two marriages becomes clear in the wake of Warwick's death, for the vast Warwick lands that came via its earldom should have been retained by Richard Neville's widow, Lady Anne Beauchamp, Countess of Warwick. Instead, as stated above, the lands were divided up between the king's two brothers and their spouses. For the countess, total alienation from her accustomed power, wealth and prestige came in the form of being declared 'naturally dead' in law, despite her being very much the opposite. This status enabled the king's brothers to claim the lands in the name of their wives. It would have far-reaching consequences though, to be felt most keenly by the next earl of Warwick a generation later. Whilst Countess Anne was therefore living a life of enforced seclusion, some semblance of peace finally fell across England, and her daughter Isabel was able to settle into life as a royal duchess and the responsibility that came with it – the production of healthy living heirs.

Isabel did not have to wait long, and on 14 August 1473 at Farleigh Hungerford Castle in Somerset, the duchess was safely delivered of her first healthy living child, a daughter, the Lady Margaret. At that very moment, no one could have guessed that nearly seventy years later this little girl would be executed as a convicted traitor to the crown, by a member of her own extended family. Unlike their first child who had died within hours of its birth, Margaret's successful birth must have been a huge relief to Isabel and George. She was robust and gave hope that male children would follow. For the fledgling Yorkist dynasty, Margaret was another legitimate daughter and a means of shoring up the future. As a child of the second man in the kingdom, she would have been regarded as a critical part of the country's future, a superb bargaining chip on the ever-changing European royal marriage market. Margaret would be recognised as a princess of the blood, although not carry that title formally. In the fifteenth century, only the daughters of the reigning sovereign were addressed as princess ahead of their given name, Margaret would instead be known as 'My Lady Margaret of Clarence'. She would, however, maintain precedence over all other women in England, save those of higher rank than herself. Eighteen months after her birth, Margaret was joined by a baby brother, Edward. In a society as patriarchal as fifteenth-century England, the delivery of healthy sons was of paramount importance to the nobility. With a son, George Duke of Clarence had his heir, which in an instant demoted little Margaret in status. How much the young toddler noticed the change is likely to be negligible, perhaps all she may have sensed was an increase in the size of her parents' retinue of servants, because a bigger household required a larger workforce. This team of attendants did not extend solely to her parents, but also upon Margaret and her brother, who would have had their own circle of servants to cater to their every wish. These Yorkist children were thus born at the very apex of society in medieval England, although their rank had not been acquired through peace and prosperity, nor would it be retained without considerable bloodshed.

Although her early years were probably very comfortable, as a member of the high nobility Margaret's own relationship with her parents was to be rather distant. Children of her station were taught to deeply revere their parents, but not to be overly dependent on their presence. Thus, whilst her mother's death in 1476 at the age of just 25 must have been unsettling, how much it actually impacted her daily life is likely to be minimal. The Duchess of Clarence's death came not long after giving birth to her last child, a short-lived boy named Richard. The exact cause of Isabel's death is unknown. George felt otherwise, and soon laid a charge of murder at the feet of one Ankarette Twynyho, a servant in his late wife's household who may have waited on Isabel during Richard's birth. George went further still, accusing another servant, John Thursby, of being behind the death of the infant Richard. Soon, both were arrested by a group of George's henchmen, tried in Warwick Castle and subsequently executed. No evidence produced by Clarence bears close scrutiny, which suggests either genuine misplaced conviction or a breakdown in understanding of reality. As a man coping with the premature death of his wife and second son, in such a short space of time, it is understandable to believe that he was not thinking coherently, but to take such an extreme course of action was certainly unusual. This has often been cited as a key factor in what began to turn the tide truly against George, although as John Ashdown-Hill points out 'there seems to be no justification for making such a link. Ankarette's trial was never mentioned by Edward IV in his case against his brother'[3] and this point is certainly telling. The unlawful execution of two people who were (in all probability) innocent of all charges, would normally have been used in a subsequent trial aimed at bringing down their accuser, but it was not. Like the downfall of most prominent people from the time, no definitive single moment can be assigned as the reason for Edward finally agreeing to the arrest of his younger brother. Historians are divided; some put forward the argument that George's planned marriage to Mary of Burgundy, which was greatly opposed by the king, pushed the latter into action[4]; others look at the supposed prophecies which abounded around England suggesting Edward would die prematurely, to be replaced by George, rather than his children by Elizabeth Woodville. Edward Hall would recall in his chronicle from the time:

> 'The fame was that the king or the queen, or both sore troubled with a foolish prophecy, and by reason thereof began to stomach and grievously to grudge against the duke. The effect of which was, after king Edward should reign, one whose first letter of his name should be a G. and because the duel is want with such witchcraft, to wrap and ill quiet the minds of them, which delete in such delusional fantasies, they says afterward that that prophesy lost not his effect, when after king Edward, Gloucester usurped his kingdom.'[5]

Whatever the cause, King Edward IV did authorise his brother's arrest, which naturally led to a trial for high treason. Whilst there was some shock that the king had authorised the arrest of his own brother, it is not difficult to appreciate that Edward felt entirely backed into a corner. In contrast to Richard, Duke of Gloucester, who at this time had been nothing but faithful to his brother and family, George had repeatedly challenged the status quo. It is my belief that this, his continued history of intransigence, created a perfect storm of suspicion, which when coupled with the rumoured prophecies, gave Edward justification to order the arrest. The king would act as chief prosecutor in George's trial, which ended with the customary sentence of death. On 18 February 1478 George was privately executed, according to legend, by drowning in a barrel of malmsey wine. Why this method of execution was adopted is one of history's great mysteries. As a member of the high nobility, George would be executed in private, and so we can't say with absolute certainty how he died. What we know to be true is that the normal manner of death would have been decapitation, which makes the peculiarity of Clarence's death all the more stark. The most believable assessment is that the king's one act of charity towards his brother had been to allow him to dictate the manner of his death. If this is true, then George was certainly living up to his reputation for rebellion, for even in death he went out with misplaced ostentation. A portrait often said to depict Lady Margaret Pole later in life shows an elderly lady, bedecked in fine 1530s Tudor apparel. The sitter wears a traditional gable hood and what appears to be ermine fur, a sign confirming the high status of its wearer. The sitter's identity is still debated, but the argument that it is indeed Margaret is given credence through a tiny detail that many may overlook. On her right wrist, the sitter wears a simple black bracelet with a single charm hanging from it – a barrel of wine.

Margaret and her brother were now orphans, royal orphans, but orphans nonetheless. They were also cash strapped, as any of the wealth their father had held immediately reverted to the crown. From the sources however, the shadow cast by their father did not extend to his children. For King Edward IV, Margaret and Edward might have been the children of an attained traitor, but they were also his niece and nephew, not by marriage, but by blood, making them as royal as the king's own children. Margaret and Edward's paths which lay ahead could, and should, have been to further strengthen their family's hold on the throne, and I struggle to see why King Edward would have wanted to change that. Young Edward, Earl of Warwick, also had another job to do for the king. Following Clarence's death, his son had become a royal ward. Wardship was commonplace among the high nobility of medieval England, but was nonetheless a rather strange set up. An appointed guardian, usually someone close to the king, was given the responsibility of raising the ward in their own household. They would be paid handsomely for the task, often benefitting from the ward's lands, which in the case of Edward of Warwick, were extensive to say the least. Thus, as recorded in the calendar of patent rolls:

> '16 Sep 1480, Grant to the King's kinsman Thomas Marquess of Dorset for the sum of £2,000 paid by him to the king of the custody of the lordship or manor of Ringwood co Southampton [and many other manors not noted here]

during the minority of Edward son and heir of Isabel late wife of George duke of Clarence and the custody and marriage of the latter without disparagement and so from heir to heir without rendering anything to the king, until he shall be fully satisfied of the said sum, finding a competent sustenance for the said Edward.'[6]

Thomas Grey happened to be the elder of Elizabeth Woodville's sons by her first marriage, and therefore a stepson of the king himself. It is unclear if Margaret ever joined her brother in the Marquis' household, but what we do know, again from the patent rolls, is that Thomas Grey was assured he would gain Margaret's wardship if her brother died prematurely, making her the heir apparent of the Clarence/Warwick line. Given the tumultuous months that led up to this, I imagine that for Margaret it would have been distressing to be separated from her younger brother, something Edward may also have felt keenly. Given medieval England's habit of not recording the whereabouts of young women, albeit high born ones such as Margaret, we can only guess at where she spent her time once Edward was separated from her. Sadly there is almost nothing in the records that gives us a very clear understanding, but as Susan Higginbotham suggests, it is probable that Margaret spent her time in the ever expanding royal nursery alongside her many female cousins.[7] Certainly one thing we can find in the records is proof that her uncle, the king, made sure she lived as a young woman befitting her rank, for in 1478 he paid 50 marks (roughly £23,000 in today's money) for 'the arrayment as for the wages of her servants'.[8] He also ensured she was suitably attired, with 90 marks spent across the years 1482/1483 on Margaret's clothing, the equivalent today of roughly £40,000. As seemed the custom for the young Margaret, she could not afford to get too comfortable with the status quo, such as it was, for in April 1483 King Edward IV became gravely ill and died shortly after. At just 40, his death was premature, but with hindsight not entirely shocking. No longer the lean, athletic paragon of kingly vitality, his natural joie de vivre had turned to dangerous gluttony, something he would pass on to his grandson in time. He was able to cling on to life long enough to make his wishes abundantly clear, naming his brother Richard as Protector of England until such a time as his eldest son, Prince Edward, reached maturity. Her uncle's death, whilst shocking, would have impacted her royal cousins far more than Margaret herself, for she now found herself in the rather familiar position of niece to the man controlling the kingdom. Until his actions to overthrow the planned inheritance of the crown, Richard Duke of Gloucester had been a dependable and well respected central figure of King Edward IV's court. After George's death, he was the most senior man in the kingdom, after the king, with a more sensible and level-headed mind than the late Duke of Clarence. We now know the oft-repeated theory that he was a notorious hunchback has some basis in fact, with his remains, which were discovered in 2012, proving considerable scoliosis of the spine, but his image as the ultimate pantomime villain is, certainly to his champions, largely a product of the Tudor propaganda machine.[9] Under his protectorship, further key figures from within the dowager queen Elizabeth Woodville's circle, notably her brother Anthony and second son by her first marriage, Richard Grey, were put to death, as was Richard's one time ally William, Lord Hastings. This, understandably, created panic in Elizabeth and she soon retreated into the sanctuary of Westminster Abbey. Her fears would be fully realised when under Richard's watch the natural order of succession was entirely ignored. Within a few short weeks of his brother's death, Richard began proceedings to have himself named king. Prince Edward, also known as the uncrowned King Edward V, was housed in the Tower of London alongside his younger brother Prince Richard, Duke of York supposedly for their protection. Known to history as 'The Princes in the Tower', neither would ever leave its walls. In a bid to discredit his brother's memory, sow doubt on the right of his nephews' claim to the throne, and by extension position himself as the natural successor, Richard soon began to use the rumoured prior marriage between King Edward IV to one Eleanor Talbot as a way of wiping the slate clean. Historians still argue as to whether there was any truth in the Talbot marriage story, but for Richard, it was all too neat and straightforward to ever look into with diligence. The supposed Talbot marriage was the perfect way of removing any descendant of his brother from inheriting the throne, thus opening it up to be claimed by the natural next in line of the right age, Richard himself.

Soon, whether cowed by pressure from Richard's army or due to genuine belief in what the Ricardian propaganda machine had put out, the citizens of England and most notably its capital, London, acknowledged Richard as their next king. Now known as King Richard III, he wasted no time in stamping his authority across the kingdom, but would also have to deal with the irksome challenge of others close to him in blood, who had an arguably greater claim to the throne of England – chief among them, Margaret, and her younger brother Edward. All being equal, after the death of King Edward IV and his legitimate children by Elizabeth Woodville, the next in line to the throne was Edward, Earl of Warwick rather than Margaret herself. For King Richard III to solidify his rule, he thus had to discredit the claim of his niece and nephew, but how to do it? The answer was simple – their father's attainder for treason. Strictly speaking, the attainder had not included the Duke of Clarence's children, but in another example of King Richard III not allowing fact to thwart his plans, he used it as leverage, claiming the children of a convicted traitor could not inherit the crown of England. Given the youth of Margaret and her brother, even if they had attempted to challenge Richard's plans it is probable they'd have lost. Thus, Richard ascended the throne under the cloud of usurpation, but like earlier usurpers, ascend it he did. Unlike the mysterious disappearance of the sons of Edward IV and Elizabeth Woodville, King Richard III chose to show off his third nephew, Edward of Warwick, giving him a starring role in a journey to the north of England. That he chose to celebrate this nephew, whilst ostensibly destroying his others, is certainly peculiar, and to Richard's modern supporters is further proof that he did not authorise the death of the two young princes. Despite his fall from grace and eventual death under the former king, the north remained loyal to the memory of Edward's maternal grandfather, Richard Neville, Earl of Warwick, and thus regarded young Edward as one of their own. In choosing to position Edward so visibly in his entourage, the new king was likely safeguarding his own presence, accurately guessing that the people of the north, with whom he was also popular, would not rise up against him if Edward of Warwick was seen to be being treated well. Margaret's whereabouts during this time are difficult to pin down, although from the records we do know that following the conclusion of the progress to the north, Margaret was joined by her brother at Sheriff Hutton Castle in North Yorkshire. Sir George Buck released *The History of King Richard The Third* in 1619, which underwent an edit by Arthur Noel Kincaid in 1979. Although Buck was writing 134 years after Richard died and does not list any sources for his work (something not unusual in a book from the seventeenth century), it is just possible that he was working from a now lost original text, and if he is to be believed, Edward of Warwick and thus Margaret were treated well by their uncle, for he says:

> 'And he kept not only alive his nephew the Earl of Warwick Edward Plantagenet son of his elder brother George Duke of Clarence but also in safety and in pleasure and was pleased that he should live in a stately and delightful house of his own.'[10]

Before later writing:

> 'I have seen accounts wherein King Richard is reported to have used tyranny against his nephew Edward Earl of Warwick son to George Duke of Clarence. It is true that he sent him to Sheriff Hutton, a godly and pleasant house of his own in Yorkshire and where this young lord had liberty, large diet, air pleasure enough, and lived in safety there.'[11]

Although mentions of Margaret from this time are fleeting, we know that King Richard III was assiduous in ensuring a continued level of grandeur was granted on his niece and nephew, for records show his ordering of the very best cloth available for their attire.[12] After this, no trace of Margaret can be found, until another seismic shift rocked the foundations of the English royal court. In the same year that King Richard III ascended the throne, 1483, conspiracies around supposed revolts began to boil over, most notably the 'Buckingham Rebellion'. As the story goes, a great many of the Yorkist establishment who had been supporters of King Edward IV began to rise up against the perceived usurpation by which Richard claimed the throne. In addition to this, whilst King Richard III had been busy cementing his rule on the kingdom, two formidable women had been secretly plotting to topple him from power and establish a change in the ruling dynasty – dowager queen, Elizabeth Woodville and Lady Margaret Beaufort, an heiress of considerable fortune from the house of Lancaster, and mother to the Lancastrian's last remaining hope, Henry Tudor. Their own machinations were well under way by the time that the Buckingham rebellion took place, so called for it was supposedly led by a former ally of the king's, Henry Stafford, 2nd Duke of Buckingham. I say supposedly, because some have suggested the duke was a mere scapegoat, and that other key figures in the uprising, Reginald Bray and John Morton, were actually its figureheads. It has also been conjectured that the inclusion of Buckingham at the centre of the conflict was to distract from the embarrassing reality that the rebellion was actually the work of an overwhelmingly pro-Edward IV (his memory and thus sons) group, or more shockingly still that beneath it all, it was two women who were its main architects. The aim of the rebellion was straightforward – topple Richard from the throne and replace him with the imprisoned Prince Edward. Once it was clear that both the prince and his younger brother were dead, the focus shifted to establishing Henry Tudor as king and having him marry Princess Elizabeth of York, which in the case of Lady Margaret Beaufort, was her own long term plan anyway. With armies gathering in Surrey, Kent, Essex and Somerset, the intention was to invade the capital on all sides and force the king out of power. Henry Tudor himself was to land in England with an army of over 3000 men, supplied by the treasurer of Brittany, Pierre Landais. The rebellion was an unmitigated disaster. Those leading the charge in Kent bolted a full ten days early, in due course outing the Duke of Buckingham as a central figure of the rebellion. Until this point he had sufficiently distanced himself from association. Its failure would thus result in only one conclusion for the duke, execution for high treason. Bad weather in the channel halted Henry Tudor's crossing, with several of his ships destroyed, and following an altercation with crown loyalists in Plymouth, he fled back across the water to the safety of Brittany.

Henry Tudor had spent a great deal of his life in Brittany, having escaped across the channel for his own safety in 1470 at the age of just 13. It came following the final downfall of King Henry VI and the re-establishment of King Edward IV, who may have taken steps to secure his hold on the throne by eradicating those with a claim. For the next fourteen years Henry would live under the protection of Francis II, Duke of Brittany, whilst his indomitable mother continued to promote him as the rightful heir to the throne of England. Once in Europe, Edward IV never seriously contemplated Henry Tudor as a major threat, and made only fleeting attempts to capture him. He was, after all, not legally entitled to the throne, for the ruling that excluded the Beaufort line was still very much in play. Having spent much of his formative years on the continent, he was considerably lacking in 'Englishness', so much so that in the early years of his reign, the king would prefer to converse in French, despite English now being well established as the language of the royal court. Henry may have had a lineage of extraordinary importance, but the man himself was somewhat less impressive. Slight, cautious and miserly, he was the antithesis of the very kingly Edward IV, whose memory would continue to cast a long shadow. As the future King Henry VIII entered adulthood it was often commented on how much he favoured his maternal grandfather in looks, as opposed to his father, something which was viewed as complimentary, rather than insulting. His shortcomings aside, Henry's mother continued to press his claim as the rightful heir of England and for anyone looking to destabilise the rule of the Yorks, Henry Tudor was an obvious candidate. Lady Margaret Beaufort was well placed to plot, as via her final marriage to Thomas Stanley, 1st Earl of Derby, a committed Yorkist, she was kept abreast of the ever-changing fortunes of the dynasty which, in time, she hoped to overthrow. Lady Margaret married Stanley in June of 1472, took a place back at court in the queen's household and had sufficiently endeared herself to Elizabeth Woodville enough to be named a goddaughter to one of the many royal princesses. Margaret's biographers, Jones and Underwood, have suggested that her final marriage was nothing more than one of practicality and convenience, for it enabled her return to the royal court, under the guise of accompanying her husband in his official business, serving the Yorkist kings. Another of Margaret's biographers, Sarah Gristwood, has speculated that the marriage began and ended with one sole aim – rehabilitation into court life, from where she could covertly plot the return of her exiled son. Given the patriarchal nature of medieval England, women, especially those high born, rarely had the luxury of acting with complete independence. Lady Margaret Beaufort was a political animal through and through, and understood the limitations her sex played in how she could operate. She would shake these off in time, but for now, that could wait. An advantageous marriage had helped her before, so why not employ that strategy again. Ever the court pragmatist, Lady Margaret rode the wave following Edward IV's death and was soon back at court as part of Anne Neville's household. Anne Neville, the second and often overlooked daughter of Warwick the Kingmaker, was now queen consort following her husband's successful bid for the throne. According to sources at Westminster Abbey, Lady Margaret was given the honour of carrying Queen Anne's train at the latter's coronation in the summer of 1483.[13] Lady Margaret's apparent acquiescence with this usurping Yorkist king and his queen belied her larger aims. It was soon evident that she had set up communication with her former employer, dowager queen, Elizabeth Woodville, who was spending her days safely ensconced in sanctuary under Westminster Abbey. Just months after playing such a starring rôle in Queen Anne's coronation, Lady Margaret negotiated the betrothal of her son to Elizabeth Woodville's eldest daughter, Princess Elizabeth of York. It is believed that the two women were connected via their mutual physician, Lewis Caerleon, who ensured the correspondence between the pair remained secret. Lady Margaret began to experience a shift in her own hopes for the future, for according to Henry VII's biographer, Polydore Vergil, she 'began to hope well of her son's future'.[14] By Christmas 1483, Henry Tudor whilst still in exile, gathered his remaining supporters together at Rennes Cathedral in the east of Brittany and declared his intention to proceed with the marriage which his mother had negotiated. Just a few months later, the king and queen were dealt an almighty blow when their son, Prince Edward, died suddenly. Despite his rank, no official year of birth was recorded for the young prince, and he could have been as young as 7 when he died. Naturally Richard and Anne reacted with heartbreak, with the Croyland Chronicle stating:

> 'On hearing the news of this, at Nottingham, where they were then residing, you might have seen his father and mother in a state almost bordering on madness, by reason of their sudden grief.'[15]

The following year, Queen Anne followed her son to the grave, probably from a severe bout of tuberculosis. By the summer of that same year, 1485, Henry Tudor was ready to make another attempt at conquering England and taking the throne. It is believed he was spurred into action when news reached his ear of King Richard III's plan to marry his own niece, Princess Elizabeth, which if true would rob him of the greatest prize he looked set to acquire should his invasion of England prove successful. He might be the last hope of the Lancastrian faction, but Princess Elizabeth was the key to securing the acceptance of the people he looked to rule, for her own lineage was unquestionably royal, and crucially, in the eyes of the populace, legitimate. The planned marriage between Richard and his niece was likely pure rumour, for rather than take her down the aisle, the king promptly sent Elizabeth north to lodge with her cousins, Margaret and Edward. Unlike his previous attempt, Henry Tudor was successful in landing on British soil, but instead of England he arrived at Mill Bay in Pembrokeshire, in the heart of lands loyal to both him and his mother. As he travelled through the Welsh Marches Henry Tudor acquired a considerable army and was soon in command of in excess of 5000 soldiers. He engaged King Richard III in battle at Bosworth Field on 22 August 1485. In what was one of England's most famous battles, Henry Tudor, a rank outsider with little tangible right to the throne achieved his mother's raison d'être. His forces, helped considerably by Lady Margaret's husband, Lord Stanley, who switched sides right before the battle started, succeeded in bringing down the king's forces and by extension King Richard III himself. If the reports from the time are to be believed, the slain Yorkist king was treated with little to no respect by Henry Tudor's army. King Richard III was cut down and likely killed through major trauma to the skull due to continued strikes to his head, probably from a halberd. Certainly the examination of his bones indicate at least eight of his eleven injuries to be directly to the skull. Following his death, the fallen king was tied naked to a horse and interred at the Greyfriars Church in Leicester. The discovery of his bones in 2012 is one of the greatest historical archaeological discoveries of the modern age. With Richard's death, so came the death and conclusion of the Plantagenet dynasty. They had governed England for over 300 years, but now was the time for change. The rule of the Tudors had begun.

Chapter 2

A Changing of the Guard

As the crown that had very recently sat atop King Richard III's head was presented to Henry Tudor, noble families up and down the kingdom could not have known that their mere existence may prove to be their eventual undoing. For Margaret Pole and the rest of her extended York family however, there could be little doubt that life would be significantly different under this new order. The newly styled King Henry VII was quick to take control of those who posed an immediate threat to his authority. From the outset of his reign, Henry Tudor would use the process of rewriting laws to help solidify his shaky control on the crown. One of his first actions was to backdate his own succession to the throne of England, having it written into law that he was king from 21 August 1485, the day before Bosworth, which meant that anyone who fought against him, but still lived, could be classed as traitors to the crown. It was a cut-throat, albeit masterful stroke on his part. A charge of treason could result in acts of attainder being raised, and with them the movement of vast swathes of property into King Henry's grasping hands. He also moved quickly to neutralise potential threats and claimants to the throne, chief amongst them, Edward of Warwick. The young earl, who was just 10 or 11 years old, was to be brought from the north to the seat of power in London, accompanied by Sir Robert Willoughby and in all probability, his sister Margaret. Polydore Vergil, known by some as the 'Father of English History'[1] for his extensive and extraordinary contemporary accounts from life in England at the time, said in his biography of the king: 'He (the King) is fearful, lest the boy should escape and given any alteration in circumstances, he might stir up civil discord'.[2] As will be seen, anxiety about his position, his right to the throne, or more accurately, lack thereof, appears to have defined much of Henry VII's character and the way he managed his reign. It was a weight his successor would also have to bear. A line of plots, both real and imagined, can be drawn from the start of Henry VII's reign through to the end of Henry VIII's. These plots had the interests of the 'White Rose' houses, those that descended from Edward III in the Yorkist line, at their core, indeed the very backbone of this story centres around the ever present danger the Poles and their contemporaries represented.

As they entered the capital, Edward and Margaret must surely have felt uneasy about what lay ahead. No longer protected by their position as unquestioned members of the royal family, they were now merely the children of a convicted traitor and a dangerous threat to Henry Tudor remaining in control. Although he could not know it at the time, for Edward of Warwick this journey towards London brought with it impending doom. Once safely under the new king's control, Margaret and Edward were put into the care of Lady Margaret Beaufort, now sporting the self-made title 'My Lady The King's Mother'. With her son on the throne, Margaret Beaufort's years of scheming had paid off, she had achieved all she hoped for. Margaret had become the second woman in the land, although this she accepted only grudgingly, reportedly walking a mere half pace behind her daughter-in-law, Queen Elizabeth, at formal occasions[3], whilst wearing clothing of the same quality and materials. We know Margaret and Edward joined Lady Margaret's household thanks to expenses being paid back to her in the winter of 1486 for having the children under her control.[4] Although there are no accounts of what Margaret and Edward thought about being lodged under the watchful eye of the king's mother, there may have been some comfort in the fact that they were joined by their cousins – the as yet uncrowned Elizabeth of York, and her sisters.[5] This comfort would not last, for soon Lady Margaret was relieved of Edward of Warwick, when the king had him transferred to the Tower of London as a prisoner. There are still questions as to why the king took the decision to imprison Edward of Warwick at this point, but it was a particularly cruel act when one considers his youth. In another example of the king shrouding his avarice with a legal blanket, he decided to right the wrongs (as he conveniently saw them) enacted against the still living Lady Anne Beauchamp, Countess of Warwick. The king would grant the return of the Warwick lands that had been divided as spoils of war between her son-in-laws George and Richard twenty years earlier. For the countess, this must have felt like waking from a very long nightmare. Alas, there was a sting in the tail that she would have to accept if she wanted the lands back – a public disinheritance of her grandson, Edward. By agreeing, all the lands that she had won back would revert to the king after her death. For the young Edward of Warwick, the only thing he was permitted to keep was his earldom, which without the lands and income that came with it, was an entirely hollow and meaningless title. What Margaret felt about her brother's incarceration is unknown, for so little in the records from this time in her life exist, but on a personal level it must have been horrifying. She had seen all too frequently that those who entered the Tower rarely left it alive. She was sufficiently adept at playing the court game though to glaze over any anger or distress she felt, at least in front of the king and his ever watchful mother. As Henry Tudor and his new queen settled into married life, Margaret became a prominent feature of the Tudor royal court; she was, after all, a first cousin of Elizabeth of York and was therefore expected to play a role in the machinations of everyday royal life. There is no evidence of Margaret petitioning the queen to intercede on her brother's behalf, although this may well have happened and not been recorded. As the queen was herself related by blood to the young earl, it is reasonable to assume that she would have rather seen him at liberty than locked away. However, Elizabeth of York's views would soon become compromised by the successes of her marriage bed. The king and queen had their first child, a boy, christened Arthur, born just thirteen months into the reign, and only eight months after their wedding. This latter detail raises the tantalising prospect that the king and queen consummated their union before marriage. It is of course also possible that the queen simply delivered her child before full term. Now that the queen had a Tudor prince in the nursery, her loyalties to the memory of the Yorkist dynasty were clouded; it had become all too personal. She had married Henry VII out of duty, but the progeny of their union now complicated matters. One hopes that her cousin's freedom was something she'd have championed, but might he then represent a danger to her infant son? Quite simply, Elizabeth of York's priorities had changed. Margaret was in attendance at the christening of the young prince[6], seen atop the list of ladies and recorded as 'my lady Margaret of Clarence', and as will be seen, she and her husband would play an instrumental role in Arthur's upbringing. The production of a healthy Tudor male heir was seen as a sign that God approved of Tudor rule, and helped solidify Henry's control of the country. This should have taken the pressure off Edward of Warwick's mere existence; sadly, it would not.

Although he kept the young boy languishing in the Tower, the king did not take any further action against Edward of Warwick for the time being. Unfortunately for the earl, despite being lodged in the most impregnable fortress in London, his famous name could be used against him, and within two years of the Tudor succession, an uprising began with the wholly innocent Edward at its fabricated core. As the story goes, a young man bearing the name Lambert Simnel, a name which may have been entirely made up given contemporary records actually calling him John, appeared in Dublin. Not long after, he was under the tutelage of an Oxford-trained priest called Richard Simmonds.[7] Spotting a resemblance between Simnel and the sons of the deceased King Edward IV, Simmonds claimed that the boy was Prince Richard, the younger of the Princes in the Tower. He soon changed his mind, and instead purported the boy to be the young Edward of Warwick. As a hotbed of Yorkist allegiance, the citizens of Dublin soon rallied around the pretender and had him crowned 'King Edward VI' at Christ Church Cathedral (the fifth King Edward we must remember was the elder of the 'Princes in the Tower'). When news reached the court in London, the decision was taken to pull the real Edward out of the Tower and present him to the populace of the city. Unsurprisingly, when the king was able to do this without any trouble, the rebellion faded to insignificance. Vergil recorded that the king:

> 'Commanded that Edward, son to the Duke of Clarence, be brought out of the Tower and led through the middle of the city to St Paul's Cathedral. This young man showing himself to everybody, as he had been instructed, and participated in a thanksgiving and the rest of the rites, and at same time had conversation with many lords and particularly those thought to be participants in the conspiracy, so that they might more readily understand that the Irish were foolishly making an uprising because of a vain thing.'[8]

This is certainly an enlightening quote, for if it is to be believed verbatim, then it should assuage some of the theories around Edward of Warwick's mental faculties. If he could hold conversation as a gentleman, with his peers and enemies ever watchful, then this would suggest, at this point at least, that his mind was sound. Despite further instances of rebellion breaking out in the north of England, King Henry managed to maintain a firm grip on the crown and even allowed Simnel, who in all probability was a mere scapegoat, to take up a position in the royal kitchens. With the young earl of Warwick now returned to his miserable existence in the Tower, the king turned his attention towards Margaret and the other York princesses still flitting about the court. To imprison all of them for merely existing would have been a far too heavy handed approach, and a wasteful one at that. In a bid to diminish the power of these remaining high born ladies, and by extension their respective kin, the king went for one of the oldest and most assured tricks in the book – marriage. Just as Elizabeth Woodville's early tenure as queen saw her many siblings married off to notable members of the nobility and gentry, Henry VII would now adopt a similar approach. He would start with the two Yorks who posed the greatest threat, these being Margaret, and the most senior in terms of rank after the queen, the eldest of her younger sisters, Princess Cecily. They were of the right age and breeding, and were to be married off to trusted members of Henry VII's court. This was broadly a smart move. By marrying the remaining doyens of the house of York off to Tudor loyalists, not only did the king neutralise threats from would-be claimants to his throne, but could position men he trusted in the households of women he felt he could not. Margaret was given in marriage to Sir Richard Pole and Princess Cecily to John, Viscount Welles. Pole was a trusted member of Henry VII's inner circle, a trust which extended to his appointment as a squire of the body. This role meant close and personal contact to the monarch, a sign of great favour, but despite this, Margaret's marriage in particular caused quite a stir in those less than loyal to the new regime. Sir Richard appears to have been a decent and loyal man, but he was grossly inferior to Margaret in status, being a mere member of the gentry class. When the time came for Perkin Warbeck to rise from the ashes, claiming to be Richard, Duke of York, he made his views on the matter perfectly clear, saying of the king:

> 'Married upon compulsion certain of our sisters and also
> the sister of our aforesaid cousin the Earl of Warwick, and
> divers other ladies of the blood Royal unto certain of his
> kinsmen and friends of simple and low degree.'[9]

Predictably, we cannot be totally sure when the marriage took place. Biographers of Margaret have put forward November 1487 as the most probable date[10], for in that same month Elizabeth of York was finally crowned and in the documentation from that day Margaret is addressed with her married surname.[11] Richard Pole, born around 1460, was older than Margaret by more than a decade; she was a girl of just 14 at their marriage, and he was aged between 27-29. Despite a less than blue-blooded ancestry, Richard Pole did have a nonetheless interesting background. Hailing from an ancient Welsh family, Pole had been brought up in Buckinghamshire where he was in possession of two manors, Medmenham, which would become Margaret's chief country residence in time, and Ellesborough. Richard was the son of Geoffrey Pole and Edith St John, and it is via his mother that the link to the house of Tudor exists. Edith St John was a half-sister of Margaret Beaufort, Henry VII's mother; the two women shared the same mother, so by extension Pole was a half-cousin of the king. Another cousin of Richard's, Sir John St John, would go on to marry Alice Bradshaw and their great-granddaughter would be Lady Jane Boleyn, nee Parker, Viscountess Rochford, wife of George Boleyn, brother of King Henry VIII's most infamous of queens, Anne Boleyn. Given the increased mention of Margaret in the contemporary records, it is clear that she and her new husband settled into life at court well. Both attended the queen's coronation and other key moments in the royal calendar. For the coronation itself, Margaret was seated alongside the king and his mother, who as custom dictated watched the action from afar.[12] The coronation, perhaps to make up for the delays that had preceded it, was a highly spectacular event. The queen, accompanied by a large retinue of ladies was taken through the city of London in a litter to Westminster Abbey to be crowned. She was bedecked in the royal colour of purple velvet, trimmed with ermine fur. Why Margaret was not chosen to accompany her cousin, but instead sat with the king is unknown. Without her presence, the queen was attended by her eldest sister, Princess Cecily of York, and two of her aunts, the dowager Duchess of Norfolk and Elizabeth, Duchess of Suffolk.

Owing to her father's attainder for treason, Margaret had no legal ownership of any land or properties at the time. She was therefore required to live at court, or, in one of her husband's households. His holdings may have been considerable, but they were not overly valuable. As the daughter of a royal duke, albeit one executed for treason, Margaret was accustomed to a certain level of grandeur. This way of living was not one her husband could hope to match, at least in the early years of their marriage, which explains some of the distaste the union was met with by York loyalists. The disparity between Margaret's upbringing and what her new husband could provide is most glaringly obvious when one compares the income received from his two properties in Buckinghamshire. Combined, these amounted to a mere £50 each year[13], against her father's one time annual income, which as Pierce notes 'at the time of Margaret's birth was estimated at an immense £6,000 a year, putting the marriage very much into perspective'.[14] So, despite the high station of her birth and rank, Margaret now found herself married to a man who was unable to come close to replicating this earlier splendour. Whilst Margaret was therefore resolved to living a more frugal existence, her husband did at least provide something else, something more sustainable and in all probability, highly welcome – stability. With ever increasing influence at the Tudor court, Sir Richard Pole was ascending through the ranks, with huge trust placed in him by the king. He was soon granted holdings in Oxfordshire and was thus in a position to maintain a respectable household as befitted his wife's status. Lady Margaret continued to be treated with reverence at formal occasions, as can be seen in the records of the Christmas festivities from 1488. In the order of precedence, Margaret remained firmly near the top, placed only behind Queen Elizabeth's sisters and peeresses of the realm.[15]

Margaret's marriage at age 14 was not uncommon in Tudor England but it was still deemed young for childbirth, already a risky business at the best of times. It is unsurprising therefore that Margaret and Richard waited until a more appropriate time to start a family, with their firstborn, Henry, arriving in 1492 when Margaret would have been roughly 19 years old. A year or two later, a second son, Arthur, joined the growing Pole nursery. That Margaret named her first two children after the king and his eldest son must surely have been in their honour. When Prince Arthur was formally installed as Prince of Wales in Ludlow, Richard, who had been appointed lord chamberlain to the young prince, naturally joined his royal charge. This elevation, to what was in effect the prince's chief advisor, was highly prestigious, for Richard would take responsibility for Arthur's day to day affairs, both publicly and behind closed doors. Ever the dutiful wife, Margaret retired from her position at court and joined her husband in serving the king's son and heir. She and Richard were granted the rights to Stourton Castle in Staffordshire, located sufficiently close to the prince's central base of Ludlow. It was here that Margaret would give birth to her third son, Reginald, in 1500. Preceding this she had also given birth to a daughter, Ursula, but alas the exact date of her birth is unknown – clearly the fecundity which had graced her forebears had extended to Margaret's marriage bed. Lady Margaret Pole, as she was now formally known, had settled into her life as the wife of a prominent member of the king's inner circle. This gave her security and position, and in return she provided her husband with a string of healthy children. Her brother's existence could not have been more opposing. Still languishing in the Tower, Edward of Warwick, having now been held prisoner for a longer period of time than he hadn't, appears as a most pitiable character. As alluded to earlier, assertions have been made about the state of his mental welfare. Edward Hall, an English lawyer and historian who, like Vergil, had a front row seat to the ever changing dynamics of the Tudor royal court famously quipped that Edward, having been held in the Tower for so long 'Out of all company of men, and sight of beasts, in so much that he could not discern a goose from a capon'.[16] Unsurprisingly, the meaning behind this quote has been the subject of much speculation, with some coming to the conclusion that it indicates a severe mental illness, which, brought on by lengthy incarceration, rendered Edward insane. The more accurate assessment, I, along with other biographers of the family believe, is that he was simply unworldly, having for so long been removed from polite society and education. During the time at which a man of his breeding would have begun to play a prominent role at court (late teens and early twenties), he was instead locked up in a cell in the Tower. Is it any wonder therefore that he would be ignorant of the ways of the Tudor court? Alas, like the earlier case with Lambert Simnel, Edward of Warwick's famous name would come back to haunt him in the shape of another Yorkist pretender – Perkin Warbeck. This next chapter would spell disaster for the impressionable and naive young man, and ultimately lead to his destruction.

Warbeck's own backstory is opaque in the extreme. His later confessions indicate an upbringing in Belgium, the son of John Osbeck, a comptroller to the city of Tournai and his wife, Katherine de Faro. According to his own retelling, by the age of 17 Warbeck had learned to speak English, and after journeying to Ireland, under pressure from the citizens of Cork began pursuing a career as the physical reincarnation of Prince Richard of York, the younger of the 'Princes in the Tower'. Where or how this story came to be is sadly lost to us, for he did not have a benefactor pushing his claim early on in the way Simnel did. Despite this, once Warbeck had sufficiently convinced those in Ireland who still clung to the hopes of a successful Yorkist uprising, he journeyed to France and then to Burgundy, where he was met and given ample support by his (would be) paternal aunt, Margaret, Duchess of Burgundy, sister of King Edward IV and Richard III. Margaret overlooked the fact she hardly knew her nephews, in fact it's possible she had only ever met them once during her visit to England in 1482. Even with her support, Warbeck did not make good on his promise to displace the house of Tudor, and like his forebear Simnel, soon felt the weight of the Tudor royal machine coming against him. The imposter was captured after those in the employ of the king surrounded Beaulieu Abbey, flushed him out, and did their duty in bringing him to justice. Despite a show trial and having to endure the humiliation of a public walk of penance, Warbeck also found employment under the king. This cavalier attitude towards his would-be opponents shows a confidence, or perhaps misplaced confidence, in the king's own rule, but that isn't to suggest that Warbeck didn't cause the king considerable problems. For a man as parsimonious as Henry VII, it must have been galling to spend nearly £10,000,000 in today's money to crush the troubles caused. Worse still, his willingness to extend an olive branch to the traitor and offer employment was soon thrown back in the king's face, for Warbeck escaped his captors, fleeing from the Palace of Westminster. Exactly why he chose to make this midnight flit is unknown, and although there is no irrefutable evidence to support his claim to be the long lost duke of York, it does seem odd that a man who was basically given a job off the back of rebelling against his king, rather than enduring the torturous end of most common traitors, should choose to abandon that. Is it *just* possible that he couldn't face life as a servant to the royal house of Tudor because he actually was who he claimed to be? The enormously successful, albeit fictional, works of Philippa Gregory include a storyline in which Elizabeth Woodville manages to smuggle her younger royal son out of England in place of a changeling, stating 'If you had two rare jewels and you feared thieves, would you put both of them in the same box?' It is a tantalising prospect, and one of Gregory's deviations from fact that feels at least passingly plausible. In any case, his escape did not last long; within days Warbeck was caught and this time, it was to the Tower that he would go, not the palace.

Within a year of his incarceration, Warbeck had developed a friendship with Edward of Warwick, and shortly thereafter a daring escape plan from the Tower was hatched. Given the likely naivety of Warwick, it is generally accepted that if there truly was a plan, that Warbeck was its mastermind. I question if there was a genuine plan because some have also proposed that it was fabricated by the government as a means of entrapping these two troublesome prisoners. Even Vergil, in an uncharacteristically critical tone said:

> 'Why indeed the unhappy boy should have been committed to prison not for any fault of his own but only because of his family's offences, why he was retained so long in prison, and what, lastly, the worthy youth could have done in prison which could merit his death all these things could obviously not be comprehended by many.'[17]

Plot or no plot, the king gathered his inner circle, and the overwhelming conclusion was that death was the only course of action for both prisoners. Another twist in the tale comes from a belief that Ferdinand, king of Spain and his wife, Isabella of Castile made it clear that in order for the planned marriage alliance between Prince Arthur and their daughter, Katherine of Aragon to go ahead, that England had to be rid of claimants for the throne. If the chronicle 'The Life of Jane Dormer, Duchess of Feria', a sort of sixteenth-century autobiography of Jane, a lady-in-waiting to Queen Mary I is to be believed, then Katherine certainly did feel guilt at what was to come for young Edward, and that this as she saw it was the cause of her later troubles in life, for it is said in the preface:

> 'She applied these miseries and disasters to have specially happened for the death of Prince Edward Plantagenet, son of the Duke of Clarence, brother to King Edward the Fourth; whom (most innocent) Henry VII. put to death to make the kingdom more secure to his posterity, and to induce King Ferdinand to give his daughter, this Catharine, in marriage to Prince Arthur.'[18]

Once it was agreed that Warbeck and Warwick would be tried, their dates in court were set. Warbeck took the stand on 16 November 1499, was pronounced guilty, and hung at Tyburn as a common criminal a few days later. Warwick, as a peer of the realm, was accorded the rights appropriate to his rank, and tried by a jury of his fellows on 21 November 1499. When the sentence came back guilty, death was the only course of action. Initially sentenced to be hung, drawn and quartered, this was instead commuted to the far more merciful death by beheading. A week later, Edward of Warwick, a young man who was likely innocent of all charges against him, was led from his cell to a scaffold outside of the Tower's walls. Mercifully, with just one stroke of the axe, he was dead. The king extended some courtesy in the burial of Edward's remains, paying for interment at Bisham Abbey, a final resting place for several of his York forebears. This action is certainly enlightening, for traditionally traitors to the crown, irrelevant of their rank, would be buried at the Tower. Is it possible that the king felt some guilt in agreeing to the young man's execution, and by having him buried with honour hoped to lessen some of that culpability? Something else had occurred when Edward of Warwick's head was removed from his shoulders – the House of Plantagenet also technically died, for it became extinct in the legitimate male line. Any remaining members of the dynasty were either female, or born through the female line, so whilst they possessed royal blood, they could not claim a royal name. Sadly, no record of Margaret's reaction to her brother's death has been recorded, but we might assume that she would have been devastated. Her brother, despite his long incarceration, had been the one remaining earthly link to her parents, but he, like so much in Margaret's life, was now gone. Margaret was now all that remained of the infamous Warwick line. Her world had shifted on its axis on more than one occasion, and soon the same would be true, for a Princess of Spain was en-route to England and Margaret, her husband and children would feature heavily in the drama that would unfold.

Chapter 3

The Princess of Spain

Katherine of Aragon was born on 16 December 1485 at the Palace of Alcala de Henares, in what was then part of Castile, but today comes under Madrid. As the daughter of the joint Spanish rulers, King Ferdinand of Aragon and Queen Isabella of Castile, she was undoubtedly one of the most important princesses in Europe at the time. Described as petite and pretty, with blue eyes and red hair, she was also a descendant of the English House of Lancaster via her mother. Interestingly, this connection upon close inspection highlights the fact that Katherine had a greater claim to the English throne than King Henry VII, for she was descended from the first two of John of Gaunt's wives whereas Henry was a descendant of his third. Known as Catalina in her home land, her name would be anglicised once arriving in England. She had been legally married to Prince Arthur before even leaving Spanish shores, for a marriage by proxy had taken place two years earlier. Margaret's husband, Sir Richard Pole, had taken the part of Katherine, grasping the hand of her bridegroom-to-be in one hand and Rodrigo de Puebla, Spanish Ambassador, in the other. On 17 August 1501 she set sail from A Coruña, a city on the northern Spanish coast. A little under two months later the teenage princess met her teenage prince, and although their immediate reactions to each other are unknown, Arthur was soon praising her virtues to both his parents and Katherine's. The full scale royal wedding as befitted a young couple who would (everyone hoped) one day rule as king and queen was staged on 14 November. A hugely opulent affair, the usually parsimonious Henry VII wanted to put on a show, for the wedding would highlight to his kingdom the stability of the Tudor dynasty, and celebrate a union with one of the most powerful families in Europe. Although no record exists, given the prominence of Lady Margaret Pole and her husband both at the royal court and in Prince Arthur's day to day life, it is highly probable that they attended the wedding. They, nor anyone at the court could have predicted that the first night Arthur and Katherine spent as man and wife together would be a major talking point over twenty years later. Whether their marriage was consummated or not, the young couple soon left the capital and took up residence at Ludlow Castle as Prince and Princess of Wales, the start of what everyone hoped would be a long and happy marriage.

Alas, disaster struck, when just five months later Prince Arthur died, possibly from the sweating sickness or tuberculosis. He was just 15 years old. Katherine, now a widow, returned to London for what would be the start of seven years of great uncertainty about her future. Given the close role Sir Richard had played in a large portion of the prince's life, it was decided he would inform the king of his eldest son's death. Although we tend to view Henry VII as a cold and unfeeling man, the passing of his heir-apparent caused him and his queen great distress. Both were said to burst into tears and took a great deal of comfort from each other's presence in the aftermath that followed. If Arthur did indeed succumb to the sweat, then it's possible the king's grief was made even worse, for it is generally acknowledged that the virus was introduced into Britain by Henry's conquering army. The light at the end of the tunnel for the king and queen, however, was the benefit of their second healthy living son, Prince Henry, and two princesses, which must have assuaged some of their fears. Both were still reasonably young and in good health, so the production of more royal children was possible. In the short time Katherine had spent as Princess of Wales, she had developed a friendship with Margaret, but this also came to an abrupt end when her husband, now surplus to requirements, returned to Wales to continue in his duties as governor of the Welsh Marches. As his wife, Margaret also left court, and returned to the role she probably treasured the most – being a mother to her growing brood of children. She did maintain regular correspondence with Katherine, now titled Dowager Princess of Wales. Like nearly all of Margaret's life experience up to this point, further misery was not far off, for in October 1504 Richard Pole suddenly died. Unlike most arranged marriages of the nobility, Margaret and Richard's appears to have been a happy one. Certainly they had no trouble in producing children and across the seventeen years that they were together, Richard gave Margaret security such as she had never known. His death must surely have been a complete disaster, not only emotionally, but for what it meant in terms of her finances and position. Without her husband's already menial income, Margaret was basically destitute. All of the money tied into the Warwick lands and titles had immediately reverted to the crown after her brother's attainder, so she could not pull on the considerable resources that this would have produced. Indeed such was the dire state of her financial affairs that she was forced to borrow £40 from the king to ensure her husband received a suitable funeral, and 'borrow' it most certainly was, for the king made it clear how the funds were to be repaid – Margaret was to return the money via profit made from her late husband's estates. As Hazel Pierce observes, given that the king was now in possession of these lands it was a rather hollow request, as Margaret would be clearing her debt with Henry VII's own money.

From being one of the most important women in the country, she was now on the fringes of the court, with little money and a large household to maintain, including her youngest son Geoffrey who had been born not long before Sir Richard's death. With few options left to her, Margaret followed in the footsteps of her aunt, dowager queen Elizabeth Woodville, and took sanctuary in a house of religion. This was a well-accepted means of support, particularly for noble widows, and as a deeply religious woman must have been a comfort to Margaret. At the very least it would ensure her children had food in their stomachs. Although there is some debate amongst historians as to where Margaret resided, evidence can be found that she joined an order of Bridgettine nuns at Syon Abbey. This evidence comes directly from the household accounts of Lady Margaret Beaufort, mother to the new king, for 'My Lady the King's mother' as she was now styled, made regular payments to support Margaret Pole. The earliest record of this comes from May 1505, seven months after Sir Richard Pole's death, where it is recorded 'Item delivered unto my lady's peace the 12th May at the Syon in gold for a reward given to Dame Margaret Pole' at a cost of 20s. That regular payments were made is clear by a later entry in the summary of expenses 1505–1507, stating 'Money delivered at sundry times to the Lady Pole towards her funding'. This act of charity from Margaret Beaufort extended further, as the records state 'Costs and exhibitions of Mistress Parot, Mistress Ursula Pole, Mistress Margaret and Jane' at a total cost of 113s, 4d, the Mistress Ursula Pole being, of course, Margaret's only daughter. These payments would continue for the rest of Margaret Beaufort's life, with the last recorded entry given just a month before her death in June 1509. Interestingly, another detail in the accounts of Margaret Beaufort's expenses highlights 'Item in reward to two women norrysse (nurses) to my lady Pole's two children that were with my Lady's grace at Syon', with a corresponding payment of 6s 8d. The two nurses mentioned may indicate wet nurses, a common fixture for any noble Tudor household. Although not proven with certainty, there has been some suggestion that Margaret Pole was pregnant during the early stages of her time at Syon. Without a confirmed date of birth for Geoffrey Pole it is impossible to be sure when he was born, but if Margaret was pregnant with her sixth child, then she and her husband would have conceived this child in the short space of time between Geoffrey's birth and Richard Pole's death. The next oldest child, Reginald, was now beyond the need of a wet nurse, so if there were two nurses, it could point to there having been two infants in the household. If there was, this sixth child did not survive long, as a later reference is made to a single nurse assigned to Margaret Pole's use.

Even sanctuary could not entirely alleviate the pressures Margaret faced financially. It is believed that Reginald's early entrance into a career in the Church was done as a cost saving exercise, and one that Reginald would grow to resent in time. It was also at this point that Margaret's eldest son, Henry, now 12, began to be spoken of more openly in court circles. After his father's death, Henry Pole had been made a royal ward, which should have seen him lodging at court and serving in the king's household, but from the records neither appears to have happened. Pierce makes a strong argument for why this was, suggesting the king did not want a young man with a very strong claim to the throne taking up a prominent position at the centre of power. Following Prince Arthur's death, the future of the house of Tudor rested entirely on the young Prince Henry's shoulders, and although he was a more robust child than his late brother, history had shown all too often that fortune's wheel could greatly alter the expected future of the crown. King Henry did not have to look very far to see this, given his own status as a rank outsider when he launched his bid for the throne. Thus, Henry Pole, a legitimate grandson of the Duke of Clarence with unquestionably noble blood, posed an enormous threat to his dynasty's future prospects. Katherine of Aragon's existence at court took an upturn when it was decided that she would marry her late husband's brother and now heir to the throne, Prince Henry. Although the king vacillated over this decision, and for a time decreed that the marriage would not take place following Katherine's mother's death, which had made her a less valuable commodity, a love match between Prince Henry and Katherine appears to have surfaced, despite their five year age gap, for following Henry VII's death on 22 April 1509, the new king, Henry VIII, made it abundantly clear that he would honour his pledge to marry Katherine, and he kept his word. Just two months into the reign, the teenage king took his late brother's wife up the aisle. Seven years after landing on English soil, Katherine had at last achieved her destiny, she was queen.

Amongst the common people, and indeed many of his nobles, King Henry VII had not been a popular monarch. Already a consummate miser, following his wife's death on her 37th birthday in 1503 he began to retreat from court, and would occupy his time by recording in minute detail the accounts of his expenses. His people would endure years of austerity, whilst the royal coffers expanded ever more. The king's obsession with money soon became all consuming, which had the opposite effect to the one he hoped to convey, for the Spanish envoy Pedro de Ayala stated 'Although the English King liked to be thought of as a great man, no one believed he was, for his love of money was too great'.[1] It was therefore a relief for many up and down the land when following his death, Prince Henry ascended the throne – it was as if a cloud had lifted from the kingdom. The country was no longer a state governed by an irascible and grasping monarch, but by a young, strapping and affable king, very much in the mould of his Yorkist grandfather, King Edward IV, whom Henry was said to greatly resemble. For many it felt like a new dawn beckoned. One venetian diplomat, Pasqualigo, practically tripped over himself in praise of the monarch, stating in a 1515 dispatch:

'His Majesty is the handsomest potentate I ever set eyes on; above the usual height, with an extremely fine calf to his leg, his complexion very fair and bright, with auburn hair combed straight and short, in the French fashion, his throat being rather long and thick. He was born on the 28th of June, 1491, so he will enter his twenty-fifth year the month after next. He speaks French, English, and Latin, and a little Italian, plays well on the lute and harpsichord, sings from book at sight, draws the bow with greater strength than any man in England, and jousts marvellously. Believe me, he is in every respect a most accomplished Prince; and I, who

> have now seen all the sovereigns in Christendom, and last
> of all these two of France and England in such great state,
> might well rest content.'[2]

The natural affinity for his mother's people rather than his father's, perhaps explains why in the early part of the reign the king was fond of and showed a great deal of trust in Margaret Pole, as well as his other Yorkist relatives, whom he treated well. His subjects could not know that their new king would grow to be even more of a tyrant than his late father. Margaret's close friendship with the new queen likely helped, and unsurprisingly she was chosen as a lady of honour in the upcoming double coronation for Henry and Katherine. With this came lodgings in the capital paid for by the king, valued at 40 marks, or roughly £18,000 in today's money.[3] For Margaret and her family, this inclusion at the centre of court must surely have been welcome, following years spent in the Tudor wilderness. At the coronation, Margaret's status was made clear when she was apparelled in cloth usually reserved for countesses – this action, possibly at the queen's behest, would prove most fortuitous in time. The king did not retract from his show of loyalty to the remaining members of the house of York, Margaret chief amongst them, for just six weeks after she performed her duties at the coronation she was granted an annuity of £100[4], the equivalent of around £66,000 today. At the same time, Margaret's eldest son, Henry, cold shouldered by the former king, was welcomed into the royal household and soon felt the benefit of the royal coffers, with expensive cloth ordered to ensure he was suitably attired. This included a great deal of black in materials such as tawny and velvet, an immediate sign of wealth given the expensive nature of dying materials at the time. Henry VIII also took responsibility for the costs of educating Reginald Pole, whom as detailed earlier Margaret had given over to a career in the Church. Now back at the forefront of the royal court, luck had finally shone on the beleaguered Pole family. Margaret may not have had the stability of marriage or the extravagant riches of her early childhood, but she and her family were certainly comfortable and for the time being, safe. This comfort clearly increased Margaret's confidence in the justness of the new king, for in 1512, perhaps also at the suggestion of the queen, she petitioned Henry VIII to restore the confiscated Earldom of Salisbury to her. As Higginbotham points out, the petition also included the only known comment Margaret made on the downfall of her brother. Although the language is markedly colourless, Margaret cleverly suggests that the actions which saw her brother executed were born out of genuine naivety, rather than premeditated guilt. In her statement to the king, Margaret said her brother 'was always from his childhood being of the age of eight years until the time of his decease remaining and kept in ward and restrained from his libertie as well in the Tower of London as in other places, having none experience nor knowledge of the worldly policies nor of the laws of this realm, so that if any offence were by him done concerning such matters specified in the said act of attainder it was rather by innocence then of any malicious purpose'.[5] The king acquiesced to Margaret's request, and in a further show of generosity proclaimed that she would have the title Countess of Salisbury in her own right. It was recorded that:

'The Replication of the Lady Margaret Countess of Salisbury to the answer of the excellent Prince Henry Duke of Richmond and Somerset. The said countess in every thing as she has said in her said title and avers everything contained in the same to be good and true and over that says that the same Edward being in our late sovereign lord his ward was in our said late sovereign lord's parliament held at Westminster the 15th January in the 19th year of his reign attainted of high treason by reason of which attainder our said late sovereign lord was seised of the said lord amongst other manors lands and tenements being of the inheritance of the said Edward late Earl in his demesne as of fee as in the right of his cousin, and after a parliament held at Westminster the 4th February in the third year of our noble sovereign lord king Henry the 8th the said countess as sister and heir to the said Edward was by account of the same parliament restored to all manors lands and tenements as the said Edward or any other person of his use were seised of and the said act of attainder utterly undone and defaced as by the same act of restitution more plainly appears Without that that our said late sovereign lord king henry the 7th was seised of and in the said manor of Cambridge with the appurtenances in his demesne as of fee in the right of his cousin otherwise or in any other manor than in the replication is alleged, or that our said late sovereign lord had any other interest in the said manor before the same attainder but only by reason of the nonage of the said Edward late Earl of Warwick as in the said title is alleged, and without that that our said late sovereign lord died seised of and in the said manor of and in any other estate than by reason of the said attainder of the said Edward or that the same manor descended unto our said noble sovereign lord king Henry the 8th but only by reason of the same act of attainder. And without that that there are any other records that entitled our said late sovereign lord king Henry the 7th or our now sovereign lord King Henry the 8th unto the said manor with the appurtenances or otherwise or in any other manor than in this replication is alleged, all which matters, etc.'[6]

In Tudor England, just as it is today, titles of the peerage were traditionally passed through the male line, which all else being equal should have meant Margaret won the title for her eldest son, but in granting the title directly to Margaret, the king created a hitherto unseen precedence. Margaret was now a peer of the realm not through marriage, but by birth, and it was not until the final stages of the 'king's great matter' that another independent peeress was created, a certain Anne Boleyn, who prior to her marriage to Henry VIII was made Marquess of Pembroke. Margaret's status was made clearer when, as a widow, it was decreed she would be a 'femme sole', that is to say an independent woman, capable and able to make her own decisions, based on her own wishes, something Henry's paternal grandmother Margaret Beaufort had also enjoyed. This independence extended to the marriage bed, with the king's approval for a union being a mere nicety rather than necessity, for Margaret was able to turn down a great friend of the king's, Sir William Compton, when he had proposed marriage, without earning the displeasure of Henry VIII.

Her titles now restored, Margaret's literal fortunes were entirely transformed. With countless acres and the many properties that oversaw these lands under her control, Lady Margaret Pole, one time traitor's daughter, was now one of the most powerful people in England. She had to pay handsomely (5000 marks) to get the title and all that came with it back, but Margaret knew this immediate expense would, in time, lead to greater riches. A record from 1513 details Margaret's first payment of £1000 towards this bill for 'Her benevolence towards the King's wars, for his high and great goodness showed unto her, as restoring her to the inheritance of her said brother'.[7] Margaret's own status, and thus her children's, was also noted amongst the nobility of Europe, for as recorded in the letters and papers of Henry VIII at the National Archives, in 1515 Sir Robert Wingfield reported to the king 'If my lady Devonshire the king's aunt, or the Lady Salisbury have marriageable daughters, thinks that the Duke of Milan would rather be joined by the king's blood than with any other'.[8] Henry Pole would not have to wait too long to be given his own title, which came in 1514, when he was made Baron Montagu, one of the subsidiary titles tied to the Salisbury Earldom. Although now a baron, he was not regarded as a senior member of the English nobility, and would have to wait until 1529 before being called to the House of Lords as representative for the Pole family. Perhaps as a sign of the king's antipathy towards Henry Pole, which became more overt as the years passed, he would remain a baron, the lowest rank in the peerage system, for the remainder of his life. He never came close to receiving a more senior peerage title, such as an earldom; a title, we should keep in mind, that was eventually conferred on Thomas Cromwell, a man without a drop of noble blood in his veins. Margaret Pole's restoration is generally seen as part of a wider movement of reconciliation from Henry VIII to those who had suffered under his father. Others who would enjoy further restorations included Sir Henry Courtenay to his earldom of Devon, to Thomas Grey, Marquess of Dorset and to James Tuchet, Lord Audley. Is it possible however that these restorations could have had an altogether more calculated motive? David Starkey has put forward a convincing theory that the king's true reasoning behind these restorations came down to his desire to go to war. Wars were expensive, fraught with uncertainty and placed a heavy burden on the common people. It was therefore imperative that the king had his nobles on side, should the time come when he would call on their ample resources to help fund his own ambitions. There is certainly evidence to support Starkey's conclusion, for when the king needed funds to subsidise a French campaign in 1527 he instructed an assessment of the wealth of ten members of the nobility. Margaret's wealth was reported as being worth £1220 per year[9], which placed her fifth on the list, ahead of the country's premier noble, the Duke of Norfolk. The figures presented should be taken with caution however, for rather like the wealthy of today who find ways to minimise the amount they pay in tax, Pierce notes that members of the Tudor nobility also downplayed their worth. Under closer inspection it was found that Margaret's income was over £1000 higher than she had first suggested. The subsidy assessments went way beyond the high nobility though, with each member of the king's chamber having their finances reviewed. At this time Arthur Pole was in the king's service, and was required to contribute £63 towards the French campaign[10], a contribution he clearly failed to make, for it was recorded that 'the subsidy levied in the King's household on Sir Arthur Pole, Maurice and Will. Butler, Piers Griffith, John Amyas, Lancaster, and Mountorgule – No sums returned, as they could not be distrained'.[11]

Margaret was soon in a position to grant her own annuities, with one very notable recipient benefitting from her generosity. In the Exchequer Treasury of Receipt a grant can be found from Margaret 'for good counsel and aid rendered and to be rendered her, to Thomas Wolcy, clerk, King's almoner, of 100 marks annuity for life, payable at Easter and Michaelmas'.[12] The document is signed 'Margret Pole', which is interesting in itself, for if it was signed by Margaret directly then it gives us some indication as to how she spelt her own name, although this can't be taken with too much fervour given the lack of standardised spelling in Tudor England. The nature of the receipt is even more interesting, for it shows a regular correspondence between Margaret and Thomas Wolsey, a man who needs no introduction in the story of King Henry VIII. It cannot be overstated how unusual Margaret's position was. Her close contact and ability to give out considerable gifts of money to men such as Wolsey is a prime example of just how significant her power was at this time. The records point to Wolsey also showing favour to Margaret in return, for in a letter from Sir Richard Sacheverell to the Earl of Shrewsbury in 1516, Sacheverell recounts that when asked by the cardinal why his son was not at court, he responded that he would see him married but knew not to who, to which Wolsey responded 'My Lady Salisbury has a good young lady to her daughter'.[13] Margaret's status as a femme sole must have also been apparent to the women with whom she spent much of her time when at court. When Henry VIII had married Katherine of Aragon she was assigned a suitably large household as befitted her station. The queen would have eight principal ladies-in-waiting, and by 1517 that included Margaret Pole. Margaret had not been part of the initial retinue of women, but when a shake-up was initiated it seems reasonable to assume that Katherine herself requested Margaret's services, given their warm history. Another new face serving the queen was Lady Elizabeth Boleyn, nee Howard. It is interesting to consider with hindsight, that Margaret, who greatly outranked Elizabeth and would thus walk ahead of her in court processions would in time be required to show deference to the younger of Elizabeth's daughters.[14]

With property in seventeen English counties as well as holdings in Wales, the Isle of Wight and even Calais, Margaret was quickly becoming one of the wealthiest landowners at the court of King Henry VIII. As was customary for members of the nobility, Lady Margaret led a rather itinerant life. She would be required to visit her extensive network of properties, all whilst maintaining some level of involvement at the royal court, which meant that she also gathered about her a huge taskforce of staff to help govern in the places she could not. Margaret would principally reside at four of her properties, Clavering in Essex, Warblington Castle in Hampshire, Bisham in Berkshire and Le Herber in the capital. This last property highlights once more the meteoric shift in Margaret's finances, for owning a property on the scale of Le Herber, a palace in all but name, in London, was not something your average noble could hope to achieve. Like the majority of Tudor buildings in London, it no longer exists, but stood on the site of what is now Cannon Street underground station. Her house at Bisham had the advantage of close proximity to her eldest son, who resided at nearby Bockmer House in Medmenham, Buckinghamshire. It was also where the remains of her brother had been interred, alongside her grandfather, 'the Kingmaker', Richard Neville. As Higginbotham points out, Bisham must have been sufficiently grand, for when Margaret was put under attainder in 1538, the king personally reserved its use for himself. Warblington Castle may well have been Margaret's favourite home, for she was actively involved in all of its development and wasted no time, once her fortunes allowed, in commissioning its restoration. Now only part of the original gatehouse remains, but at one time, under Margaret's watch, a magnificent Tudor home had risen from the ashes, fitted at great expense and showcasing to anyone visiting that Margaret and her family were a true force of power in England. There would be no illusion as to whom the house belonged to, for Margaret proudly displayed her family crest on everything from altar cloths, bed hangings and in windows. Further evidence of her wealth was displayed in several large cupboards filled with venetian glass and gold and silver plate. Margaret would count the king and queen, but also Margaret Beaufort as overnight guests. Various items were recovered in 1538 during the Pole family's downfall which bore the pomegranate sigil associated with Katherine of Aragon and the portcullis of the Beauforts, which suggest they had been gifts from the royal family to Margaret, or passed down to her when times had been tougher. The fact that the castle was made using brick, then a highly expensive material, confirms the great cost that went into its creation. Its loss during the Civil War that engulfed the court of King Charles I is maddeningly frustrating, because in its creation we had a prime example of Margaret's own tastes and proof of the splendour in which she was able to surround herself. Given the lack of artefacts still in existence today and one, perhaps two, images of Margaret that were taken during her lifetime, the loss of Warblington removes the chance for us to see firsthand how she lived. Our only method for gaining some insight into how the castle once looked is to refer to the report produced in the 1630s by Warblington's then owner, William Luffe. He explained:

'The site of the principle Manor House of Warblington is a very fair place, well moated about, built all with bricks and stones, and is of great receipt, built square, in length 200 feet and in breadth 200 feet, with a fair green court within, and buildings round the said court, with a fair gallery and divers chambers of great count, and four towers covered with lead, with a very great and spacious hall, parlour, and great chamber, and all other houses of office whatsoever, necessary for such a house, with a very fair chapel within the said house, and the place covered all with tiles and stones; and there is a fair green court before the gate of the said house, containing two acres of land, and there is a very spacious garden with pleasant walks adjoining, containing two acres of land, and near to the said place, groves of trees containing two acres of land, two orchards and two little meadow plots containing eight acres, and a fair fishpond near the said place, with a gate for wood and two barns, one of five bays, the other of four bays, with stables and other outhouses.'[15]

If Luffe's assessment is accurate, then it is clear that aside from being a huge property, the house benefitted from ample and highly opulent grounds.

Although Margaret's significant wealth and position was now restored, which one would imagine she should have felt grateful for, a case arose which highlights an obstinacy around further lands Margaret felt were rightfully hers. This lack of tact and at times grasping behaviour from the countess, would earn her the king's displeasure, particularly as under closer inspection, it would appear that the king did indeed have a greater right to the lands in question. The disagreement surfaced following the death in 1528 of one of Henry's great favourites, Sir William Compton. The lands were, according to Margaret, tied to the Salisbury earldom, but to the king's mind belonged to the dukedom of Somerset. Compton had been the steward of these lands, with the properties of Canford and Deeping being granted to Henry Fitzroy by the king, and Winterbourne to Queen Katherine. A member of Margaret's household wrote to Henry's council, explaining that her willingness to pay the king 5000 marks for the return of the lands, which she felt were hers, included those now in question. At this point, some of the fees Margaret had promised to pay were still outstanding, with her advisors suggesting that this would be concluded should the lands be returned to her in full. Margaret was already significantly behind in the agreed term by which these funds would be paid, the date of 1523 having long passed.[16] Compton, we must remember, had once asked for Margaret's hand in marriage, only to be turned down. Margaret's councillor states in his letter that 'She [Margaret] took the profits until the late Sir Will Compton, for that he obtained not his purpose of her in marriage according to his suit, surmised to the King that they belonged to the dukedom of Somerset'.[17] In short, the letter makes the rather flimsy claim that Compton doctored the king's right to these lands as revenge for Margaret not agreeing to his proposal. It is certainly intriguing that Margaret did not raise the question of Compton's unwillingness to hand over these lands whilst he lived, but as Hazel Pierce notes, 'she was careful not to attribute such a vengeful motive to him until safely after his death'.[18] To understand whether Margaret did have a superior claim over the disputed lands, we must consider the way in which land would exchange hands or be appropriated. Whilst land and property could be gifted or inherited, it could also be seized, were the land's owner to suffer an act of attainder.

If the latter, then any property or land would typically revert to the crown, and thus be at the disposal of the sitting monarch to do with as they saw fit. Margaret's restoration to the Salisbury earldom made provision for her to receive lands and properties that went with it, but crucially only those held at the point at which her brother had been attainted. Properties such as the manor of Ware, which had at one time belonged to Anne Neville and thus firmly in the Warwick line, had, after Bosworth, been given by Henry VII to his mother Margaret Beaufort. Margaret Beaufort would retain the property till the end of her days[19], which upon her death went to the king. Margaret Pole's claim to the property was thus weaker. Despite this, the king would allow her to retain its possession, perhaps in an attempt to placate Margaret's claims to other properties. Unsurprisingly, the countess was not going to be bought off that easily, and would continue to push her suit, even going so far as to present her rights to the manor of Canford directly to Fitzroy[20], an action which would have undoubtedly got back to the king. Although Margaret no doubt felt the justness of her cause, her actions come off as both ill-judged and grasping. That Margaret behaved no differently to her peers, that she acted in her family's interests and sought steps to ensure their continued power and influence, is undoubtedly true. This doesn't counteract the fact however that she knew the safest course of action was to defer to the king's wishes. To do anything else was foolish in the extreme.

Evidently, Margaret's ongoing battles with the king did not tarnish her image amongst the nobility, in fact the greatest indication of Margaret's changed position at court resides in her household being seen as an excellent place for high born young women to take up residence. Rather like the finishing schools made popular in the Edwardian era, the households of prominent nobles in Tudor England provided an excellent place for young girls to mix and hone their social skills, a Tudor social scholarship of sorts. Whilst not as grand a placement as that of the queen's retinue, as a countess with royal blood Margaret's household would still have been highly desirable, especially as she also had sons of marriageable age. It was customary that some of the women who made up Margaret's retinue of attendants would be of her own kin. As expected, Margaret had followed convention, for by the time of her fall from favour in 1538, five of her granddaughters had roles in her household: Winifred, daughter of Henry, Baron Montagu;

Mary and Margaret, daughters of Sir Arthur Pole; Margaret Stafford, a daughter of Ursula Pole; and Katherine, daughter of Sir Geoffrey Pole. This close knit community of cousins would have also had the hopefully positive outcome of greater familial loyalty and trust, of good and respectable social mores. Others who would serve Margaret Pole included Johanne Chomeley, the wife of William Chomeley, who had formed part of the Duke of Buckingham's household; this appointment is likely to have occurred after the duke's downfall. Another was Anne Ragland, the wife of one of Baron Montagu's retainers. The extent to which the Pole family's fortunes had been transformed is evident from the scale of the household which Margaret alone kept, not to mention the households her children also enjoyed. This would include a comptroller, who was responsible for Margaret's finances, a steward who maintained general order, as well as three chaplains, six gentlemen waiters, two clerks of the kitchen, six yeoman of the chamber, two men of the wardrobe and two marshalls of the hall. She also had a wide retinue of grooms, cooks, porters, bakers, a brewer, a tanner, a laundress and a further ten gentleman servants. Margaret, like her noble contemporaries, thus maintained a sort of royal court in miniature, greeting guests seated below a canopy of state. Although her household appointments were typically filled by extended members of Margaret's own family and kin, she, like other noble widows, would also source talent from elsewhere. One such appointment was Sir Christopher More, a well-established member of the Court of Exchequer, who came on as her surveyor. Like other great nobles and indeed the royal family, Margaret also kept a fool. The records do not tell us whether Margaret's was a natural fool, that is to say someone who was born with severe mental difficulties, or whether they performed the role as an act, a sort of sixteenth-century take on a standup comic. Henry VIII famously kept a fool called Will Sommers, who was important enough to the king to be featured in the well-known 'family of Henry VIII' portrait which hangs in the haunted gallery of Hampton Court Palace. The Tudors had an altogether more accepting outlook on mental illness than might be expected. In an age of fervent religious belief, some argued that the mentally ill were of a purer heart. As Tracy Borman points out, the great Dutch philosopher, Desiderius Erasmus, would lean on the teachings of St Paul, that 'all men are fools before God, and the foolishness of God was wiser than man's wisdom'.[21]

As Margaret adjusted to her new status as Countess of Salisbury, her relationship with the queen, which had always been close, continued to prosper further; indeed two of the properties, Brettis Manor and Perbright Manor, that were now assigned to Margaret, had hitherto been in the ownership of Katherine of Aragon.[22] Furthermore, the manor of Chilton Foliat in Berkshire was also granted to Margaret, with a promise that 'if the sad manor of Chilton Foliat or any part thereof be taken from the possession of the said Queen by any prior right or title the King shall grant her other property of equal value'.[23] Margaret and the queen had lived through the uncertainty of Henry VII's reign and had also shared the bond of widowhood for a time. Both of their lives had been transformed via the ascension of Henry VIII and so it is no surprise that their friendship would be life-long. Given Margaret's background and breeding, she acted, as Hilary Mantel observed, as something of an ornament for the king. She was, after all, a living embodiment of the Yorkist dynasty and as Pierce notes was 'intelligent, unquestionably virtuous, traditionally pious, and possessed an easy familiarity with the convoluted etiquette of a royal court'.[24] In other words, Margaret was what we might now call 'old school', she understood how things worked and was a safe pair of hands for the king to lean on. This was a woman who was as noble as it was possible to be, and despite enormous turbulence throughout her life, had remained strong and ostensibly loyal to the house of Tudor. Their friendship may have been strong, but Katherine of Aragon's position as queen was only assured provided she gave the king healthy sons, something over which she had very little control. Devastatingly for the queen, the prolific baby-making machines that were the king's forebears had not extended to their own marriage bed. A year into the union she was delivered of a stillborn daughter. Not long afterwards a prince, Henry, named for his father, came into the world, only to die a little under two months later, to be followed by two further stillborn children. Princess Mary's arrival in 1516, whilst not the much desired male heir, but undoubtedly healthy, was therefore a huge comfort to the king and queen. Margaret was confirmed as a godmother to the infant princess, as was another living embodiment of the once great house of York – Catherine, Dowager Countess of Devonshire. Born Princess Catherine, she was the last surviving child of Edward IV and Elizabeth Woodville, and thus a great-aunt to Henry VIII. As the daughter of a one-time king, Catherine possessed what is arguably the most royal pedigree of any courtier alive under Tudor rule, a precarious position to be in. Thankfully, she was well respected and well liked. Her eldest son, another Henry, was especially close to the king, having 'been brought up of a child with his grace in his chamber'.[25]

Princess Mary's christening a few days later was recorded in detail and gives us some insight into the spectacle that surrounded this little girl. A reference to Margaret appears, stating she was present for the bishopping, another term for the confirmation of a child.

> 'From the court gate to the church door of the Friars was railed and hung with arras; the way being well gravelled and strewed with rushes. At the church door was set a house well framed of timber, covered with arras, where the princess with her godfather and godmother abode. There she received her name Mary. Then they entered the church, which was hung with cloth of needlework garnished with precious stone and pearls. She was preceded by a goodly sight of gentlemen and lords. Then followed the bason, borne by my lord of Devonshire, supported by Lord Herbert; the Lady Dorset bearing the Chrism. The Lord Chamberlain followed, with the Lord Steward on his right. Then the canopy, borne by Sir David Owen, Sir Nich Vaux, Sir Thos Aparre and Sir Thomas Boleyn, under which was the Princess, borne by the Countess of Surrey. The princess was assisted by the Duke of Norfolk at the head, and the Duke of Suffolk at the feet. Next the Lady Katharine, the Duchess of Norfolk etc. The Lord Cardinal godfather Lady Katharine and the Duchess of Norfolk godmothers at the font. The Countess of Salisbury at the bishopping. Then Te Deum sung by the King's chaplain.'[26]

Margaret's position as a key figure in the life of the infant princess was made official in 1520, when she was named as Lady Governess. Mary's household had been set up the year prior, and was normally based at Ditton Manor in Buckinghamshire. The king's expenditure on his daughter's upbringing came in at £1400 per year[27], the equivalent of over £700,000 by today's standards. If Reginald Pole is to be believed, the king and queen personally visited Margaret to ask her to take up the post, with the queen in particular imploring Margaret to acquiesce, which naturally, she did. Her role was made clear in a record from 13 May 1520, for she is titled 'Margaret Countess of Salisbury, Governess of the Princess Mary'. The king gave clear instruction to Margaret that Mary was to be educated as befitting a noblewoman of the time, connecting as Barbara Harris points out, that piety and female virtue went hand in hand. Margaret was instructed to ensure 'honourable education, and training in all virtuous demeanour. That is to say, at due times to serve God'.[28] This would be the start of a lifelong bond between Margaret and her young charge, who would come to think of the countess as her 'second mother'.[29] Not long afterwards, the king and queen set sail for France, where they would meet with the French king and his court at one of history's most lavish and arguably pointless exercises – 'The Field of the Cloth of Gold'. For nearly a month, the English and French royal courts continually attempted to outdo each other in a series of balls, feasts, games and contests. Two of Margaret's sons, Henry and Arthur, were part of the English retinue and actively engaged in the revelries that took place. Margaret's daughter, Ursula, was also recorded as being in attendance, despite being in the fourth month of her first pregnancy.[30] Arthur is also named as one 'of the noblemen and others appointed to attend upon the King and Queen at the interview with the French king'.[31] They were joined by their cousin, Henry Courtenay, 1st Marquess of Exeter, taking part in a joust, a favourite pastime for male members of the nobility. With their team clad in blue and white, bearing a sigil of a female hand pouring water onto a man's burning heart. As ever with Tudor England, the iconography used in such court activities deliberately evoked almost Arthurian chivalry. Arthur Pole won praise for his skill in the lists, bringing home one of the prizes handed out.[32] Back in England, Princess Mary, now established at Richmond Palace, held court on her parents' behalf. As she had been betrothed since the age of 2 to François, Dauphin of France, son of the French king and queen, Mary's overall welfare was not only the concern of the English royal court but also that of France. Accordingly, three men of the French king's trusted circle were sent to England to visit the young princess. Their report back provides an insight into the running of Mary's household and the respect accorded to Margaret Pole.

'On 28th June came the three gentlemen of France whose arrival they had notice from the Cardinal; and on Saturday after dinner, as tide was commodious for them, they being well accompanied by the Lord Barnes, Lord Darcy and others visited the Princess at Richmond. There were with her divers lords spiritual and temporal; and in the Presence Chamber besides the lady governess [countess of Salisbury] and her other gentlewomen, the duchess of Norfolk her three daughters the lady Margaret wife to the lord Herbert, countess of Worcester, the ladies Grey and Neville, the lord John's wife and others. She welcomed the French gentlemen with most goodly countenance, proper communication and pleasant pastime in playing at the virginals, that they greatly marvelled and rejoiced the same, her young and tender age considered.'[33]

The Tudor court was one which ran with strict protocol and hierarchy. With Margaret being mentioned first and notably addressed as standing beside the princess, the inference here suggests that behind Mary, Margaret was seen as the most important woman in the room. This is at odds with the accepted order of precedence, for in the next sentence we see that the Duchess of Norfolk was also present – then, as now, a duchess outranks a countess. Margaret's role as governess clearly elevated her standing beyond the norm, though her royal blood may have also played a role. For now, it seemed as if Lady Margaret Pole, and by extension her children's lives were destined for ever increasing royal favour. Alas, just a year into her appointment as Princess Mary's lady governess, everything would come crashing down. Margaret was removed from her position, her sons expelled from court, or worse imprisoned. The next chapter of the Pole family's destiny would be tied to the connections of kinship they shared with some of the most powerful members of court, none more so than Edward Stafford, 3rd Duke of Buckingham.

Chapter 4

The Pole Family at Court

In conjunction with her position as Lady Governess to the Princess Mary, Margaret Pole continued to solidify her family's prospects at the royal court, carving out roles for three of her sons and building solid alliances with other noble and gentry families. Her only daughter, Ursula, also began to benefit from close association to the king, and was officially recognised as a member of his family, as evidenced from 'a warrant to the Great Wardrobe for a gown of tawny velvet to the King's cousin Ursula Poulle' found in the national archives.[1] It was during this time that Margaret became one of the most powerful figures at the court of Henry VIII. Putting the queen aside, Margaret was one of the very few women who could wield what we might call 'soft power'. She was in a position which enabled her to speak and act on a level with the great male peers of the realm. We must be cognisant that the court was deeply patriarchal, so this level of both independence and position set Margaret apart from the other ladies of her time. Where they would be required to try and influence those close to the king and queen in the hope of advancement, Margaret by contrast enjoyed this status by virtue of who she naturally was. Like her male peers, she was one of those coveted to help advance the plight of others with ambition, and naturally her family and close kin would be those to whom she would pay most heed. Henry Pole, Baron Montagu, had been a courtier for some time, having received a knighthood for his involvement in the king's 1513 war with France, which saw the English occupation of Tournai take place. He was also kept busy in the maintenance of manors which he had inherited following his father's death. An indication of Henry Pole's growing importance in the governance of his mother's lands can also be seen, for he sat as a justice of the peace in five counties, Dorset, Wiltshire, Somerset, Hampshire and Sussex, with Geoffrey Pole also serving in the latter two.[2] Justices, sometimes known as Commissioners of the Peace, were elected representatives who would dispense summary justice locally, ensuring good governance in their area – local policemen before such a thing was known. Typically filled by sons of key noblemen or loyal bannermen, this role would have given Margaret's sons ample experience for when, particularly in the case of Baron Montagu, they themselves would be called upon to sit in judgement on trials tied to the crown.

Clearly Arthur Pole's success in the tiltyard of the Field of the Cloth of Gold had not been a fluke, for in 1516, the same year that he joined the king's household as a squire of the body, he was recorded once more as taking part in jousts, with great success. Given the king's own penchants for jousting, it is probable Arthur's apparent successes caught his master's eye. Squires of the body were personal attendants to the king, and thus a highly coveted role for any young man looking to rise through the ranks at court. The annuity paid by the king was for life, at £33 6s. 8d.[2] Evidently, Arthur performed his duties with aplomb, for just two years later he was promoted further to a gentlemen of the privy chamber, a position hand-selected by the king, which would provide greater access to the monarch than the vast majority of the court. The role was in effect, akin to a servant, something to a modern ear that sounds like an undesirable role, but for Tudor England was highly coveted. To serve the king, even if nobly born, was deemed a huge honour. Arthur also had the advantage of overseas court experience, albeit fleetingly. Two years before he joined the king's household, he had been part of the English retinue of courtiers who travelled to France alongside Princess Mary, the king's beautiful younger sister, for her marriage to the old French king, Louis XII. As the marriage only lasted for three months Arthur's stay on the continent was not long, but would have provided invaluable insight into the machinations of the court of England's great rival. Once back in his homeland, Arthur made good contacts amongst his peers, and was known to take part in a spot of gambling, for he is recorded in the accounts of his and the king's cousin, Henry Courtenay, as having played a round of shuffleboard with the marquess.[3]

One of the most established means of advancement in Tudor England was through advantageous marriage. As a member of the high nobility, Margaret would have understood this perfectly, and accordingly sought out marriages for Henry, Arthur, Ursula and George. Reginald, as a member of the Church, was not expected to marry. As heir apparent to the Pole dynasty, the intended marriage for Henry was naturally of the highest importance, although Arthur and Geoffrey also made matches appropriate to their rank. They may have been Margaret's second and fourth sons, but the allure of the royal blood in their veins was enough to net both men good matches. Arthur would marry Jane, daughter of Sir Roger Lewkenor and Eleanor Tuchet, a daughter of John Tuchet, 6th Baron Audley. The baron had been a one-time great supporter of King Edward IV, having defected from the Lancastrian cause when imprisoned in Calais by the Earl of Warwick. He had fought alongside the king in at least three of the war's battles – Mortimers Cross in 1461, Barnet in 1471 and in that same year, the conclusive battle of Tewkesbury, which finally crushed the core Lancastrian faction. Baron Audley would also serve the next king, going on to become the Lord High Treasurer for Richard III in December 1484.[4] It seems reasonable to assume that Jane, a granddaughter of such an ardent York loyalist, felt like an entirely natural choice for marriage to one of Margaret Pole's sons, both in terms of breeding and ancestral ties. As Jane and her sister were the only children of Sir Roger, they were joint heiresses to his entire estate. She also came with considerable wealth in her own right, having previously been married to, and subsequently widowed by, Sir Christopher Pickering of Ellerton, by whom she had a daughter, Anne. On her first husband's death, his wealth would revert to her and their young child. Her fertility proven and riches assured, Jane was a fine prize indeed. Arthur and Jane would have four children, a son, Henry, born around 1525 and three daughters, Jane, whose date of birth is unknown, Margaret in 1527 and finally Mary in 1529. Putting the successes of their marriage bed aside, we do not have much insight into how well Arthur and his wife actually got on. What we do know however, is that Arthur struggled to maintain a good relationship with his father-in-law. In October 1522 he wrote a letter, to an unknown recipient, in which he hoped that the Earl of Arundel would change his mind and come to his aid in a dispute over lands Arthur felt should have come to him from Sir Roger. In it he says:

> 'Sir, I am much obliged for the trouble you took with me when I was in Sussex. The King has written to the earl of Arundel to further my cause, and to you to deliver the letter. I beg you will also deliver the other that he sends to my father-in-law, though I know it shall be a great trouble

unto you to meddle with such a man; howbeit you know his conditions best of any man. If I cannot recompense you before I die, I hope the King will, for he will be very glad if I obtain my purpose. When I told him how the earl of Arundel handled me, he was greatly miscontent, and told me to speak to Mr. More to devise a sharp letter to him; but More thought it better to send him a loving letter first. I trust the Earl will now do all he can, as the King writes so favourably. The King thinks my father-in-law unmeet, considering his age and small experience in the wars. If the Earl can bring my father-in-law to consent to let me have his lands to farm at the value at which they were assessed before the commissioners, which is far more than they are worth, then you shall say the King desires my father-in-law's letter, to let me have the land for 300 marks yearly, he retaining the manor of Cratton, as he himself promised to the King. I leave the matter to your discretion, as you know best what to do.'[5]

Without knowing who this letter was intended for, we cannot be sure how it was received, but it clearly highlights a fractious relationship between Arthur and his father-in-law, which must have been disappointing considering their ancestors' closeness. That the king himself waded into the disagreement, and proposed what we must assume to be Sir Thomas More also getting involved, suggests it was taken seriously by those at the top.

Geoffrey would marry Constance, daughter (and co-heiress) of Sir Edmund Pakenham, a gentleman usher in the queen's household. Just a few years into the marriage, Geoffrey's father-in-law died, which saw his fortune divided between Constance and her sister Katherine much sooner than had been expected. Although this would net Geoffrey additional properties across both Hampshire and Sussex, and by extension strengthen Margaret's hold across the south of England, rather like his elder brought Arthur, there is evidence which alludes to a fractious relationship with his in-laws. The will of Sir Edmund makes one sole mention of Geoffrey, when it states that Constance would receive 'ten pounds which I paid to her husband Geoffrey Pole'.[6] Familial custom of the time dictated that once married into a family, sons or daughters-in-law would typically then be addressed as such. The somewhat cold 'her husband' would suggest that the family wanted to distance themselves from association with Geoffrey, as if by not naming him more affectionately, it created a distinction in their interests and his. This is compounded further, for also in the will is the presence of Sir Edmund's other son-in-law, Edmond Mervyn, who is referred to fondly as 'my son'. Hazel Pierce puts forward a compelling argument that the reason for this lack of warmth towards Geoffrey, who was well known for being both affable and popular, is that his burgeoning financial woes, which would in time turn disastrous, had invoked his father-in-law's vexation. It would have been natural for Sir Edmund to have grave concerns that his daughter's fortune could be compromised by her fiscally inadequate husband, and so he perhaps took steps to safeguard his family's future. If so, it was sage reasoning, for Geoffrey's financial problems would follow him throughout his life.

As referenced earlier, the marriage of Henry Pole was of the most importance to Margaret. As her heir apparent and therefore the expected future Earl of Salisbury, the choice of his wife was essential to get right. Margaret would arrange a marriage to Jane, daughter of George Neville, 5th Baron Bergavenny. As a maternal great-great-great-granddaughter of John of Gaunt, son of King Edward III, Jane Neville had a tincture of royal blood in her veins, which naturally enhanced her suitability on the marriage market. Upon closer inspection of Jane's ancestry, she could also trace a direct descent to this same king via her mother, making her unquestionably noble from both sides of her family. This also means that Henry Pole's great-grandmother, Cecily, was a brother to Jane's great-grandfather, Edward. Once again, this highlights the complexity of the bloodlines which descend from King Edward III. The marriage would thus join two families whose descent was as grand as each other's, another solid link in the ever expanding web of Plantagenet dynasts. As this union was the highest in profile, we have considerable evidence available on how it was contracted, which highlights Margaret's own formidable negotiation skills. The indenture, which in effect outlined the terms and conditions of the union, is extensive, and although no fixed date can be put forward as to when the marriage took place, we can say with some confidence that it was between 1515 and 1519. The indenture is dated '8 July 7 Hen VIII [1515]', the inclusion of the seven here dictating that it was the seventh year of the king's reign. The crux of the negotiation came down to the siring of healthy sons by Jane Neville, although significant attention is also given as to who would be picking up the tab for food and drink. Both parties would, to use modern parlance, split the bill, but any materials needed for the outfits to be worn by bride and groom would be picked up by their respective families. Grants of money and land would be gifted to the newlyweds, but also Margaret herself. The National Archives at Kew hold the indenture in its entirety, as part of the private and confiscated papers seized following the family's downfall. It is stated that:

> '£200 to the use of the said Countess during her life without impeachment of waste and after her death to the performance of her will for 10 years next after her death and after the said 10 years to the use of my lord Montague and his heirs of his body. Also of £100 by year to the use of my lord Montague and Jane his wife and the said heirs of the said Lord Montague.'[7]

It was also written into the agreement that the children of the couple, and more importantly their gender, would impact how money would cross paths between the two families. All eventualities were considered, with Margaret on the receiving end of lands and money if Jane died without giving Henry Pole children, with the reverse occurring should Henry Pole die before begetting children from his wife. It was also made clear that 'If the said lord [Henry Pole] have no issue male or they happen to die then payment to cease and repayments to be made by the said countess of what is paid hereof'.[8] Thankfully for both families, the virility of the York dynasty held true, for Henry and Jane had three, possibly four, children: Catherine, Henry and Winifred, the potential fourth being a second son, Thomas. Thomas Pole is only fleetingly mentioned in a couple of sources, both of which suggest he was born around 1520, married one Elizabeth Wingfield, and died in early adulthood without having had children. Given the lack of standardised birth and death registrations at the time, it is entirely possible that there was indeed a fourth child of the house of Montagu, but as no reference is made by Montagu himself, or indeed by Margaret, his existence is at best sceptical. The Montagu family would be primarily based at Henry Pole's favoured home of Bockmer House. Montagu would continue to have a loving and close relationship with his mother, and although Margaret was the de facto head of the Pole family, Henry was the family's official representative from a court perspective. His brother Reginald's secretary would confirm as much, stating he (Henry) was 'the chief stay of his family'.[9]

The other major marriage that Margaret would negotiate would be that of her daughter. Although Tudor England was a deeply patriarchal society, it was often the job of daughters of the nobility to bring greater prestige to their family name, for on the whole daughters would marry 'up', that is, they would wed the sons of noblemen of higher rank than their parents. This was certainly true of Ursula Pole's union, for Margaret had contracted her daughter in marriage to Henry Stafford, only son of Edward Stafford, 3rd Duke of Buckingham. Interestingly, the marriage itself was first suggested to the duke by Cardinal Wolsey[10], although Ursula was not the only prospective high born daughter-in-law on the table. Buckingham and Wolsey had initially wanted to wed Henry Stafford to the daughter of the Earl of Shrewsbury. The duke had coveted this potential bride for his son years earlier, but had made too great a demand of the dowry she would come with, which was beyond the scope of Shrewsbury's finances.[11] This was not unusual, for the nobility of England would often have intentions grander than their coffers could allow. This ultimately took the Shrewsbury match off the table, and so Buckingham agreed to the union with Ursula Pole. This marriage would, all being well, in the fullness of time see Ursula become Duchess of Buckingham, a title which would have meant she outranked all members of her family, including her mother. After royal dukes, the dukedom of Buckingham was the grandest in England, followed closely by that of Norfolk. Like Margaret Pole, the then Duke of Buckingham was descended from strong Plantagenet blood, being the son of Katherine Woodville, a sister of Queen Elizabeth Woodville, thus he was a nephew by marriage to King Edward IV. He was also descended in the legitimate, albeit female line from King Edward III. Henry VIII, we must remember, also descended through an illegitimate line. In Buckingham, this royal-but-not-royal status engendered a man of supreme arrogance and entitlement, but little tact, which in a court as volatile as King Henry VIII's was extremely dangerous.

Buckingham, as a member of the old and well established high nobility, had no time for men of lowly origin, who had risen through the ranks by virtue of their talent, as opposed to their birth. Like his comrade, Thomas Howard, 3rd Duke of Norfolk, he greatly resented upstarts such as Wolsey who continued to gain ever greater power with the king, which in turn diminished the cache typically enjoyed by men of his creed. A union between the Stafford and Pole families was therefore entirely suitable, and strengthened ties between two of the country's premier houses. If the king, who would have been required to provide assent to the marriage, held any reservations about two Plantagenet members of his court marrying, he did not voice them at the time. Ursula was around the age of 15 at her wedding, her groom a couple of years older. She came with a dowry worth 3000 marks, the equivalent to over a million pounds by modern standards, which was to be topped up by a further 1000 marks 'if the Countess [Margaret] gets back certain lands from the King'[12], the lands here being those debated between Margaret and the king on behalf of William Compton discussed in the preceding chapter. Margaret would also gift the couple properties in the south-west of England. Clearly the fecundity which blessed those of Yorkist descent extended to Ursula and her husband, for during their marriage she would give birth a staggering fourteen times – seven boys and seven girls. For the first couple of years of Ursula's marriage she would have been known as the Countess of Stafford, for her husband took on the secondary courtesy title of Earl of Stafford from his father. This would all change however following the Duke of Buckingham's arrest, and later execution, which greatly threatened the safety of the wider Pole family. Although they had worked together, and as referenced earlier had agreed upon the Buckingham-Pole marriage, the distaste Buckingham felt for Cardinal Wolsey was reciprocated, and given the latter's unwavering loyalty to the king, such enmity had scope to turn deadly for the duke. Buckingham has often been cited as one of the very few men who may well have been guilty of the crimes he was convicted of, at least under the laws of the day. In the spring of 1521, the cardinal officially moved against the duke, ordering his arrest with a trial set for 13 May. According to the evidence brought forward, the origins of his downfall lay in the failings of the royal marriage bed. It was said that once it became clear that the king and queen's union would not provide a healthy male heir, talk sprang up as to who would be the natural successor to the crown.

Three men of Buckingham's own household, Charles Knyvet, the duke's surveyor, John Delacourt and Robert Gilbert, were questioned at length, and according to them, Buckingham saw the answer to the question quite plainly: the rightful heir would be himself. He was also reported as saying to his son-in-law, Ralph, Earl of Westmorland 'There be two new Dukes [Norfolk and Suffolk] created in England, but that if anything but good should happen to the king, he, the Duke of Buckingham was next in succession to the crown of England'.[13] To imagine, let alone openly speak of the king's death was treason, a legal technicality that would help undo Anne Boleyn some years later.*

If he did indeed suggest that he should be the next king, and if the reports from his household are to be believed – that he threatened to kill the king himself – then he was most certainly guilty of high treason, which was a one way trip to the executioner's scaffold. Treason by the spoken word alone was not a new concept under English law, but would come into play most forcefully under the rule of Henry VIII, particularly when Thomas Cromwell began his process of reinterpreting, or simply rewriting, England's laws. Significantly, the king felt concerned enough about the rumours to order a full investigation, even examining some of the witnesses personally. This, we must remember, came many years before the king's more tyrannical side would gain full exposure. He was, by and large, still a reasonable man, who did not turn on people for slights real or imagined. Buckingham was a major member of the nobility, the first of his ilk to be brought low under the king. The duke was arrested on 8 April 1521 and shortly thereafter tried by seventeen of his peers. The sentence of death, a foregone conclusion, was read out by Thomas Howard, 2nd Duke of Norfolk who according to Hall did so with tears streaming down his face.[14] Buckingham was beheaded on 17 May 1521. According to an eyewitness account, the executioner took three strokes of the axe to sever his head.[15] Buckingham had not been the

---

* A major piece of evidence brought against Anne Boleyn in May 1536 was that she had spoken of the king's death, for she supposedly said to the courtier Henry Norris after he explained that he was waiting to marry 'you look for dead men's shoes, for if aught came to the king but good, you would look to have me'. In other words, you wish to marry me when the king dies.

only person caught up in the fallout. Henry Pole and his father-in-law, Lord Bergavenny, who himself was son-in-law to the duke, had also been implicated. The two men were imprisoned under a suspicion of misprision, for failing to reveal Buckingham's treasonous behaviour.[16] Although Montagu was released without punishment, Bergavenny's imprisonment would last for nearly a year. It would result in his being called to the king's bench in February 1522, where he was stripped of office and ordered to sell his home, Birling Manor, to the king. He was then fined a further 10,000 marks, minus the value of Birling, again payable to the crown. This may have financially crippled him, but at least he kept his head. Bergavenny's release would have a longer lasting negative impact on the overall success of Montagu and his wife's marriage, however. When Margaret Pole had negotiated the marriage alongside him, Jane and her elder sister Elizabeth, wife of the Earl of Bridgewater, had been joint heiresses to their father's entire estate. In 1519, Bergavenny had married for the third time, and at the age of approximately 50 began producing no fewer than eight further children, three of whom were sons. This greatly reduced the value of Jane's planned inheritance. What had once been a valuable commodity on the marriage market for Margaret Pole's firstborn, was now set to return little gain. Like the marriage of her daughter, this was not the glittering future everyone had hoped for.

An easy and perhaps close relationship between Buckingham and Montagu is clear, for following the formal attainder against the duke, his household accounts were reviewed, detailing that he had 'Lost a game of cards to Lord Montague' for which he had paid £65 2s 9d[17]; the same bill makes mention of payments to his daughter-in-law, Ursula. Although he would not join his brother in prison, Arthur Pole also had a brush with danger when he instructed Lord Leonard Grey to 'write concerning the imprisonment of the duke'. Not long after the news of this broke, Arthur was expelled from the court, his closeness to the king counting for little. Margaret managed to sufficiently distance herself from the storm, with Richard Pace, a diplomat at the royal court, stating 'the matter is under debate because of her nobility and goodness'.[18] The Pole family's closeness to Buckingham now became highly problematic, and was not helped by the duke directly, for he said of Margaret's brother's death 'God would punish it, by not suffering the King's issue to prosper'.[19] It is this, and their closeness to Buckingham, which no doubt played a role in implicating the Pole family in the affair. It is of course entirely plausible, however, that it was mere guilt by association. Certainly the close ties to a man convicted of treason had the ability to reopen old wounds, and was sufficient enough reason for Margaret to be removed from her post as governess to the Princess Mary. Ursula Pole's own glittering future was also now in tatters. As the daughter of a countess and daughter-in-law of a duke, Ursula had developed a taste for finery, which is evidenced through the inclusion of expensive materials such as damask, ermine fur and velvet in her wardrobe inventories.[20] For the foreseeable future, however, she would be required to endure a more frugal existence, as under the attainder of her father-in-law, his many estates, which would in time have come to her husband, now reverted to the crown. It is interesting to note, however, that the lands and revenues drawn from Buckingham's attainder, valued at £5000 (over £2,500,000 by modern standards), would be divided up between the king and men he felt he could trust implicitly, which included Sir Edward Neville, the brother of George, Baron Bergavenny, and Sir Nicholas Carew, a close ally of the Pole family. This would suggest that the king's actions against Buckingham were reasonably concentrated to the duke's family and nearest kin, and that for now, the wider 'White Rose of York' families remained quite removed from the scandal. It was during this time that, as referenced in the preceding chapter, Margaret would take in her granddaughter, Margaret Stafford, as a means of lessening the strain placed on Ursula and her husband.

Mercifully for all concerned, the king, at least at this stage of his reign, did not hold onto a grudge for too long. Following his release from prison, Montagu joined his brother Arthur in the king's campaign into France in 1523. They would go under the command of the king's oldest and arguably greatest friend, Charles Brandon, Duke of Suffolk. Although the campaign itself was largely ineffectual, Arthur clearly impressed the duke, for he was knighted by Suffolk on 1 November that year.[21] Montagu was also recorded as being in attendance at the Christmas celebrations, in which he joined the king, Suffolk and the Earl of Devon in the traditional festive jousts.[22] In 1522, Ursula and her husband were given a smattering of the lands and property in Stafford, Chester and Salop (modern day Shropshire), that had been revoked in the late duke's attainder.[23] Although this enabled them to live to a respectable standard, if not to the level of grandeur they had previously enjoyed, it would ultimately prove to be insufficient. As Ursula and her husband's household exponentially grew, through the many children that they had, their situation would, in time, become dire. By 1529, Lord Stafford had begun to petition for greater restoration of lands seized by the crown in the wake of his father's downfall. His letter to the king provides a fascinating insight into the financial difficulty that he and his wife supposedly endured, and the response given by the king's then chief minister, Cardinal Wolsey, highlights his own frustration with the ongoing saga. At this stage, Stafford and Ursula had been granted 500 marks of land to live on, but the former complained that they were undervalued. From the records, his plight was perceived as being one of ungrateful greediness by Wolsey, who suggested he accept them as they were, but also said to give him time to push the matter further with the king, in the hope of securing greater financial returns. When Stafford continued to push the matter however, Wolsey effectively threatened him, saying 'he should either be content with the lands, or he should have none at all, but the King's high displeasure'.[24] Usually a man of composure, such a heavy handed rebuttal suggests that by this stage the cardinal had suffered quite enough from this grasping nobleman. It would not be the last of Wolsey and Stafford's interactions though, for the latter had spent a great deal of money refurbishing a house in Sussex in which he had lived for three years. Stafford was compelled by the cardinal to sell it and break up his household in order to fund somewhere for himself, his wife and their then seven children to live, having supposedly boarded at a nearby abbey for over four years.[25]

Directly following Buckingham's downfall, Margaret Pole spent much of her time away from court at her many country houses, waiting for times to change. By 1522 she had begun to receive New Year's gifts from the queen, a positive sign. However, she would not be fully enveloped back into the royal fold until reappointed to Princess Mary's household, again in the role of Lady Governess. This took place in 1525. Mary was 9 years old and, as Prince Arthur had been under the reign of Henry VII, she was sent to the Welsh Marches to govern in her father's name. Although the king did not formally acknowledge Mary as Princess of Wales, the inference was clear for all to see – Mary was acknowledged as the king's uncontested legitimate heir, for now at least. This is not to say other candidates were also spoken of, mostly notably Henry Fitzroy, the king's illegitimate son by Elizabeth 'Bessie' Blount, whom he had chosen to greatly ennoble as Duke of Richmond and Somerset. The Richmond title was especially grand, for it was the first creation of a Richmond dukedom, having hitherto been an earldom (two rungs down from a duke in peerage seniority), and was particularly symbolic as it had been the title held by the king's paternal grandfather. Fitzroy was also given the responsibility of the north of England, in effect replicating the role Mary would execute in Wales. To be separated from her parents at a young age sounds appalling to a twenty-first-century ear, but for Tudor England this was entirely normal, particularly for someone of Mary's status. As governess, it was natural that Margaret would join her and run the princess's day to day existence in Wales. The experience must surely have conjured up a considerable sense of deja-vu from her time spent with her late husband under Prince Arthur's short lived tenure as Prince of Wales. Margaret was easily the most senior female member of Mary's 300-plus strong entourage, and was joined by Bishop John Voysey who was made Lord President of the Council, Lord Dudley as Mary's chamberlain and Lord Ferrers as her steward. These four figures were, in effect, the household management, but as their young charge was female, the bulk of responsibility landed with Margaret. The household became a sort of court in miniature, with all the pomp and ceremony exhibited at the central royal court, mirrored at Ludlow. The king and queen gave strict instructions to Margaret on how Mary was to be looked after, detailing everything from what she should be fed to how frequently she was to pray, what languages she should learn and how often she should take exercise. A letter from the queen during Mary's time at Ludlow shows us not only the close bond that existed between mother and daughter, despite the separation, but also the high esteem in which the queen continued to view Margaret, for she signed it off saying 'It shall be a great comfort to me to see you keep your latin and fair writing and all. And so I pray You to recommend me to my Lady of Salisbury. At Woburn this Friday night, Your loving mother, Katherine the Queen'.[26]

After three years spent in Wales, Mary's household was packed up and returned to the capital on what should have been a temporary move. They could not know it at the time, but Mary's retinue would never return to the Marches. Margaret's role, itinerant as ever, did not disappear; instead a new court would be set up for the princess near to her parents, again with the Countess of Salisbury at its helm. Thanks to a detailed letter from Venetian Ambassador, Mario Savorgnano, who visited Mary's household, we have a fascinating insight into how Mary spent her days, but more significantly it contains a physical description of Margaret. The letter reads:

'Next we went to another palace, called Richmond, where the Princess, her daughter, resides; and having asked the maggiordomo for permission to see her, we spoke to the chamberlain, and then to the governess, and they made us wait. Then after seeing the palace we returned into a hall, and having entered a spacious chamber where there were some venerable old men with whom we discovered, the Princess came forth accompanied by a noble lady advanced in years, who is her governess, and by six maids of honour. We kissed her hand, and she asked how we had been in England, and if we had seen their Majesties, her father and mother, and what we thought of the country; she then turned to her attendants, desiring them to treat us well, and withdrew into her chamber. This Princess is not very tall, has a pretty face, and is well proportioned with a very beautiful complexion, and is 15 years old. She speaks Spanish, French, and Latin, besides her own mother-English tongue, is well grounded in Greek, and understands Italian, but does not venture to speak it. She sings excellently, and plays on several instruments, so that she combines every accomplishment. We were then taken to a sumptuous repast, after which we returned to our lodging, whither, according to the fashion of the country, the Princess sent us a present of wine and ale (which last is another beverage of theirs), and white bread.'[27]

A royal cousin of the princess, Margaret Douglas, daughter of Margaret Tudor, Queen of Scotland and thus a niece of the king, would join Mary's entourage, and from here a lifelong friendship between the two women would develop. Such was Margaret Douglas's loyalty to Mary that when, years later, Mary had become queen and for a time lodged her younger sister Elizabeth in confinement, Margaret Douglas quickly (and intentionally noisily) refitted her apartments, which was directly above where Elizabeth was held, in a callous bid to stop the young girl from sleeping. Although Mary's life at this time must have seemed idyllic, it would not last, for the king continued to be troubled by his lack of a legitimate male heir. Mary may have been a princess, with the love of the common people, but that could not mask the fact that to Henry's mind, women were unfit to rule. His desire for a son became the king's great obsession, and with the appearance of a young, glamorous and seductively dark eyed courtier, Mary's future and that of Margaret and her family, would once more undergo a colossal shift in fortune.

Chapter 5

The Scandal of Christendom

'The King had been caught in the snare of unlawful love
with the Lady Anne'

Sir Geoffrey Pole

Anne Boleyn. A name which after nearly 500 years' distance continues to throw up a cacophony of varying opinion. Arguably the most famous 'other woman' in history, she would go from being the younger daughter of a middling noble, to King Henry VIII's great obsession, his second wife, the catalyst for the English reformation, mother of Elizabeth I, and most infamously, the first queen consort in English history to be executed. Despite this notoriety however, she remains something of an enigma. Historians still openly debate when she was born, with the years 1501 and 1507 being most consistently put forward, placing her at either around 28 or 35 years of age at the time of her death. Such fundamentals as how she looked also remain uncertain, for in the wake of her momentous fall from grace, save for a damaged medal, all known portraits of Anne from life were destroyed. From the smattering of descriptions we do have, something of the woman can be pieced together though. According to reports she was petite, with a small bosom, an oval face, long dark brown hair and eyes that were almost black in colour. Her complexion, referred to as 'swarthy', was what we may now call olive skinned. The contrast she presented to the pale skin, blue eyes and blonde hair that were always in vogue at the English royal court was therefore stark. Anne spent her formative years on the European continent, serving first Margaret of Austria, before being called to join the household of Henry VIII's younger sister Princess Mary, following her marriage to King Louis XII of France. Following the French king's death and the return of Mary to England, Anne transferred to the household of the new queen, Claude, wife of King Francis I, with whom she would stay for nearly seven years.[1] This period of Anne

Boleyn's life, although only fleetingly recorded in a smattering of letters, would entirely mould the woman who would later be described by her biographer Eric Ives as 'the most influential and important queen consort England has ever had'.[2] Although Anne came from ambitious stock, no one could have predicted just how far her star would rise. The Boleyn family's elevation to prominence would be a defining chapter in the relationship between the king and the Pole family. As Anne Boleyn ascended and Katherine of Aragon's power waned, those close to the latter would feel its pinch. How Anne Boleyn came to be the second wife of King Henry VIII, and indeed her downfall after just three years of marriage, is still hotly debated by historians around the world. What cannot be overlooked however, is the shift in both power and favour that the Pole family would undergo during Anne's moment in the sun. This is not to suggest that Anne was the sole reason for the Poles perpetually volatile relationship with the king, indeed some of their own activity was as detrimental to their cause as that of the new queen, not to mention the colossal transference of power in the political landscape of the time, with the ever increasing influence of Thomas Cromwell. At the crux of the issue was the very nature of the Pole family's religious beliefs and their fierce loyalty to Katherine of Aragon, and by extension, her daughter, Princess Mary. Like the other 'White Rose of York' families such as the Courtenays, the Poles, as we have seen, were conservative by nature. Religious reform was anathema to their way of thinking, which would in time put them on a collision course with the king's second wife, and his wily chief minister. Although not as openly hostile to Anne Boleyn as Gertrude Courtenay, Marchioness of Exeter, Margaret Pole would be put under intense scrutiny during the ascent of Anne as Henry VIII's second queen, whilst her sons, ostensibly advancing the plight of the king and his new love, would have to put duty to the crown ahead of their own morals.

The king's decision to part with Katherine of Aragon, contrary to popular belief, was not at the insistence of Anne Boleyn. The notion that she sauntered into the king's life and demanded he make her his queen is largely inaccurate. It is true that she would become central to 'the king's great matter', but she alone was certainly not its architect. Exactly when Henry VIII began to seriously consider leaving Katherine of Aragon can only be guessed at. Katherine's last pregnancy, which had resulted in a stillborn daughter, was towards the end of 1518. This would suggest that thereafter the royal marriage had become sexless, or more likely that the queen had entered the menopause. She was five years older than the king, making her over middle-aged by the standards of the time. We know the king was continuing to court mistresses with the birth of his illegitimate son Henry Fitzroy in the summer of 1519. Even though the boy was born out of wedlock, his robust health and crucially, gender, was a source of great rejoicing and comfort for the king. Fitzroy was living proof (to Henry's mind) that the problem lay not with him, but with the queen. He *could* have sons. This fact would be germane to the king's actions, for thereafter, he would begin to question the very validity of the marriage. So, what was to be done, what could be done? Despite the religious turbulence of the latter half of the reign, Henry was at heart a deeply religious man. He would live, and die, in the Catholic faith, albeit one of his own devising at the end. Let us not assume that this was feigned. He believed he was divinely appointed by God, and so his lack of sons by the queen, surely, as he saw it, pointed to some impediment in the marriage. To annul the marriage would, the king hoped, be the easiest course of action, but on what grounds could he hope to achieve this? As a European royal princess with staggeringly powerful relations across the continent, not to mention deeply beloved of the English people, the king's decision to break from Katherine would have to be watertight. Henry would lean on scripture, obsessing over clauses in the book of Leviticus which stated 'You shall not uncover the nakedness of your brother's wife: because it is the nakedness of your brother' (18:16), which goes on to say 'If a man shall take his brother's wife, it is an unclean thing: he has uncovered his brother's nakedness. They shall be childless' (20:21). That the king had a daughter, and was thus not childless, he chose to overlook, conveniently deciding that the meaning laid out by Leviticus was intended to apply solely to male children.

Anne Boleyn had been recalled to the English court as part of the intended marriage treaty to her distant cousin, James Butler. The purpose of the marriage was a political one. The hope was that the union would end an ongoing dispute between Anne and James's fathers over the title and estates of the earldom of Ormond. The king, not wanting to provoke a potential civil war in Ireland, proposed the marriage himself. It would ultimately come to nothing. The reason for the breakdown of the negotiation is sadly lost to us, although we can say with some confidence that this wasn't because the king had already fallen for Anne; in truth he hardly knew her. Thus, Anne Boleyn arrived back at the royal court, and made her entrée on 4 March 1522. A pageant, known as the *Château Vert*[3] (Green Castle) had been staged to welcome the Imperial Ambassadors to England, in which notable ladies of the court played the roles of different virtues. The scene was famously recreated for television in Showtime's popular retelling of Henry VIII's reign *The Tudors*, but the element in which the king 'claims' Anne Boleyn is fictitious. Mary Boleyn, Anne's elder sister, would take on the role of kindness, whilst Anne would land the role of perseverance, a virtue which would in time, turn out to be phenomenally apt. In a further twist of irony, two other women who made up the party would eventually become some of Anne's fiercest critics – her former mistress, the king's sister, Princess Mary, now Duchess of Suffolk following her controversial marriage to the king's oldest friend Charles Brandon, who played the role of beauty, and Gertrude Courtenay, who took on the role of honour. Another notable figure was Jane Parker, playing constancy, who would eventually become the sister-in-law of Anne and Mary Boleyn. Boasting charm in abundance and noticeably continental behaviour, Anne soon proved exceptional from the other ladies of the court. She was fashionable, quick witted, vivacious and extremely intelligent. Outspoken and emotionally immoderate, Anne could dance, she could recite poetry, she loved the prospect of debate, Anne was a rare breed for Tudor England indeed. Lancelot de Carles, a French poet and diplomat would famously quip that Anne was 'so graceful that you would never have taken her for an Englishwoman, but for a French woman born'. Anne also possessed a well-hidden but nonetheless burgeoning commitment to religious reform, something we must remember that was abhorrent to the likes of Margaret Pole, her family and the other conservatives at court.

In short, Anne Boleyn stood out.

She had hoped to marry Henry Percy, heir to the earldom of Northumberland, a marriage which would have been highly advantageous, but Henry Percy's father would not agree to the match, and nor would the man in whose household Percy was serving – Wolsey. Thomas Wolsey's role in blocking Anne Boleyn from marrying the man of her choice would be the start of a fractious relationship between the two. In time, Wolsey's own failure to recognise the danger Anne could pose to his authority would be his prize mistake. With her desired marriage quashed, Anne took up a position as lady-in-waiting to Queen Katherine, and it is during this time that four years after arriving back in England, she finally caught the king's attention. He had previously had a sexual relationship with Anne's elder sister Mary, with some speculating that her children may have actually been the king's, rather than Mary's husband, William Carey. In 1526 however, all the attention had shifted solely to Anne. The king made several overtures, requesting that she become his official mistress, assuring her that he would put aside all other women in the kingdom to have her. At this point therefore, we must assume that the king had an all-encompassing passion for Anne Boleyn, but did not think of her as a suitable wife, and answer to his son-less prayers. Unlike her sister who gave in easily, Anne would remain firm in her refusal to become Henry's *maîtresse-en-titre*. It is easy, with hindsight, to say that even then, Anne was holding out for a bigger prize, perhaps recognising how quickly the king disposed of those he had won too quickly. Reginald Pole would certainly echo this, when in 1533 he said Anne had refused to sleep with Henry knowing 'how soon he was sated with those who had served him as his mistress'. The king would bombard Anne with letters expressing his ardent love, even doodling their initials inside a love heart, evoking the behaviour of lovestruck teenagers. As Anne's responses to these letters are lost, we cannot be sure how she reacted or felt about what was happening. Either way, the exchanges would be the start of a seven year legal battle which would irrevocably alter the political landscape and identity of England.

The first public sign that the king had begun proceedings to investigate the validity of his marriage came in May 1527. He was ordered to come before Cardinal Wolsey (take the term 'ordered' loosely here, given it would have been the king pulling the strings, but was required to maintain a front of law abiding civility) to answer the accusation that he had unlawfully married his late brother's widow. In that same month, Henry and Anne made their first joint public appearance together at a ball held in Greenwich Palace. At this time, the queen remained largely in the dark about the seriousness of her situation, and Lady Margaret Pole dutifully kept up her role as Princess Mary's governess with aplomb. At the start of the year she had accompanied Mary to court, when marriage discussions between the English and French were serious enough that envoys from the French court made the journey to conclude negotiations. Two grooms had been offered up to wed the 11-year-old princess, King

Francis I himself, and his far more suitable second son, Henry, Duke of Orléans. The latter option was ultimately decided as being the better choice, with the two formally contracted to be married shortly after the end of the visit. This, like the other marriages her father had negotiated, would never come to fruition. The duke would famously wed a niece of Pope Clement VII, Catherine de Medici, a few years later.

With uncharacteristic reserve, Wolsey decreed that he would not declare the royal marriage invalid on his own, but instead suggested canvassing the opinion of lawyers and theologians on the justness of the king's cause.[4] He dutifully set off for France, hoping to gain traction with those of influence in Europe. It was during this time that the king finally opened up to Katherine about his troubled conscience, insisting they separate for the good of the realm, and their own souls, for he said they had been living in sin. According to the Imperial Ambassador, Inigo Mendoza:

> 'The Queen, bursting into tears, and being too much agitated to reply, the King said to her, by way of consolation, that all should be done for the best and begged her to keep secrecy upon what he had told her. This the King must have said, as it is generally believed, to inspire her with confidence and prevent her from seeking the redress she is entitled to by right, and also to keep the intelligence from the public, for so great is the attachment that the English bear to the Queen.'[5]

To make matters worse for the queen, the actions of her relatives on the continent did more to damage her relationship with the king, at least at this stage, than Anne Boleyn ever could. Armies under the control of Katherine's nephew Charles V, Holy Roman Emperor, had sacked Rome, imprisoning Pope Clement VII. The action was widely condemned at the English court, and when coupled with the Emperor's own inconsistent support of England's interests, greatly diminished the value of Katherine of Aragon to England as queen, at least in the eyes of the king. It also made what Wolsey and the king had initially hoped to be a simple matter of annulment all the more challenging, for the very man who could have granted an annulment, the Pope, was held prisoner by the queen's nephew. Although she maintained the great respect and love of the people, to Henry she was now a barren burden, even if he did, in all probability, still have deep affection for her. We must not forget how new and thus vulnerable the Tudor dynasty was. There were many people still living who could well recall King Edward IV, the power of the Yorkist dynasty, and crucially, its vast offspring – Margaret Pole of course being one. Conversely, those bearing the name of Tudor could be counted on just one hand. Margaret was 10 when her uncle had died, and if we include the uncrowned King Edward V into the mix, Henry VIII was the fifth monarch she had known in her own lifetime. Margaret had seen usurpation happen before, what was to stop it happening again. What was to stop a son of her's from being instrumental in such an act, or sons of the countless other Plantagenets prominent at court? For a man such as Henry VIII, to not have a legitimate son was not only a personal problem, but a political disaster. The king knew all too well that there were many about him with claims to his throne, and that the only assured method of avoiding civil unrest was to finally have legitimate male heirs to protect his dynasty. Quite simply for the king, he had to remarry.

Misjudging how his wife would react to the situation, the king instructed Katherine to retire from public life and take up residence at a nunnery. Understandably, the queen who had always loved her husband dearly, was heartbroken, but that did not stop her own pride from coming to the surface. Having been hitherto a deeply obedient wife, she now refused to accept what was asked of her, insisting she had not known Prince Arthur carnally, and that her marriage to the king was valid in the eyes of both God and the Pope. Her refusal to accept the king's wishes would result in banishment from court and being separated from her daughter. Had Katherine acquiesced to the king's demands then there is an argument that life would have been easier, particularly for the princess, for it would have ensured Mary remained in the line of succession. Mary's own fierce loyalty to her mother would in turn have dire consequences in the relationship she held with her father. The queen also flouted Henry's request to 'keep the intelligence from the public', for she promptly instructed her servant Francisco Felipez to travel to her nephew to make him aware of the situation. Despite an attempted arrest by the king, Felipez achieved his task and alerted Charles to what was happening back in England. Responding without haste, not only to his aunt, but also the king and the Pope, the Emperor threatened that 'We cannot desert the Queen, our good aunt, in her troubles and intend doing all we can in her favour'.[6] It was also at this time that the king sent his secretary of state, William Knight, to Rome to secure a papal dispensation which directly impacted his planned marriage to Anne Boleyn. The crux of the dispensation was that it would allow the king to marry the sister of a woman he had previously had a carnal relationship with, and by extension, allow that woman to marry him in turn. The inference here is incredibly clear. Henry's well known affair with Mary Boleyn could have been a stumbling block in his road to marrying Anne Boleyn. It placed Anne within the first degree of carnal affinity to the king, a technicality we must keep in mind that Henry was using as justification for his split from Katherine.

By the summer of 1528 the Pope was free from the clutches of Emperor Charles, but still ostensibly at his mercy. A swift acceptance of the English king's heart's desire was thus not one he could allow, and so the aged Cardinal Campeggio was ordered to travel to England to act as proxy for the Pope, where he would hear the case put forward by the crown, and the queen, respectively. It was during these court meetings that one of Katherine of Aragon's most memorable actions as queen took place. She and her husband had been called to Blackfriars to sit before a court ordered to examine the validity of the marriage. Although stage-managed to a fault by Wolsey, the cardinal could not control how the queen would act, or indeed what she would say. Entering the court, the queen proceeded past the assembled crowd and judges, past her own canopy of state facing the king, instead falling to her knees directly in front of her husband as he sat enthroned. The contemporary writer George Cavendish, famed for his biography of Wolsey, recorded Katherine as saying to the king:

> 'Alas, Sir, where have I offended you? Or what occasion have you of displeasure, that you intend to put me from you? I take God and all the world to witness that I have been to you a true, humble and obedient wife, ever conformable to your will and pleasure. I have been pleased and contented with all things wherein you had delight and dalliance. I never grudged a word or countenance, or showed a spark of discontent. I loved all those whom ye loved only for your sake, whether I had cause or no, and whether they were my friends or enemies. This twenty years and more I have

been your true wife, and by me ye have had divers children, though it hath pleased God to call them out of this world, which hath been no fault in me. And when ye had me at the first, I take God to be my judge, I was a true maid, without touch of man; and whether it be true or no, I put it to your conscience.'

The queen concluded her speech by saying 'and if ye will not extend to me so much indifferent favour, your pleasure then be fulfilled, and to God I commit my case'. Katherine then rose from her kneeling position, turned and left the room, despite the court crier requesting her return. She had played her trump card, and she had won. Campeggio, left with no other choice, adjourned the court to Rome. For Wolsey, this was the end of the road. By October 1528, the cardinal was in open disgrace, having for the first, and last time, failed in his duty to get the king of England what he wanted. He was forced into relinquishing the Great Seal of office, and was shortly replaced by Thomas More as Lord Chancellor.

As the situation continued to boil over, Margaret Pole did all she could to shield the princess, and given Margaret and Katherine's closeness, it must also be assumed that the countess was both outraged and deeply saddened by what was happening to her dearest friend. The family would also have to endure grief much closer to home during this time, for Arthur Pole, Margaret's beloved second son, died. Without a recorded date for his birth or death, we can only speculate as to his age when he breathed his last. It seems shocking that the son of a countess, particularly one of royal blood, could slip from the pages of history without such fundamental information recorded, but, at this time such matters were not set down as standard practice. It is this same reason that, as referenced earlier, Anne Boleyn's own date of birth remains a mystery. The situation would remain the same until 1538, when Cromwell brought in reform that required local parishes to conduct detailed recordings of baptisms, marriages and burials. There are clues however which allow us, with relative conviction, to confirm that Arthur died some time in 1527/1528, and certainly no later than the summer of 1532. Certainly he is last recorded in the records on 20 March 1527 as being part of the king's household.[7] Hazel Pierce puts forward the theory that Arthur fell prey to the sweating sickness pandemic which raged through England in both 1526 and 1528. A highly virulent and often deadly disease, it could famously kill in a matter of hours. Both Anne Boleyn and her father Thomas would contract the infection, making rare recoveries, whilst Thomas Cromwell would lose his wife and two daughters, Anne and Grace, to a bout in 1529. Pierce hones in on these years because Margaret Pole chose to record a new will during this time, an action which would have been necessary with the death of one of her children. As custom dictated, Arthur would be interred at Bisham, resting alongside his notable forebears. In the wake of her son's death, Margaret and Montagu made stringent efforts to protect the inheritance of Arthur's three children, Henry, Mary and Margaret, and by extension, their own interests. The goal was to block Arthur's widow Jane from remarrying, correctly fearing that if she did, further children would no doubt come along and be detrimental to the provisions set out for Arthur's children. Jane herself would complain that Montagu had been particularly adamant that she enter a vow of chastity. The Pole family's fears were confirmed, when in August 1532, Jane did indeed remarry, to Sir William Barentyne. Not long afterwards, she gave birth to their son, Drew. The situation was made worse still, when, just like George, Baron Bergavenny had done earlier, Sir Roger Lewkenor also remarried, producing three more children, which watered down the planned Lewkenor inheritance further still. Yet again, the marriages which Margaret had worked so hard to contract for her children did little by way of long term financial gain. Even though Bergavenny's new brood of children negatively impacted Montagu and his heirs financially, they were evidently still on good terms. In the spring of 1532, Bergavenny had enfeoffed (a system in which lands are granted between parties in exchange for their pledged service) to 'Sir Henry lord Courtenay, marquis of Exeter, Sir Robert Ratclyff earl of Sussex, Sir George Hastings earl of Huntingdon, Henry Stafford Lord Stafford, Sir Henry Pole Lord Montague, Francis Hastings son and heir apparent of the said Lord Montague, and assigns to the use of the said Sir George Bergavenny his heirs and assigns forever, with a view of fulfilling the will of the said George of the manor or lordship of Birling and many other lands'.[8] That Montagu's heir apparent, Henry, was especially marked out suggests Bergavenny was attempting to maintain a steady flow of revenues in the direction of his grandson. The other big light at the end of the tunnel was that marriage contracts for Margaret's grandchildren were also being concluded at this time, shoring up the next generation of Pole dynasts, and as ever, expanding their influence and financial security. One particularly advantageous match was made between Montagu's daughter Catherine, to Francis, Lord Hastings, eldest son of George, Earl of Huntingdon (two men also enfeoffed by Bergavenny), a union which would in time see Margaret's granddaughter follow in her footsteps, and become a countess. Later down the line, Henry Hastings, Montagu's grandson via Catherine, was also treated well at the royal court. Just a year older than Henry VIII's longed-for son, Prince Edward, he was personally invited by the king to join the prince at his studies.

Until quite late into the many years of the king's great matter, Princess Mary would continue to be treated with great deference. Her household, though smaller than before, was still considerable, and she was recorded as being in attendance at the Christmas celebrations of 1529 and 1530, by which time Anne Boleyn was queen in all but name. As distasteful as the Pole family felt about the ascension of the Boleyns, duty would have to come before honour, for the king chose to not only lean on Wolsey, but also important members of his court in his attempts to be rid of the queen. The Pole men would feature prominently, as would their kin, the Courtenays. Even so, their dislike for the task was evident, with Geoffrey Pole stating the king was 'in the snare of unlawful love with the lady Anne'.[9] Had such talk got back to the king, it could have spelt disaster for the Pole family. It is at this time that Reginald, Margaret's third son, reappeared. Unlike his brothers who had been married off and built careers at court, Reginald, having been given over to the Church in his youth, had only one natural future. Deeply devout, he attended Magdalen College at Oxford before being granted the deanery of Wimborne Minster in Dorset by the king himself. By 1521, Reginald was ready to leave England and continue his education overseas. His first stop was Avignon in the far south of France, but disliking the climate, he enrolled at the University of Padua, with the bulk of his tuition fees also covered by the crown.[10] Reginald took pains to ensure he did all well by the king whilst studying, and soon built up such a positive reputation that he was nicknamed 'the nobleman from England'. His good conduct and dedication to work ensured that Reginald remained in favour with the king and queen, and given the king's willingness to cover the cost of his education, suggests Henry put great stock in his cousin's future prospects. The king, at this stage at least, was clearly a good judge of character, for at Padua, Reginald gained access to a wide circle of acquaintances, who were as religiously devout as they were cosmopolitan. He struck up close friendships with the leading lights of Renaissance Italy, including Gianpietro Carafa, who would later become Pope Paul IV, and Gianmatteo Giberti, chief minister to Pope Leo X. He also met two women who would become life-long friends, Vittoria Colonna and Giulia Gonzaga, both of whom were deeply committed to reform within the Catholic Church. Reginald's apparent ease with which he found both friendship and respect within the zenith of Italy's elite, suggests a man of considerable charm and intellect. He would return to England in the summer of 1526, but having been out of the country for such an extended period, appears to have struggled with the deeply volatile nature of life at court. Claiming that his studies would progress more quickly away from all this distraction, he sought permission to return to the Carthusian Monks of Sheen Priory where he had spent much of his childhood. Not long after, he was chosen as Dean of Exeter Cathedral, but by 1529 Reginald was ready to leave England's shores once again. He obtained permission to study at the University of Paris, but unfortunately his planned trip took on an altogether more challenging turn. Ever a man to turn a situation to his advantage, the king decided his academically gifted cousin could do more than merely study in France, Reginald could be of use in the ongoing 'great matter'. Henry would entrust Reginald to attempt to gather support for the divorce. In his later, highly controversial attack on the king, known as *De Unitate*, Reginald would claim that he was initially reluctant to take on the job. He supposedly wrote to the king, insisting he was too inexperienced for such a task and begged the king to find an alternative.[11] Whether true or not it didn't matter. The king had decided, and thus Reginald was duly sent to France with clear orders to fulfil. He would be required to meet with leading theologians of the time to debate the matter, and, Henry hoped, persuade those with influence to look kindly on his wishes. Evidently, the king was correct in his assessment, for Reginald was able to return to England having achieved his task. The University of Paris was won over by the argument and issued a statement in support of the king's planned annulment.[12] As mentioned, Reginald would later claim that he found the commission to his distaste, and that the act had been greatly against his conscience. However, as this was said at a time when he had entirely forsaken the king, his words should therefore be treated with caution. Certainly in 1529 it would not have been politic to speak against the planned annulment, and with the memory of the Duke of Buckingham's fall still fresh in memory, Reginald's actions in Paris were another step to restoring the Pole family name. He made one fleeting appearance at court when landing back on English soil, then retired back to his house at Sheen.

Reginald may have been a man of the Church, but he had not formally taken holy orders. This technicality meant that should the situation arise where an advantageous marriage be put forward, he could, should he wish, be free to accept it. This loophole in canon law would come to haunt the Pole family in time. In November 1530 the king approached Reginald with a spectacularly grand offer, namely the archbishopric of York, which had until quite recently been held by Cardinal Wolsey, prior to his death. For a man ostensibly committed to the work of the Church, it is natural to assume that Reginald would have leapt at such an office. Such a role would have made him the second most senior churchman in England, but, shockingly, he declined. Is it possible that Reginald knew taking on the role would irrevocably block him from a future advantageous marriage proposal? At first he had intimated that he would accept the offer, and had told his brother Montagu as such. He was then duly brought before the king to conclude matters, but would later state in his own words:

> 'The king gave me to understand, on my arrival, that he had been anxiously expecting me; but when I attempted to set forth the case in a sense favourable to his wishes, not merely did I hesitate and fail to make my meaning clear, but I thank the Divine Goodness my tongue was so tied and my speech so obstructed that not one word could I utter of all that I had intended; and when I did find my voice, it was to oppose by every argument the cause I had been summoned and expected to defend. There is no need to dwell in this place on the astonishment and agitation of the king. I attempted some sort of apology, but he cut me short, and having given me to understand how deeply he was offended, he burst away into his own room, closing the door behind him with a furious clang, and leaving me outside, bathed in tears.'[13]

Although he does not say it, reports soon leaked that the king had to restrain himself from thumping his cousin. Chapuys would also discuss the matter in a letter to Charles V, in which he wrote:

> 'The son of the Princess's governess who refused the archbishopric of York because he would not adopt the King's opinions, could not obtain a licence to study abroad until the other day. He told the King that if he remained here he must attend Parliament and if the divorce was discussed he must speak according to his conscience. On this the King immediately gave him leave to go, and promised to continue his income of 400 ducats and to allow him to retain his benefices.'[14]

This measure of willingness to turn a blind eye to Reginald's views on the divorce is highly irregular. Usually a man of minimal forgiveness, perhaps their kinship in blood counted for more than your average courtier, or maybe the king feared Reginald would represent too much of a standard around which other conservatives could lean. Unlike the other notable dissidents such as Sir Thomas More and Bishop Fisher, Reginald had a large and powerful noble family, who shared a close kinship with the king and countless other notable families. Reginald being out of the way, with all royal favour and revenues intact, was perhaps a safer course of action than forcing him to remain. And so, as Chapuys reports, Reginald was given leave to depart England's shores, retaining the revenues he had received from his various Church appointments. Once safely ensconced in the protection of overseas supporters, Reginald gave way to his feelings on the king's divorce, making it clear 'that he would not come till the King had returned to the obedience of the Church'.[15] Although he wouldn't have guessed it at the time, Reginald would not set foot onto English soil again for over twenty years.

As representative of the Pole family at court, Lord Montagu had been elevated to a position within the House of Lords. This had occurred on 1 December 1529, with the court herald officially acknowledging his admittance to this most illustrious of posts. Not long after, Montagu would be required to sign his name to a petition brought before the court, by the king, in May 1530. The petition, by now likely the work of Cromwell, urged the Pope to finally agree to the king's request for an annulment. It was hoped that further weight would be added to the entreaty if it was seen to have the backing of both the clergy and nobility of England. Geoffrey Pole, now becoming something of a liability for his loose tongue, would say of the petition that 'all wise, virtuous and good men and faithful were against the King's purposes both in his unlawful marriage and also the forsaking of the authority of the pope'.[16] Later in the year, no doubt spurred on by the Boleyn faction who remained hostile to Wolsey, the king moved decisively against his former right hand. He ordered Wolsey's arrest, which would likely have ended in the cardinal's execution were it not for his own natural death on the road to London to face trial. Whilst her sons were doing their part in support of the annulment, Margaret, although not openly speaking out against the planned Boleyn marriage, continued to support the beleaguered Queen Katherine and her daughter as best she could. Margaret would not be the only senior female member of the nobility to do so. The divorce and the change in religious policy was felt by many of the great and good across England, and some of the fiercest opponents to the Boleyn marriage were high-status female members of court. Chief amongst them and highest in rank was the king's younger sister, the Princess Mary, Duchess of Suffolk. She was joined by Elizabeth, Duchess of Norfolk and Gertrude, Marchioness of Exeter, who all remained fiercely loyal to Katherine of Aragon. The Duchess of Norfolk was particularly open in her distaste for Anne Boleyn, despite the fact that the queen-in-waiting was her niece, albeit via marriage. So committed was she that it is believed the duchess secretly conveyed letters, hidden inside oranges, that came from Italy to the queen, who in turn shared them with Eustace Chapuys, Imperial Ambassador and staunch opponent to the Boleyn marriage. According to Chapuys, the duchess had also confided in him that her husband had declared Anne would be 'the ruin of all her family'.[17] Gertrude, a lady-in-waiting to the queen was soon dismissed from her service, according to Chapuys, at the insistence of Anne Boleyn. Her husband, Henry Courtenay, would also fall foul of the king and his queen-in-waiting, being ejected from the privy chamber for supposedly 'serving the queen too faithfully.'[18] The situation was viewed with some seriousness, for the king personally placed his cousin under house arrest and ordered the interrogation of the marquis's household.[19] Things would escalate further when servants of the Courtenays were supposedly overheard saying that the Marquis was the natural heir apparent. Such talk, and movement against a member of Margaret's extended family was detrimental to all remaining Plantagenet descendants; it smacked of the earlier troubles caused by the downfall of the Duke of Buckingham. Once again, the fallout had the capacity to create unwelcome suspicion on those who made every effort to downplay their natural birthright.

As this played out, Margaret would try to minimise the impact the king's actions would have on the young princess. By 1531, however, it was becoming entirely clear that Mary had to be told the truth. By now she was a teenager of 15, precocious, forthright and smart. She would have been all too aware of the changes happening within her father's court and her parents' marriage, which put great strain on her own life. Mary was notorious for regular bouts of ill health and was often described as painfully thin and pale. Her highly irregular menstrual cycle caused problems throughout her life and points towards endometriosis, which Mary's doctors at the time simply brushed off as her 'usual troubles'. The princess became prone to bouts of hysteria and what would now be characterised as depression. She looked on in horror as everything she had grown accustomed to, slowly but surely eroded away. It is no surprise that later in life, when she ascended to the throne as queen in her own right, that she would act so vociferously to right all the wrongs she felt had been done in her youth.

In July 1531, the estranged relationship between the king and queen reached its conclusion. At Windsor Castle, Henry and Anne rode out on a hunting trip without the former saying goodbye to his wife. Henry and Katherine would never see each other again. After knowing each other for thirty years, there wasn't even a proper goodbye. Just a few weeks later, Katherine was also saying what would turn out to be a final goodbye to her daughter Mary, for the king had ordered their separation, with Mary's household set up in Richmond and the fallen queen at The More, a home of the former Cardinal Wolsey. As 1532 dawned, Katherine's reduced position was made yet more stark, with the king not sending her a new year's gift, something he had continued to do even as Anne Boleyn grew in ever greater influence. Although it had been suggested that Margaret was also left off the list of new year's gifts, this is incorrect, for a record from 1 January 1532 states 'to the ladies including Margaret Lady Salisbury gilt crosses, cups, salts, a lee pot, casting bottles and goblets', going on to also mention Montagu and his brother-in-law Baron Stafford as receiving the same.[20] Even at this late stage in the game, Katherine maintained resolute in her refusal to accept what was happening to her. This mantra of keep calm and carry on could only last so long though, and one of the first instances when we see Katherine of Aragon openly acknowledge the presence of Anne Boleyn, and the severity of her position, arose when the queen was asked to formally part ways with her royal jewels. Knowing all too well that their destined owner was the very woman who, to her mind, was destroying everything she held dear, she retorted that it 'would be a great sin to allow her jewels to adorn "the scandal of Christendom"'.[21] Usually a woman of much poise and composure, this is a rare example of the queen's fury at what was happening to her. It must also be considered that Katherine had an altogether more meaningful reason to not part with the jewels, for had she done so, it would have been an open acceptance that she was not their rightful owner, and by extension, rightful queen and her daughter, princess. The symbolism these precious items held was therefore central to Katherine's stance on the entire affair. Relinquishing them was something she simply could not countenance. Alas, a direct summons from the king was not something to be trifled with, and obedient as ever, the queen would eventually agree to their return. The jewels were to be used at a highly significant meeting that was due to take place between the king and his French rival, Francis I. In September 1532 Henry took steps to raise Anne Boleyn's status in spectacular fashion – she was granted the title of Marquess of Pembroke, in her own right. The spelling of the title tells of its uniqueness, for the male version is a Marquis, and the female equivalent, enjoyed by Gertrude Courtenay for example, was Marchioness, her title we must remember being received by virtue of her marriage. As 'Marquess', Anne held this title independently, the only other woman in England to enjoy such status was, of course, Margaret Pole, a fact that would no doubt have irked the latter.

Anne's elevation to the peerage was a means of making her a more palatable choice for the king's intended wife. Just weeks later, Henry and Anne set sail for France accompanied by 2000 members of the royal court and household. Members of the nobility always travelled with their own servants, which no doubt attributed to this vast number. One notable attendee was Montagu, who himself was joined by twenty members of his staff.[22] The sojourn in Calais was viewed by contemporaries as a political triumph, particularly for Anne, who played her part with complete aplomb. Her affinity for all things French no doubt played a massive part in the charm offensive. It isn't too hard to imagine that for Anne, this was her moment to show off literally everything she had ever learned, all the style, charisma and glamour, which she exuded in spades, could be put to perfect use. Her private audience with the French king, and the support his government was willing to provide to the intended marriage was an enormous confidence boost to the king and his would-be wife. Interestingly, Montagu had an entirely different take on the success of the meeting, and took great risk in writing to his brother Geoffrey, telling him to visit Katherine of Aragon and to relay the news that 'nothing was done at that meeting touching the marriage with the lady Anne, and that the King had done his best but the French king would not assent to it'.[23] Whilst Montagu's reading of the meeting is at odds with the generally accepted successes it produced, he was accurate to say that there were limitations to what King Francis could agree to. He may have given time to meet with Anne Boleyn, and for all we know, he may very well have genuinely liked her, but Francis, who remained loyal to the Church in Rome, was, in effect, caught between a rock and a hard place. This, of course, would be semantics to Henry and Anne. Sufficiently assured of her future, Anne would finally give way to the lust that had built between her and the king. After seven long years, the couple, perhaps en-route back to England, finally lay together, possibly conceiving their first child that very day.

A few weeks later, the newly appointed Archbishop of Canterbury, Thomas Cranmer, a fellow reformist and chaplain to the Boleyn family, declared the marriage between Henry and Katherine invalid. Bishop John Fisher, one of the very few willing even at this stage to stand firm against the king's separation from Katherine was arrested, and given into the hands of Stephen Gardiner, who, ironically, would grow to be one of the fiercest supporters of Katherine's daughter later in life. Henry duly married Anne, in secret, on 25 January 1533. Despite the obviously growing belly of his new queen, the marriage was kept secret until Easter Sunday, 13 April, in which Anne appeared 'loaded with diamonds and other precious stones, and dressed in a gorgeous suit of tissue'.[24] The new queen would be crowned a few months later on 1 June 1533. As a prominent member of the nobility who had, albeit in a small way, aided in making Anne queen, Montagu and his family were almost certainly in attendance, for his son-in-law Francis had been made a Knight of the Bath on the eve of the coronation; a great honour. Geoffrey was also present, recorded as a server at the banquet that had followed the service. It is probable that Ursula Pole was also in the crowd, given the prominence of her marriage and kinship to the king. As best we can tell, Margaret was not present, a fact which must have stung the king; she was, after all, a living embodiment of his mother's family. Like Thomas More, who also remained absent, by deigning not to attend Margaret set a dangerous precedent around which others could follow. As an incredibly senior member of the nobility, her presence was therefore both expected, and appropriate. To not attend was a major social faux pas, highlighting, in case anyone wasn't already aware, how Margaret felt about the festivities. There is of course the possibility that she had been barred from the celebrations, but given the presence of other notable female courtiers, this seems unlikely, for we know from the records that some of Margaret's peers became directly involved in the coronation procession. For example, as she made her way to Westminster Hall, Queen Anne's litter was followed by 'seven ladies in crimson velvet turned up with cloth of gold and tissue and their horses trapped in gold'.[25] One of these ladies was Gertrude Courtenay, Marchioness of Exeter, a woman who had hitherto been one of Anne's outright enemies. If Gertrude was there, then surely Margaret had been given an invitation, which if true points to her being absent as a conscious decision. In a mirror image of the uniqueness of the queen now sat enthroned, the ceremony would, in itself, break with tradition. A major variation lies in the crown used for Anne Boleyn's investiture as queen. She would be crowned with the crown of Saint Edward, which was only ever used to crown a reigning monarch, not their consort. Such an honour had never been seen before, or used since. Exactly why Anne was singled out in such a grand way remains a mystery.

The king had his new wife. Anne Boleyn had her crown and a child in her belly. Katherine of Aragon was an exile and Princess Mary was now viewed as a bastard. With the tragic loss of Arthur Pole aside, Margaret and her family had largely avoided too much hardship during this time. After a near decade long battle, Henry and Anne could finally ease into married life. The king had held up his end of the bargain, now was the time for Anne to return the favour. She needed to provide the much desired legitimate male heir. Her desires would turn to disasters.

Chapter 6

Ainsi Sera, Groigne qui Groigne

'Let them grumble, this is how it's going to be'
Queen Anne Boleyn

Brimming with characteristic confidence, and more than a touch of arrogance, 'Ainsi sera groigne qui groigne' became one of Anne Boleyn's mottos. She would adopt it prior to her marriage to the king, but its tone and choice of words made her intended actions abundantly clear. Those at court, such as the Poles, who still held a flicker of hope for the restoration of Katherine of Aragon, and her daughter Mary, were wasting their time and energy, not to mention acting in direct contravention to the wishes of the king. The rather crude nature of Anne's adopted motto spelt out that anyone who fought against her position as queen was a mortal enemy, and to go against her, was tantamount to treason. Although it is often suggested that the marriage between Henry and Anne began to break down almost from the moment that it was concluded, this is far from accurate. Their relationship was undoubtedly tempestuous, one of sunshine and showers, but until relatively late into Anne's reign she maintained a powerful hold over the king. Even for the queen's many detractors, her end was one that no one could have seriously contemplated, and yet, after just three years of marriage, Henry VIII would bring down his second wife in spectacularly ignominious fashion. The queen aside, the years 1533–1536 were a period of continued civil unrest and sweeping reform across nearly all of the legislation in England. This juncture, which would see the king go from a broadly popular monarch to the tyrant of memory, laid the foundations for the troubles that would, in time, rip apart Lady Margaret Pole, Countess of Salisbury and her family.

Margaret, despite her closeness to the fallen queen and Princess Mary, was evidently in good enough graces with the king and his new wife at the start of Anne Boleyn's reign. In the new year's gifts of 1533, given by and to the king, Margaret received a 'gilt cup with a cover freeman weighing 22oz'[1], and in return she gave the king 'two pieces of camericke'[2] (cambric), a type of high quality linen cloth. As Anne Boleyn settled into life as England's new queen, watching with much anticipation as her belly continued to grow, the awkward reality of there already being a living royal princess became a matter which needed addressing. Anne, more so than anyone but the king, hoped that the child she carried would be the much desired male heir, but even if it wasn't a boy, the time had come for Princess Mary's new status to be made clear, a process which would start with the surrendering of her royal jewels and plate. As Margaret was still in control of the princesses' household, the task of providing these items fell upon her shoulders. Thomas Cromwell, now in a position of untrammelled power, instructed John, 1st Baron Hussey, Mary's chamberlain, to work with Margaret in the transference of the goods. According to Hussey, Margaret was less than willing to part way with the items. Writing on 21 August 1533, he said:

> 'I thank you for your kindness; advertising you that on the King's command and your letter that Mrs. Frances Elmer should have the custody of the Princess's jewels, I spake with my lady governess to have an inventory made, and the jewels delivered as the King desired. On calling for an inventory, to charge her that had the custody of them and her executors, none could be found. The most that I could get my said Lady to do was to bring forth the jewels and set my hand to the inventory she had made. But she will not deliver the jewels to Mrs. Frances unless you obtain the King's letters to her in that behalf. Would to God that the King and you did know what I have had to do here of late.'[3]

Recalling her once obstinate behaviour to the king over disputed lands, Margaret now refused to part ways with Mary's collection of plate, insisting that it was all needed on a day-to-day basis. As a means of perhaps softening the blow this would have when fed back to the king, Margaret would further instruct Hussey that if Henry ordered the handover of the items, that replacements should be provided beforehand. On 7 September 1533, following her confinement at Greenwich Palace, Queen Anne gave birth to a healthy child. Much celebration erupted at court and in the city, but there was an undeniably muted tone to the festivities, for Anne had done no better than her predecessor; she had given birth to a daughter. The king would, to use modern parlance 'style it out'. He acknowledged through clenched teeth that the baby was healthy, and that he and Anne had enough youth on their side for more children to follow. This was certainly true of Anne, who if born, as many believe, in 1507, placed her at just 26 when she gave birth. She had fallen pregnant with relative speed, so there was nothing to suggest she couldn't once more. The baby was named Elizabeth, in honour of both her grandmothers. Just three days later, she was christened amongst much pomp and splendour. In a move which must surely have been deliberate, John Hussey was chosen as one of the men to carry the canopy of estate over the infant Princess Elizabeth, alongside her uncle, George Lord Rochford, Lord Thomas Howard and William Howard, 1st Baron Howard of Effingham. On 1 October 1533 the king's first daughter, Mary, was told that she was to no longer use her princess title, but be known as 'the Lady Mary, the king's daughter'. Henry VIII had, however, arranged for her household to continue under Margaret Pole's watch, with a further 162 members of staff. The king hoped that providing Mary with her own establishment, away from court, with the calming and reassuring presence of Margaret would appease his daughter. Unfortunately for the king, that was to reckon on Mary being a soft touch, and he was wrong. Every inch her mother's daughter, Mary refused to accept the loss of her royal title and used such heavy words against her father that even the dependably loyal Chapuys felt she had overstepped the mark.[4] As the king could not bring Mary to heel, he took steps to reduce her status further, to essentially force her into capitulation. Within a few weeks, Mary's once grand and costly wardrobe depleted to such a degree that she was described as 'nearly destitute of clothes and other necessaries'.[5] Anne Boleyn's uncle, the Duke of Norfolk, travelled to meet with Mary in December 1533 at her home, Beaulieu Palace. She was informed that her household was to be broken up, and Margaret Pole dismissed from her service. Worse still, Mary was to transfer to the household of her infant half-sister, at Hatfield, in the capacity of a servant. Reporting directly from the scene, Chapuys, very much on the side of Mary, described what happened in detail, saying:

'The duke of Norfolk went himself to the Princess, and signified her father's pleasure that she should attend Court, and enter the service of his other bastard daughter, whom the Duke deliberately, and in her presence, called princess of Wales. Upon which princess Mary replied: "That is a title which belongs to me by right, and to no one else", after which she addressed to him many gracious, honest and very wise remonstrances, all tending to show that the proposals the Duke had brought from the King were both strange and unfitting. Which argument on the part of the Princess the Duke was unable to combat, so much so that he said to her that he had not gone thither to dispute, but to see the King's wishes accomplished, and his commands executed, namely, that she should be removed to the house taken for the bastard. Upon which the Princess, seeing that all her arguments and excuses would be of no avail, asked for half an hour's time to retire to her private chamber; where she remained, as I am given to understand, all the while, or nearly so, occupied in drawing out the protest whereof I once gave her the words. Thus, should she in any way be compelled by force or persuaded by deceit to renounce her rights, marry against her will, or enter a cloister, no prejudice should result to her hereafter. When she came out of her room the Princess said to the Duke; "Since such is my father's wish, it is not for me to disobey his injunctions; but I beg you to intercede with him that the services of many well deserving and trusty officers of my household may be rewarded, and one years wages at least given to them". After this she asked the Duke how many of her own servants she would be allowed to retain and take with her. The answer was that as she would find plenty of servants to attend on her where she was going, no great train of followers was needed. Accordingly, the Princess set out on her journey, accompanied only by very few of her household. Her governess, daughter of the late duke of Clarence, and the King's near relative – a very honourable and virtuous lady, if there be one in England – offered, I hear, to serve the Princess at her own cost, with a good and honourable train of servants, but her offers were not accepted; nor will they ever be, for were the said lady to remain by the Princess they would no longer be able to execute their bad designs, which are evidently either to cause her to die of grief or in some other way, or else to compel her to renounce her rights, marry some low fellow, or let her fall prey to lust, so that they may have the pretext and excuse for disinheriting her, and submitting her to all manner of bad treatment.'[6]

What Chapuys reported were no idle threats. Margaret knew from her own experience that being a princess of the blood counted for little when monumental changes in governance took place. In a bid to downplay her own natural birthright, Margaret had herself been married off to a man far beneath her in status; she knew the same could come of her beloved teenage charge. It is unsurprising therefore that Margaret offered to continue in her post, at her own cost. Norfolk, a man with few redeeming qualities, clearly felt enough confidence in his own position to threaten the princess with violence, informing her that were she his daughter, he would smash her head against a wall until it was as soft as baked apples. The psychological impact this period had on Mary's already fragile state likely did life-long damage. Never a particularly robust woman, the pressure and the trauma she endured would manifest in continued bouts of illness and depression. By her twenties, she had lost many of her teeth, something that can be triggered following chronic periods of stress. Unfortunately, for as long as Anne Boleyn stood beside Henry VIII, the outlook for Mary seemed bleak. This is not to suggest that Anne herself was directly responsible for Mary's ill treatment, in fact, time would eventually tell that it was undoubtedly the king behind the actions taken against his eldest daughter. For Mary personally though, it isn't hard to see that she could not, and would not, acknowledge Anne as the rightful queen of England. It was made clear however that if she continued to act in defiance of her father, her life would be in danger. And so, just like that, Margaret and Mary were separated. The brief period during the downfall of Buckingham aside, Margaret had been almost constantly by Mary's side. Their relationship, in the absence of Katherine of Aragon, had become extremely close, a constant that would have been of huge comfort to a girl whose life had been even more volatile than Margaret's in her youth. The annoyance the king felt at his daughter and Margaret would not wane with the passing of time, if anything Henry would become more vociferous in his treatment of Mary as she continued to act in contravention of his wishes. When, for example, she fell ill in 1535, Chapuys delicately suggested Margaret return to Mary's side to aid her recovery, at which point the king snapped back that Margaret was 'a fool, of no experience, and that if his daughter had been under her care for this illness she would have died, for she would not have known what to do'.[7] Given the king's involvement in Margaret being appointed to Mary's household when she was an infant, his outburst rings hollow, for he knew well that Margaret was more than experienced. The ongoing realisation of how unpopular his marriage to Queen Anne was, made starker by the lack of a legitimate male heir, perhaps explains the king's heightened susceptibility to rash outbursts.

Now separated from Mary, Margaret and her family could, all being well, retire to a quiet life in the country, something one suspects that Margaret, now in her sixties, must have welcomed with open arms. Unfortunately, fresh brushes with danger were never far away and would start for the Pole family almost as soon as the crown had been placed atop Anne Boleyn's head. The Poles natural conservatism and commitment to Katherine of Aragon's cause, had led to their association with Elizabeth Barton, known to history as 'the Holy Maid of Kent'. A conservative Catholic nun, she claimed to have divine visions which would allow her to predict the future. Such was the strength of her conviction, that she soon convinced some of the most prominent churchmen in the country of her skills, with both Bishop Fisher and Archbishop William Warham[8] as her supporters. Barton would eventually count the great Thomas More as another of her advocates. Whether she ever personally met with Lady Margaret Pole remains unclear, however Barton was not a new figure at the Tudor court, for she had held a meeting with Cardinal Wolsey as far back as 1528 and had also met privately with the king. She had grown in greater infamy during the final stages of the planned annulment, and the king's marriage to Anne Boleyn. Barton was open in her hatred of the king's second wife, and was happy to make her feelings clear, stating that if he married her 'the vengeance of God should plague him'.[9] She was particularly bold in the threats made against Henry directly, warning that he would 'die a villain's death'[10], and that she had seen the king having a place reserved for him in hell.[11] The belief in prophecies, of visions from God, for good or for ill, was a very real thing in Tudor England. We must remain cognisant of this fact when assessing the seriousness in which Barton was taken. Bishop

Fisher would personally remind Cromwell of the bible's teachings that 'God never acts without first warning his prophets'.[12] Given the king's naturally superstitious nature, he may well have been anxious about the revelations, which perhaps explains why he allowed the nun to remain at liberty for as long as she did. By the autumn, however, enough was enough, and Elizabeth Barton was finally arrested. It was at this point that things became dangerous for Margaret Pole and her family. Under questioning, Barton revealed the extent of her courtly connections, naming Margaret as one of those she had been in contact with. A Franciscan friar, Hugh Rich, who was arrested alongside Barton, also named Margaret, claiming he had repeated Barton's prophecies to the countess directly.[13] Like Barton, Rich had also made strong courtly connections, and was in close proximity to Lady Mary, for he was the guardian of an Observant house which was directly next door to Mary's main residence of Richmond.[14] Unsurprisingly, the list of court figures who had been meeting with Barton made up the conservative, anti-Anne, pro-Katherine faction. This group, ever supportive of Lady Mary, as she was now known, would suffer further for their association to the king's elder daughter, when Barton stated that Mary 'should prosper and reign in this kingdom and have many friends to sustain and maintain her'.[15] The implication being that these 'many friends' were made up of the conservative faction who had given credence to Barton's prophecies, Margaret Pole unquestionably amongst them. Barton would also say that 'no man should put her [Mary] from her right that she was born unto'[16], an action which had the capacity to incite rebellion against the king's continued reduction in the status of his first born. Although Henry VIII had a deep rooted belief that women could not rule, the love and respect Lady Mary engendered in the common people suggests that to them, her sex was not an issue. Just because the king had brought in sweeping religious reform across the country did not mean that everyone adopted it overnight. Save a few pockets of burgeoning conviction in religious reform, which were mostly concentrated around the capital, England remained devoutly Catholic. This also meant fierce loyalty to the daughter of Katherine of Aragon, and her interests. Another figure who had put great stock in the young prophetess was Gertrude Courtenay, Marchioness of Exeter, with the two communicating on several occasions. In fact such was the closeness between Barton and the Courtenays that even Katherine of Aragon was said to 'fear for the marquis and marchioness of Exeter, and the good bishop of Rochester, who have been very familiar with her.'[17] Certainly the relationship between Barton and Gertude appears to have been stronger than that of Barton and Margaret, but given the kinship of the Courtenays and Poles both through blood and disposition, they were open to being tarred with the same brush. Thankfully, although questioned at length, Margaret's connection to Barton appears to have been minimal. Gertrude however felt it prudent to write to the king to beg for his forgiveness, an action which suggests a much greater level of involvement in the scandal. Katherine herself had resolutely refused to ever meet with Barton, and as Pierce notes, she likely instructed Margaret that Mary was also to never meet directly with the prophetess. Another argument surrounding Barton is that Cromwell used the fallout against her as a means of tightening the net around his court opponents. Correctly guessing that their loyalties remained with Katherine and Mary, Cromwell could use this in the context of association to Barton. The disgraced nun would act, in effect, as the gateway to a trap in which Cromwell hoped senior courtiers would fall. Given Cromwell's ability to forward plan and outmanoeuvre those around him, this theory does hold credence. We must keep in mind that Cromwell's incredibly divisive plans for the dissolution of the monasteries would be abhorrent to the likes of the Poles and Courtenays, who apart from their own devout adherence to the traditional Catholic faith, also benefited financially from the copious amounts of Church land within their territories. Discrediting them in the eyes of the king at this stage could have long term benefits for the future. The idea that Cromwell enacted this trap is contemporary and has its roots in a missive from Chapuys, in which he says 'Many think, and even believe, that those who now have the Nun in their power will make her accuse many people unjustly that they may thus have the occasion and the means of revenging themselves upon those who have supported the queen'.[18] As Pierce observes, historians have corroborated Chapuys' sentiments; the late Professor Garrett Mattingly suggesting that Cromwell merely used Barton as a form of bait, not interested in the nun directly, but 'aimed at larger game than monks and friars. He aimed at the Marchioness of Exeter and the Countess of Salisbury, Katherine's two chief friends among the ladies of the higher nobility'.[19] Cromwell, perhaps better than any other courtier of his time, understood that the king's persistent sense of insecurity could be weaponised when needed.

Following her arrest Barton confessed that she was a fraud, although in a rather lame attempt to minimise her culpability suggested that God had told her to lie. She was found guilty of treason and sentenced to death by hanging. On 20 April 1534 Elizabeth Barton was executed at Tyburn. For good measure, five of her chief supporters, including Hugh Rich, died alongside her. Following the execution, Barton's corpse was decapitated and her head placed on a spike at London Bridge, giving her the dubious honour of being the only woman in history whose remains would suffer such a great indignity. It was around this time, perhaps brought on by the stress of the past year with the separation from Lady Mary, or more probably through her advancing age, that Margaret Pole was taken ill. She was by now in her early sixties, considered advanced in age by the standards of the day. Henry, Baron Montagu was concerned enough for his mother's health that he felt it prudent to write to the Pole family's relatives, the Lisles, to make them aware. Arthur Plantagenet, Lord Lisle, and his wife, Honor, were another offshoot of the Plantagenet dynasty, Lord Lisle being one of the many illegitimate children of King Edward IV, making him a cousin of Margaret's. Despite his bastardy, Lisle was a well-liked member of the court, and was particularly close to the king, who in his youth opined that Lisle had 'the gentlest heart living'.[20] Made Viscount Lisle in 1523, Arthur and his wife spent a number of years in Calais, with Arthur acting as Constable. Honor Lisle had been one of the ladies of the court who attended Anne Boleyn when she first travelled to Calais alongside the king in 1532. In his letter to Lady Lisle, Montagu says 'My Lady my Mother lies at Bisham, to whom I made your ladyship's recommendations. I assure you she is very weak, but it was to her great comfort to hear of my lord and your ladyship'.[21] Whatever the cause of Margaret's illness, she would soon overcome it, and by the spring of 1534 was sufficiently well enough to resume her duties of patronage to those in need. Given her prominence within the now disbanded household of Lady Mary, it was natural that those who had been part of that retinue would turn to Margaret in the hope that she could help provide gainful employment. Accordingly, Margaret wrote to Lord Lisle to try and secure a role for Richard Baker, who had been part of Mary's household, saying:

'Mine own good Cousin, in my most hearty manner I recommend me unto you, and to my Lady, your wife, being glad to hear of your good health: praying you that where my friend Richard Baker is by your favour appointed to the King's service in Calais, it may please you to be a good lord unto him, and rather for my sake, in all such things as ye may do him favour therein. For I do not but that ye shall find him an honest man, and meet to do the King's service. And thus I pray Jesu preserve you in good health, and prosperous, to his pleasure. At Bisham, the fifth day of March, by your loving cousin, Margaret Salysbery.'[22]

In the spring of 1534, Lady Mary was declared illegitimate via the parliamentary act of succession. The purpose of the act was to make it entirely clear that the children of Anne Boleyn, Elizabeth and the much desired but as-yet unborn prince, were to be recognised as the heirs of Henry VIII. With the passing of the bill, all of Henry's subjects were also expected to approve it. Although in his heart he remained loyal to Katherine and Mary, Henry, Baron Montagu had been present when the bill had been passed, and like the rest of his family, willingly took the oath. In the autumn of that same year, a further bill was brought forward, the Act of Supremacy, which sought to recognise the king as the head of the Church of England. Loyalty to the Pope was now loyalty to a foreign power, loyalty to a man who did not sit on the throne of England. In other words, not recognising the act was not recognising the authority of the king, an act of treason. Undoubtedly the work of Cromwell, who faults aside, was a spectacularly gifted lawmaker, the bill had its legal basis in the introduction of new treason laws. These laws were redrafted to make both thoughts and language against the king a capital crime. Bishop Fisher and Thomas More had been arrested earlier in the year for refusing to add their names to the act of succession, resulting in their imprisonment in the Tower. When presented from his cell with the Act of Supremacy, More famously quipped that the bill was like being presented with a double edged sword, for 'if a man agreed to it he would lose his soul, but if he refused it, he would lose his earthly life', a statement which suggests that More knew that there was only one realistic outcome. Within a few months of the bill's passing, the first victims, those who had refused to accept it, met their grisly fate. A group of devout churchmen, they were tried before a jury which included Montagu. Found guilty, they would suffer the full horrors of a traitor's death, being hanged, drawn and quartered at Tyburn. Such a spectacle, although not uncommon, was made all the more consequential because of the victims' positions as men of the Church. Chapuys would later report that those close to Queen Anne had watched the spectacle unfold. Attended by the zenith of the Tudor court, both the Duke of Richmond, the king's illegitimate son, and the Duke of Norfolk, the queen's uncle, were present. Anne Boleyn's own father and brother were also said to have been in the crowd. Just weeks later, the first of the high profile victims met their end, with John Fisher's execution on 17 June 1535. Aged 65, he was an elderly man by the standards of the time, but his refusal to align with the king's wishes would ultimately lead to his demise. Whilst undoubtedly a devout servant of the Church, the bishop was not completely, to use a pun, holier than thou. Evidence suggests that he backed, or at least gave assent to, actions aimed at bringing down the king. Ever watchful of movements at court, Chapuys soon wrote to his master, the Emperor Charles, informing him that:

'That excellent and holy man, the bishop of Rochester, told me some time ago, the Pope's weapons become very malleable when directed against the obdurate and pertinacious, and therefore, it is incumbent upon Your Majesty to interfere in this affair, and undertake a work which must be as pleasing in the eyes of God as war upon the Turk. Indeed, should there be a question of coming to a rupture it would not be amiss for Your Majesty to try by all possible means to have at your court, or elsewhere under your power, the son of the Princess' governess, the daughter of the duke of Clarence, upon whom, in the opinion of many people here, the succession to the crown would by right devolve. Owing to the said duke's great and singular virtues, her son [Reginald] is now studying at the Paduan University, to which circumstance may be added that being closely related to this king, both on the father's and mother's side, he and his brothers might easily lay claim to the succession to the kingdom. For this reason the Queen wishes for marriage in that quarter as much, or perhaps more than in any other, and the Princess herself; far from refusing it, would, I have no doubt, gladly give her

94

consent. The youth and his brothers have many relatives and allies beside a very numerous party whose affections Your Majesty might by such means easily gain, and thus secure those of the rest of this nation.'[23]

In this letter, Chapuys encapsulates everything that Henry VIII feared. Not only did the ambassador openly suggest the Emperor wade into, as he saw it, the ongoing problems in England, but he then stressed the significance of Margaret Pole's family both dynastically, and potentially, the role they might play for the future of the realm. By referencing the scale of the Pole family's courtly connections, their popularity and influence, Chapuys unwittingly put a price on their heads. With Fisher dead, Sir Thomas More was next in the firing line. He was tried in July 1535, found guilty and duly sentenced to death. Although Montagu was called to sit in place as a juror, he failed to appear. The reason for this may have been illness, for he was reported to be unwell not long after the trial. Such was the degree of his sickness that a report from John, Lord Hussey to Lord Lisle stated Montagu be 'sore sick or dead'. Whilst there is nothing to suggest Montagu was not genuinely unwell, it was certainly well timed, conveniently explaining his absence from a trial in which the man sitting in judgement was held in high regard by the Poles. Thomas More had had dealings with the Pole family for many years, and was known to have deep respect for Margaret, once describing her as 'noblest and best of women'. Following his death, Montagu would be the recipient of More's extensive library of books, taking 'much pleasure reading of them'.[24] More would famously approach his death with humour and steadfast bravery. Upon noticing the dilapidated state of the scaffold on which he was to die, he would utter perhaps his most famous quip, 'I pray you Mr. Lieutenant, see me safe up, and for the coming down let me shift for myself'.[25] He then told the crowd that he died 'the king's good servant, but god's first', before being dispatched with a single blow of the axe. The deaths of Fisher and More were met with anger by the common people, and as is so often the case, the men would become more dangerous for the king dead, than alive, achieving the status of sainthood almost as soon as they were executed. More would be one of very few people whom the king would later admit regret at having killed. Although outwardly compliant to the king's wishes, the deaths of More and Fisher would have been met with horror by Margaret, her family and extended

95

kin. As the two lone voices in a sea of assent to the Boleyn marriage and progeny, More and Fisher represented the interests of Katherine and the Lady Mary, of an England now in tatters. Their deaths all but quashed any significant dissent against the Boleyn marriage; those who had chosen not to join them had, to use modern parlance, made their own beds and now must lie in them. This is not to suggest that Mary herself became any more compliant. She maintained a fierce opposition to Anne Boleyn as queen, the royal supremacy and most significantly the reduced status she and her mother were asked to assent to. In the wake of Fisher and More's deaths, Katherine and Mary reopened correspondence with the Pope and the Holy Roman Emperor, imploring them to send aid in support of the Catholic faith, and by extension their own interests. Writing to Chapuys, Mary said:

'I would dare ask this favour of you, that you dispatch forthwith one of your men, an able one and possessing such information, to the Emperor, and inform him of the whole, and beg him, in the name of the Queen, my mother, and mine, for the honour of God, and the considerations above mentioned, to take this matter in hand, and provide a remedy for the affairs of this country. The work itself will be highly acceptable in the eyes of God, and no less glory will be gained by it than by the conquest of Tunis, or even that of Africa; begging you in the meantime not to forget to solicit permission for me to live with my mother, or else obtain leave for her to come, or send her people to visit me. I should very much wish to write to His Majesty in my own hand, but not knowing how to thank him in due measure for what he has already done for the Queen, my mother, or for myself, and on the other hand, fearing lest those who are constantly watching me should get hold of the letter, I have hitherto been unable to accomplish my wish, though I find some consolation and comfort in the idea that you yourself will supply the want, and do and say in my name what is proper and fit.'[26]

That Mary felt the need to caveat the likelihood of the letter being intercepted, explains clearly both her sense of unease and awareness that she was acting contrary to her father's wishes. As the situation played out, Margaret and her family sensibly chose to ride out the storm and pray for better days. The king's second marriage may have turned their world upside down, but this was not a family for whom peace and quiet was a particularly abundant commodity. That Margaret took time away from court during Anne's tenure as queen is clear from the sheer lack of information we have on her during this time. One of the few examples of when Margaret did resurface, was to openly rally against an appointment to the priory of Bisham which sat within her lands, which based on Margaret's response, was done without her approval. Barlow was a notable reformist, undoubtedly in Cromwell's employ, and was also under the patronage of Queen Anne. The queen and Cromwell combined made for a formidable opponent, and so Margaret was forced into a corner – Barlow was named prior, and Margaret and her family no doubt smarting, simply had to accept it. It was also around this time that John Helyar, Margaret's personal chaplain, suddenly left English shores. William Tyndale was fast becoming the megastar of religious reform; reform which was abhorrent to the likes of Magaret, her family and her kin. The reasons as to why he chose to leave will be discussed at a later stage. What is important to keep in mind is that the departure caused disquiet with Stephen Gardiner, Bishop of Winchester, who promptly wrote to Cromwell saying that Helyar left 'in such fashion and manner as I like not'.[27] Such a statement would suggest Helyar and the wider circle around the Pole family, just like the family themselves, were being watched, and their actions judged in an automatically suspicious light. Stephen Gardiner, despite being a man of the cloth, was a master par excellence at recalibrating his views to suit the times he found himself in. A quality that we would now recognise as pure self-preservation, it was broadly at odds with other men of his creed. Consider for example, that such was his likely feigned conviction for the Act of Royal Supremacy, that he published a treatise, *De Vera Obedientia*, in avid support of it. One hopes that the irony of this action was not lost on Gardiner as he placed the crown onto the head of Queen Mary I eighteen years later.[28]

Henry, Baron Montagu was by now a well-established and exemplary courtier. He appears smart and diligent, and would maintain warm relationships with other noblemen of the court, particularly with those who also carried Plantagenet blood. This is most overt in his dealings with the Marquess of Exeter, with evidence pointing to a close and genuine friendship between the two men. They were of roughly the same age, had very similar backgrounds, and each carried the weight and expectation that came with being the eldest born son of a noble house. Montagu's private chaplain, John Collins, once overheard his master praise the marquess as 'a man of very good mind and courage', later describing Exeter as Montagu's 'assured friend'.[29] Another close friend of Montagu's, despite a considerable age gap, was his mother's cousin, Arthur Plantagenet, Viscount Lisle. Thanks to the sheer wealth of information held in the famous Lisle letters, we know that regular correspondence between the two men was maintained for several years, with Montagu informing Lisle that 'no kinsman he hath he shall be more assured of to do him pleasure'.[30] By contrast, Montagu's younger brother, Geoffrey, was more frivolous, less astute and unguarded in his behaviour. As Pierce notes, aside from his role as a justice of the peace, Geoffrey would never achieve a position of particular note. This is unsurprising, for his financial difficulties were becoming well known and did not engender confidence in his courtly abilities. However, in many respects, this wasn't entirely Geoffrey's fault. The burden of not being the eldest son was a constant issue for noblemen of the court, and made worse through the expected convention that noble houses would strive to produce as many children as possible. Consider Katheryn Howard's father, Lord Edmund Howard, for example. He was consistently strapped for cash, whilst his elder brother, the Duke of Norfolk, lived like a king. Being the son of a peer was undoubtedly advantageous, but acted, as it still does today, under a rule of primogeniture which placed a financial burden on anyone but the heir apparent. As we have seen, Geoffrey's monetary difficulties impacted the success of his relationship with his in-laws, and appears to have been a relatively constant struggle, being once forced into asking a friend to lend him £5. Geoffrey would also find himself in debt to the king, which appears to have been cleared through a generous gift of £40, roughly £18,000 by modern standards, from Cromwell to Geoffrey.[31]

One member of the Pole family who did remain politically active during this time, was Reginald. His scholarly approach to life had served him well, being fluent in Greek and of course Latin, and not to mention a basic understanding of Hebrew. Still safely ensconced in Italy, Reginald had begun to write what would eventually become his most infamous work. Known colloquially as *De Unitate*, its full title was

Pro Ecclesiasticae Unitatis Defensione, or *Defence of the Unity of the Church.* Although the size of a small book, it was intended to be nothing more than a personal communication between Reginald and the king, in response to questions asked of Reginald by the latter. In February 1535, a chaplain of the king's, Thomas Starkey, wrote on behalf of his master to Reginald, to clarify Pole's views on the two most significant aspects of Henry VIII's life at this stage: the marriage to Anne Boleyn and the authority of the Pope, or as Henry now called him, the Bishop of Rome. Although Reginald informed Starkey that he needed time to consider his response, he did not suggest it would be contrary to the king's wishes. Indeed he felt compelled to write to Cromwell, informing him that 'you will do me the greater favour to assure his Highness of my readiness to do him service at all times; for I count whatsoever is good in me next to God to proceed of his Grace's liberality in my education, which I esteem greater benefit than all the promotions the king gave to any other'.[32] That Reginald felt it prudent to highlight the king's role in his education suggests it was something that Henry had taken great interest in maintaining. The irony is that as these words were written, Reginald had begun work on *De Unitate*, which when completed, was as opposed to Henry VIII's will as it was possible to be. This duplicitousness makes Reginald a difficult man to root for. By the time he had written to Cromwell, his opinions must surely have been decided on, so why lie, when months later he would come out so forcefully against the king's policies. The content and fallout from *De Unitate* will be covered in the next chapter.

Towards the end of 1535, the first major cracks in the royal marriage began to appear. They came from an unlikely source, Anne Boleyn's own uncle, the Duke of Norfolk. Although ostensibly his niece's elevation to queen of England was a great coup for the Norfolk family, a strained relationship between the queen and her prickly uncle was evident. According to Chapuys, Norfolk would vocalise his frustrations to Montagu, stating that 'he was held in no esteem due to the malign influence of Anne Boleyn, and Henry's eye, which had strayed towards an unidentified young lady, had now strayed away from her in the direction of a cousin of Anne Boleyn'.[33] This cousin of the queen's is almost certainly one of the Shelton girls, either Margaret, known to history as Madge, or her sister Mary. Madge was known to be particularly close to her royal cousin, but still found herself on the receiving end of

Anne's famously tart tongue. When the queen discovered Madge had been doodling flowers in her prayer book she 'wonderfully rebuked her for defacing it with such wanton toys'[34] a reminder that for all Anne's reformist leanings, she was every bit as pious as her contemporaries. This piety, whilst admirable, didn't really matter to the king, what mattered was that Anne had failed in the primary goal of her marriage – there was still no prince in the royal nursery. Her misfortune was compounded and made all the starker through Anne's own forceful personality. The king prescribed extravagantly to the contemporary notion that a wife should in all ways be subordinate to her husband's will. Anne's temperament, whilst thrilling as a would-be mistress, was grating in a wife. She could not curtail her naturally forthright manner, and she struggled to look the other way as the king conducted his extramarital affairs. Simply put, Anne continued to be Anne. The beleaguered queen would enjoy a brief injection of a more solidified position at the start of 1536, when on 7 January, Katherine of Aragon died. Having been ill for some time, she passed away, aged 50, at Kimbolton Castle, probably from a form of cancer. No steps had been taken to allow her daughter to visit, and so the former queen had died surrounded by her still loyal ladies, professing to her dying breath that she was, and always had been, the king's true wife and uncontested queen of England. Given Katherine's position as persona non grata, how Margaret and her family reacted to the news is not recorded, but it can be said with some certainty that it would have been nothing short of devastating, for Margaret in particular. They had been friends for decades, sharing the horror of Prince Arthur's death, the shared understanding of widowhood, and most significantly, how it felt to be entirely left out in the cold by the Tudor court machine. When news of Katherine of Aragon's death reached London, the king and queen appeared bedecked in yellow. Although some have suggested this was the colour of mourning in Spain, and that the decision was therefore deliberate, this does not hold true, for the colour of mourning was the far more appropriate black. Henry and Anne's attire must surely therefore point to their treating the occasion as one of celebration. For the king, the death of his first wife removed the fear that Katherine's nephew, Emperor Charles, would invade England, a fear which according to Chapuys the king freely vocalised, saying 'God be praised, the old harridan is dead, now there is no fear of war'.[35] For Queen Anne, she was safe in the knowledge that now, finally, she was the only living woman in England who could claim the title of queen. At a feast, the king paraded the young Princess Elizabeth around in his arms, his wife looking on with pride and confidence in her position, for she was once again pregnant, and as ever, everyone hoped that this would finally be the much desired boy.

Anne's victory would be short lived, for in a twist of fate, on the very day that Katherine of Aragon was laid to rest in Peterborough Abbey disaster struck. Anne Boleyn 'miscarried of her saviour'.[36] The foetus she carried was sufficiently far enough along to confirm that it was, devastatingly, male. The story that she was 'delivered of a shapeless mass of flesh'[37] came up years later in the work of Nicholas Sander, a Catholic propagandist, and should be taken with extreme caution. In all probability, the queen had suffered just as her predecessor had, delivering a premature, stillborn, albeit normal, child. When one factors in the unbelievably intense pressure upon Anne to deliver a healthy male heir, and the age's rudimentary understanding of obstetrics, it is unsurprising that such disasters would occur. Anne herself suggested that the traumatic shock just days earlier when the king had suffered a severe jousting accident, in which he had been knocked unconscious for two hours, brought on the miscarriage. Although the loss of her son is for many the final nail in the coffin for Henry and Anne's relationship, this isn't quite accurate. The miscarriage undoubtedly hampered Anne's position, and gave heart to her many opponents, but the couple themselves soon reappeared in public, Anne having apparently rebounded in the king's favour. A certain Jane Seymour was now on the scene, with the king paying her court through small gifts, which according to Chapuys led 'to the intense rage of the concubine'.[38] At this stage at least, the king's actions were likely flirtations, rather than seeking Jane out as potential wife number three. Outwardly the king was still in support of his second wife, and loyal to the honour of their daughter. This was felt keenly by another court conservative and close friend of the Pole family, Sir Nicholas Carew. Carew dared Will Sommers, the king's fool, to refer to Anne as a ribald or whore, and name the Princess Elizabeth a bastard. The king was said to be so apoplectic that he threatened to kill Sommers with his bare hands.[39] Carew understandably kept a low profile thereafter, but by the middle of spring, the ever turbulent royal court, and the marriage of Henry and Anne, would utterly implode. The relationship between Henry and Jane Seymour had continued to develop apace, with Chapuys happily orchestrating meetings with those, such as the Poles, who viewed with anticipation the prospect of 'Queen Jane'. Henry, Baron Montagu was one such guest, informing the ambassador that 'after many complaints of the disorder of affairs here, told him that the concubine and Cromwell were on bad terms, and that some new marriage for the king was spoken of'. Geoffrey Pole would also dine with Chapuys, as would the Marquess of Exeter.[40] Whether at this stage the king had actually decided to part with Anne and replace her with Jane is still hotly debated, as are the reasons for her downfall. What we do know, is that as late as 18 April 1536, literally one month and a day before the queen would be executed, the king orchestrated a situation in which Chapuys would finally come face to face with Anne, and be required to pay her reverence. A mass was held, with Chapuys escorted to the service by Anne's brother, George, Lord Rochford. Until this point, the wily ambassador had managed to never actually meet with the woman he so despised, the woman he called the concubine. However, as the king and queen arrived, Chapuys had been manoeuvred into a position which entirely blocked him from leaving. Some would say a simple bow to the queen is hardly cause for celebration, but the symbolism behind it meant everything to the king, and particularly to Queen Anne. As the Imperial Ambassador, Chapuys was the Emperor's official representative in England. To bow to Anne was to recognise her as queen, to recognise the invalidity of the marriage with Katherine of Aragon and the bastardy of Lady Mary. Such an action was one Chapuys and the Emperor had resolutely refused to countenance. This gesture, at least at this stage, suggests the king was still fiercely championing his second wife. Ironically however, this may very well have been the thing that freed the king, as he saw it, from Anne Boleyn. Whilst others refused to acknowledge the marriage, the king, petulant as ever, would remain dogmatic in his insistence of its validity. Now as this ultimate opponent had finally been made to acknowledge Anne as queen, did Henry feel he could let her go? Certainly after this display, the queen's once powerful hold over the king began to wane with every passing day. Henry VIII had torn up his constitution, he had executed old friends, he had quite literally created an entirely new religion in England for this woman, and yet to the king, she had not delivered on her promise. For all her fame, Anne Boleyn herself remains something of a mystery, and yet, the very nature of Jane Seymour helps us form a more definitive image of Henry VIII's most controversial consort. Like a pendulum, the king swung from one extreme to another. Where Anne was bold, clever and seductive, Jane was meek, plain and religiously conservative. At the very least Jane seemed like she wouldn't be any trouble.

On 2 May 1536, Queen Anne Boleyn was arrested at Greenwich Palace on charges of adultery and high treason; contrary to popular belief, no accusation of witchcraft was ever levelled against her. Exactly why the queen was arrested is the subject of countless studies and debates among historians. Overwhelmingly she is viewed as someone who suffered a gross miscarriage of justice, with very few historians believing she was actually guilty. The most consistent argument in attempting to understand her downfall resides in the breakdown of Anne's relationship with Cromwell, alongside her not providing the king with a son, which created the perfect storm in which Anne would fall. We should be under no illusion that had Anne Boleyn successfully delivered male heirs, she would have been absolutely secure. Alongside the queen, a total of seven men, including her own brother, were arrested. Their supposed crime – adultery with Queen Anne. Once conveyed to the Tower, Anne would be lodged in the same apartments that had been hers at the coronation just three years earlier. A trial was set for 15 May 1536. Three days prior to that, Viscount Rochford aside, four of the men arrested alongside Anne would be tried, found guilty and sentenced to death; the sixth and seventh arrestees, Sir Thomas Wyatt and Richard Page, escaped without charge. The queen must surely have known then that there was only one possible outcome when the time came for her to take the stand. As Anne Boleyn stood in Westminster Hall, the realisation that her husband had actually authorised this spectacle must have shocked the queen to her core. The king had sent dukes and earls to trial, he had sent chancellors and churchmen, but Anne's case truly was a first. Never before had a queen been tried on the orders of the king, there simply was no precedent to follow. Although Anne put up a sturdy defence, the verdict of guilty was a foregone conclusion. One of those appointed to judge the queen was Henry, Baron Montagu.[41] In a cruel twist of fate, another of the jurors was Henry Percy, Earl of Northumberland, the very man Anne had hoped to marry years earlier.

Clearly the stress of sending a woman to her death, whom he likely knew was innocent of all charges, was too much for the earl to bear, for upon delivering his verdict he collapsed and had to be helped from the room. The sentence itself was read out to the astonished audience of over 2000 spectators by the Duke of Norfolk, who as Earl Marshall of England presided over the case. It would be his job to sentence his own niece to death. When the verdict was proclaimed, the queen was said to have remained completely resolute, her face didn't move, despite what must have been abject terror, for the verdict read out 'that thou hast deserved death, and thy judgement is this: that thou shalt be burned here within the Tower of London on the Green, else to have thy head smitten off, as the King's pleasure shall be further known of the same'.[42] Mercifully, Anne was soon informed that she would be given the much swifter death by decapitation.

The grisly spectacle was conducted on 19 May 1536, two days after the men who had been sentenced to death alongside her met their ends. Elegant to the last, Anne Boleyn approached the scaffold every inch the English queen, shunning her preferred French hood for the traditional English gable, a mantle of ermine fur, a fur the reserve of royalty, draped over a simple dark grey, possibly black, gown. She addressed the crowd, which despite Sir William Kingston, Constable of the Tower's attempts to minimise, still counted around 1000. Her speech followed the custom of the day, with Anne praising the king, whilst cleverly hinting at her own innocence, stating 'if any person will meddle of my cause, I require them to judge the best'.[43] Anne would kneel upright to await the executioner's blow. Exactly why Henry chose to authorise the use of a sword rather than the traditional block and axe remains unclear. Some say Anne requested it, others that the king used it as an act of mercy, for the sword was said to deliver a much cleaner and more assured result. It is certainly interesting that such a (dubious) honour was not given to Katheryn Howard a few years later, when her guilt was almost undoubtable, for she would endure the horror of the clumsier axe. Perhaps this was Henry's own small way of recognising that Anne was innocent? Repeatedly reciting the prayer 'To Jesus Christ I commend my soul; Lord Jesu receive my soul' the expert executioner from Calais called aloud in French for his sword, a diversion tactic, causing the queen to turn her head towards the noise. As she turned, the executioner swung down, killing the queen with one swift blow. Anne Boleyn, the scandal of Christendom, the great passion of the king's life, now lay in a pool of her own blood, a tiny figure, brought low on what are generally accepted to be made up charges. No doubt loath to admit it, even Chapuys was forced to concede that 'no one ever showed more courage or greater readiness to meet death than she did'.[44] Although Thomas Cromwell had played a monumental role in bringing Anne down, his assessment of her following the execution, perhaps sums up this most enigmatic of queens most succinctly – 'intelligence, spirit, courage'.[45] Despite the considerable preparation that went into Anne Boleyn's execution, astonishingly no coffin had been provided. A spare arrow chest was found, and it was in that, that the very first queen in English history to suffer execution, was interred.

With wife number three already in the wings, and a much more placid and traditionally minded one at that, the Pole family must surely have felt some relief at Anne's destruction. Better days must be on the horizon?

Chapter 7

De Unitate

'Not like a human being, but a wild beast'
Reginald Pole

The Pilgrimage of Grace was the most significant and troubling period of civil unrest that Henry VIII had known during his reign. Large swathes of the north of England and pockets within the Midlands would come out in revolt against the king's actions, although openly would profess their issue was not the king himself, but his councillors, with Thomas Cromwell and Archbishop Cranmer as their prime targets. This points to the key grievance of those rising up, for at its core, the pilgrimage looked to address the break with the Catholic Church. It also provided what could have been the one true opportunity the Poles and the other White Rose houses, such as the Courtenays, had at overthrowing Henry VIII, and yet no such action took place. Baron Montagu could have raised the county of Hampshire, and the Marquis of Exeter the west of England. The combined forces would have plunged the south into chaos, opening the capital to the northern rebels with ease. Instead, the Poles, the Courtenays and the rest of their kin remained outwardly loyal. Based on Margaret Pole's adherence to the memory of Queen Katherine, and the interests of Lady Mary, it is probable that she and her family secretly sympathised with the pilgrims' plight, but as ever, fidelity to the king would come before family honour. Both Henry, Baron Montagu and Geoffrey Pole were required to provide men who would fight against those raising arms; Montagu providing 200, to Geoffrey's feebler 20.[1] The Marquess of Exeter would also be a key figure alongside other senior noblemen in bringing the rebels to heel. Although the downfall of Anne Boleyn gave the Pole family much to rejoice in, the fallout from her short lived reign had far reaching consequences to the detriment of Margaret and her kin. The speed at which the fallen queen had gone from being the most powerful woman in England to a convicted traitor was staggeringly swift. Just seventeen days divided Anne's arrest from her execution. It highlighted how readily the king could turn on those he held dearest. The men who had been executed alongside Anne Boleyn included some of the king's oldest friends, most notably Henry Norris, his long term groom of the stool. This callous disregard for loyalty must have been disconcerting to witness, even for Anne's many detractors, for it showed quite simply that nobody was safe. The king of old, the buoyant, young and easy going 'man of the people' was now a distant memory. Anne Boleyn's death would not bring about an immediate return to Papal authority, nor would it see Lady Mary restored as princess. Everything that the Pole family had been pinning their hopes on would become ultimately fruitless. The idea that all would be 'as it was' could not have been further from the truth, a fact which highlighted with spectacular fashion that Anne may have been the instigator for change, but that this change had not died with her. Simply put, the religious upheaval in England which the White Rose of York families so deplored would not be thrown out purely because its catalyst was now dead. If anything, the changes would become more radical, for its chief facilitator, Cromwell, grew in even greater power, now that his one-time ally, turned bitterest rival, was destroyed. He would push forward with ever increasing verve the controversial dissolution of the monasteries, which put him on a collision course with powerful and long standing supporters of the king, and more dangerously still, invoke the ire of many of the common people. In fact, the Pole family would go through even greater scrutiny not long after Anne Boleyn's execution, which would sow the seeds for their eventual downfall. The family had hoped that things would become more safe, more stable, but instead, the court exploded into a chorus of hearsay, with the political explosion of the Pilgrimage of Grace, destabilising the hitherto warm relationship between the king and his people. The emergence of Reginald Pole as a highly vocal critic of the king would place a dangerous spotlight on Margaret's family, and although they would not know it at the time, this rebellion against the king would act as a precursor to the affair which tore the Pole family apart – The Exeter Conspiracy. The two are inexorably linked, one feeding into the other, lighting the fire which pushed the king into bringing down his own extended family.

Anne Boleyn's body was barely cold when King Henry VIII and Jane Seymour were officially betrothed. Their marriage took place a few days later on 30 May 1536.[2] Although repeatedly viewed as the original 'plain Jane', Henry's third wife was not so placid as to be concerned with challenging the king on his estrangement from his eldest daughter, Lady Mary. Rebuffed, Henry instructed Jane to 'solicit the advancement of the children they would have between them'.[3] The king's comments to Jane highlight perfectly that the driving force behind his daughter's unhappiness had always laid with the king, and not Anne Boleyn. Indeed the fact that nothing changed, not in policy or in the position of Mary within the royal family, confirmed quite plainly that the ongoing fissure was between the king and anyone who continued to defy him, daughter or otherwise. Rather like Margaret Pole and her contemporaries, Mary had naturally assumed that the destruction of 'the great whore' would right all the wrongs, as she saw it, in England. Her hopes were folly. Mary was not going to be treated any differently now that her despised stepmother was dead. Even with Anne Boleyn permanently out of the picture, Mary was still in danger. Her familiarity to the conservative faction at court, and most starkly in her closeness to Margaret Pole, now had the very real capacity to create an even greater storm of suspicion against both her and her supporters. The great and the good of England were now, more than ever, under close watch. Cromwell plainly alludes to this, informing Mary on 11 June 1536 that 'If you do not leave all sinister counsels, which have brought you to the point of undoing, I take leave of you forever, and desire you to write to me no more'.[4] Despite the monumental role he played in bringing her mother low, Cromwell had hitherto been on relatively good terms with the king's eldest daughter, but even he had a breaking point. The 'sinister counsellors' Cromwell refers to must surely mean Mary's chief champions, the Poles being high on that list. Ever the king's loyal servant, Cromwell kept a watchful eye on all senior courtiers, with a web of contacts, spies and informants across all of King Henry's territories, and as will be seen, in the households of his foreign enemies also. It is likely that Cromwell himself felt a natural distaste for the Pole family as well as their contemporaries, the Courtenays and the Lisles etc. They were his natural enemies in nearly all facets of life. He was the base born son of a blacksmith from Putney, with zero noble blood, but an abundance of skills which through hard work found good use on the continent, and now at the royal court. A ruffian jack-of-all-trades, his rise through the ranks was thus through merit, as opposed to birth. These experiences gave Cromwell a more well-rounded view on the world, an understanding of how society was truly built. He understood human nature, and crucially recognised how the nobility were a constant threat to the king, even if professing outward loyalty. By contrast, Margaret and her contemporaries clung to the past with ever increasing desperation, watching as the world they had been a part of, and continued to prop up, slowly eroded away. For Cromwell, Margaret and her ilk were dinosaurs, with excessive pride and too much influence, whilst for the nobility, Cromwell was an upstart with no right to even be in the same room as them, let alone place burdens on how they chose to operate their lands and finances. Cromwell's rise to power did however provide untrammelled access to all the great houses of England, and so the nobility would be required to play host. The Marquess of Exeter had once been obliged to receive Cromwell at his home in Surrey, an event at which Geoffrey Pole was also in attendance. The marquess gave Cromwell the customary gifts, in this instance a coat and wooden knife, before tipping a wink to Geoffrey and telling him 'Knaves rule about the king, I hope to give them a buffet one day'.[5] Cromwell's prize mistake, however, would be to become too grand, too assured of his security, which, like much of the Tudor court, would lead to his eventual undoing.

That a warm relationship existed between the king's third wife and Margaret Pole is clear, almost from the moment Jane became queen. This is unsurprising, for as already referenced, the new queen was keen to rebuild relations with Lady Mary, something Margaret would have championed keenly. For the king however, Mary's rehabilitation would not start until she submitted to his will, and swore to the Act of Supremacy. Up until this point, Lady Mary had sufficiently dodged ascribing her name to the document, a fact unsurprising given that it would see her accepting her own bastardy, and the invalidity of her parents' marriage. Finally, broken down by constant pressure, and after assurance from her old friend Chapuys, Mary added her name to the hated bill, signing without even reading its content. This may have troubled Mary's conscience, but she soon felt the benefits of her capitulation. Instantly restored and recognised by all as the king's daughter, she was invited back to court, given the right to select her own servants and provided with a vast and costly wardrobe.[6] Interestingly, however, Mary chose not to reappoint Margaret to her household[7], but why? Whilst it's entirely reasonable to surmise that now, aged 20, Mary had simply outgrown the need for a governess, it's also credible to assume that being finally returned to her father's confidence made Mary more circumspect in her choice of retainers. It would not be politic to appoint someone Henry, and Cromwell for that matter, viewed with suspicion. Mary's biographer, David Loades, confirms that of the twenty-five members of staff appointed by Mary, twenty-one had served her before.[8] This alone acts as proof that there was no issue in Mary bringing back one time servants, which certainly makes Margaret's exclusion noteworthy. Mary's reunion with the king took place shortly after her return, their first meeting in around five years. Although not making up part of Mary's household, her return to court was soon followed by Margaret's, the latter no doubt keen to catch up with her long-term charge. The lack of appointment to her household aside, a close bond between Margaret and the king's elder daughter was still clear, as evidenced through the traditional new year's gift giving, from Margaret to Mary, which was maintained during this time. The bond between Margaret and Mary was also something the common people of England were aware of. In an age centuries before mass media, before the notion of celebrity was even a thing, the nobility of England provided star power. Margaret, as a countess with royal blood and high in the esteem of Lady Mary, was an instantly recognisable figure. This is clear from her return to London, for according to the Bishop of Faenza 'On the return of Margaret to court, it being supposed that the Princess was in her company, a crowd with 4,000 or 5,000 horses ran to meet her'.[9] Evidence that for all her father's actions, Mary remained deeply beloved of the people.

In June of 1536, Queen Jane would begin to build out her own household, and with it her retinue of servants.[10] Although the centre of power in Tudor England was inexorably tied to the king, and thus the court was highly masculine in nature, one of the few areas of court life in which women had some degree of agency was in their ability to promote or provide assistance to other women looking for roles within the queen's household. As one of the most powerful women in England at the time, Margaret was naturally sought out to aid in securing roles for well born young ladies. That the very nature of this role was one viewed as inherently female, is felt clearly in an exchange between Henry, Baron Montagu and the Lisles. Honor, Lady Lisle, who appears to have been a rather forceful and frankly irritating figure, kept up a steady stream of gifts and letters towards key figures in England, all with the end goal of hopefully securing her daughters with positions at the court of Queen Jane. Lady Lisle's agent in London, John Husee, told her plainly that it was 'no meet suit for any man to move such matters, but only for such Ladies and women as be your friends'.[11] Montagu explained that he would defer the request to his mother, imploring her 'to do her best', before adding to Lord Lisle that his wife would see her wishes 'sooner take effect'[12] if she wrote to Margaret Pole directly instead. Even at a distance of nearly 500 years, one can almost picture Henry Pole rolling his eyes in bewilderment.

At the very point that Margaret was hoping to rebuild trust in the king, *De Unitate* would arrive in England. The news of Anne Boleyn's execution was now widespread across Europe, which begs the question, did Reginald choose this moment to deliver *De Unitate* deliberately? Did he hope it would be auspicious timing, aimed at landing before the king, fresh from the end of his hated second marriage, forging a pathway to reconciliation with Rome? If Reginald hoped *De Unitate* would encourage this, it was foolish to the point of idiocy, for its contents were explosive in the extreme, and did no favours for the Catholic cause or more crucially, his family's position at court. *De Unitate* was a deeply critical, explosive and highly personal attack on the king. Relations between the king and his wayward cousin had been steadily breaking down for some time, with the Act of Supremacy as the overriding bone of contention. When Henry VIII forwarded a sermon in support of the Act of Supremacy, Reginald dryly informed his friend, Contarini, that 'the King has sent me some books to instruct me in the opinion he wishes me to adopt; ordering me, at the same time, to say exactly what I think'.[13]

Reginald clearly took this literally, for in *De Unitate* he compared Henry to the despised ancient Roman Emperor Nero, and most damningly he openly called for the Holy Roman Emperor, Charles V, to invade England. As Higginbotham covers, Reginald informed the king that 'You have squandered a huge treasure; you have made a laughing-stock of the nobility; you have never loved the people; you have pestered and robbed the clergy in every possible way; and lately you have destroyed the best men of your kingdom, not like a human being, but a wild beast'.[14] The 'best men' Reginald refers to being Thomas More and Bishop Fisher. Reginald also made his feelings on the divorce from Katherine of Aragon abundantly clear, referring to the separation as a 'lying affair'.[15] To make matters worse, Reginald would also profess

111

the innocence of his long executed uncle, Edward, earl of Warwick, an action which highlighted Reginald's own royal bloodline. With no son in the royal nursery, Henry VIII's dynasty remained deeply uncertain. Sly reminders such as those given by Reginald, thus had the capacity to be deeply troublesome for the safety of both the Pole family, and the wider network of Plantagenets still at court. Unsurprisingly, the king did not respond well to *De Unitate*, with one report suggesting Henry threatened to make Reginald 'eat his own heart'.[16] Margaret's return to court had been brief. After spending some time with Mary, the king and his new wife, she departed for what was hopefully a quiet life in the country, basing herself most regularly at the castle of Warblington.[17] Given the highly volatile nature of court, it isn't too difficult to assume that a quiet life in the country was exactly what Margaret coveted, being now, as she was, elderly by the standards of the time. *De Unitate* put pay to that, with the king soon calling for Margaret to personally visit him to hear what her traitorous son had to say. In what must have been a spectacularly uncomfortable meeting, the king read aloud Reginald's words against him. Immediately pulling rank, Margaret met with her eldest son Montagu, with the two fleshing out a path forward, a process of intense damage limitation. Montagu informed his mother that for the safety of the family, they were to entirely renounce Reginald as a traitor, which Margaret did willingly. She soon wrote to her wayward son, imploring him to take back his words and remain loyal to the king, saying:

> 'Son Reginald, I send you God's blessing and mine, though my trust to have comfort in you is turned to sorrow. Alas that I, for your folly, should receive from my sovereign lord such message as I have late done by your brother. To me, as a woman, his Highness has shown such mercy and pity as I could never deserve, but that I trusted my children's services would express my duty. Trust me, Reginald, there went never the death of thy father or of any child so nigh my heart. Upon my blessing, I charge thee to take another way and serve our master, as thy duty is, unless thou wilt be the confusion of thy mother.'

Margaret would then tactfully remind Reginald of the education he owed to the king's sponsorship, telling him 'who have brought you up and maintained you to learning but his Highness?'[18] We must remain sceptical of how much Margaret actually believed her words. Like others of the time, this was, in all probability, pure lip service to the king, but an action necessary to try and limit culpability of the wider Pole family. Indeed the letters that both she and Montagu wrote would be screened by the king's council before making their way to Italy. Montagu was under no illusion as to the danger his brother was inflicting, stating 'the king, to be avenged of Reginald, I fear will kill us all'.[19] Time had repeatedly shown that outward obedience to the king, even at personal cost, was the safest course of action. Accordingly, Montagu would parrot his mother's words, but with even greater fervour, informing Reginald that:

'At time convenient, I spoke with the king, who declared a great part of your book so at length that it made my poor heart so to lament that I had lost mother, wife, and children it could no more have done, for that had been but natural. But you, to show yourself so unnatural to so noble a prince, of whom you cannot deny next God you have received all things. And for our family, which was clean trodden under foot, he set up nobly, which showeth his charity, his clemency, and his mercy. I grieve to see the day that you should set forth the contrary, or trust to your wit above the rest of the country, whose mind you will perceive from him whom you bade read your book. If there is any grace in you, now you will turn to the right way, and then we may reckon it was the will of God that your ingratitude should show the king's meekness. He has borne your slanders more patiently than the poorest in the country could do, and is contented that your friends should instruct you of what moves them, as I know those who are learned have done. I, for lack of learning, could never conceive that laws made by man were of such length but that they might be undone again by man, for what seems politic at one time, by abusion proves at another time the contrary. Therefore, gentle Reginald, let no scrupulosity so embrace your stomach but that we, which be so knit in nature and so happily born under so noble a prince, may so join together to serve him, as our bounden duties require. It is incredible to me that by reason of a brief sent to you from the bishop of Rome you should be resident with him this winter. Learning you may well have, but doubtless no prudence nor pity, but showeth yourself to run from one mischief to another. And then farewell all bonds of nature, not only of me, but of all mine, or else instead of my blessing they shall have my curse. But utterly out of hope I cannot be that ever superstition should so reign in you that you would so highly offend God to lose the benefits of so noble a prince, your native country, and whole family.'[20]

It is clear from Margaret and Montagu's words that they took the situation very seriously. An uncomfortable reality for Margaret, however, was that she had given her son entirely over to the Church, and he was now using that experience as impetus in his fight against the king. Had Reginald been raised in England, alongside his brothers and sister, it is likely, if not certain, that he would have treated the safety of his family's welfare more seriously. Removed as he was, both emotionally and physically, the backlash of his actions would mean little for Reginald himself. Indeed even with the words of his mother and brother no doubt ringing in his ears, Reginald would continue in his obstinacy towards Henry VIII. It would appear he was either so blinded by his own certainty that it manifested as outright arrogance, or he attempted to rewrite the way in which his works had been received by the king. After hearing of Henry VIII's response to *De Unitate*, Reginald fired off a letter to his friend Cardinal Gasparo Contarini, telling him that:

'The messenger by whom I sent my book delivered it into the hands of the king, then he was ordered to return at the top speed with letters and commands of which the substance is as follows. The king was not displeased with what I had written, but since, in a good many, or rather in almost all particulars, my view appeared to differ from his own, it would gratify him very much to discuss the matter with me in person. This was his pretext for summoning me back, and he himself wrote me an exceedingly sharp letter to the same, not so much inviting as commanding me without evasion or delay, to return at once to my country and to his palace, that we might communicate with each other freely upon certain

Right: Portrait believed to be Lady Margaret Pole, Countess of Salisbury. The small wooden barrel charm, which may act as an indication of the portrait sitter, can be seen hanging below her right wrist.

Below: The remains of Farleigh Hungerford Castle, Somerset. Birthplace of Margaret Pole.

Portrait of George, Duke of Clarence, father of Margaret Pole.

Sketch of Edward, Earl of Warwick from the Rous Roll. This is the only extant image of Margaret's brother.

King Edward IV, the first Yorkist king and uncle of Margaret Pole.

Above: Tewkesbury Abbey, Gloucestershire, the resting place of Margaret Pole's parents – George, Duke of Clarence and Isobel, Duchess of Clarence.

Left: Queen Elizabeth of York, the first Tudor queen consort, mother of King Henry VIII and cousin of Margaret Pole.

Right: England's most infamous monarch – King Henry VIII.

Below: Photograph of a writ sent to Thomas Wolsey by Margaret Pole. Margaret's signature is visible at the bottom: 'Margret Pole'.

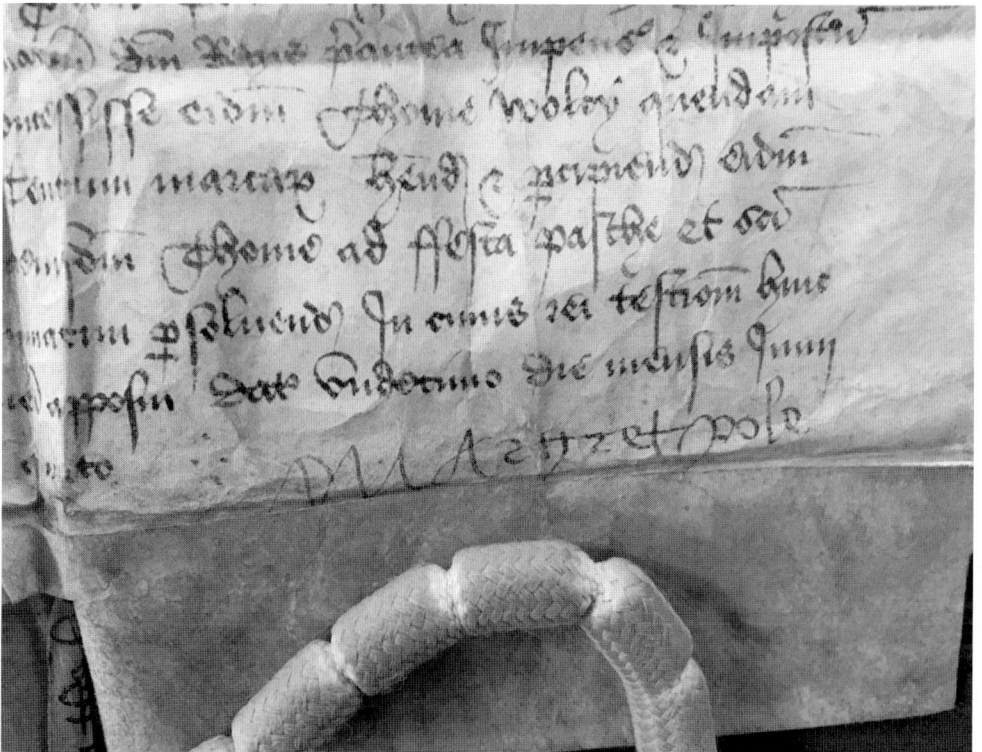

Edward Stafford, Duke of Buckingham.

Queen Katherine of Aragon.

This sketch, by Hans Holbein, is believed to be a contemporary sketch of Anne Boleyn, which if so gives us a true indication of what Henry VIII's most controversial wife actually looked like.

Fitz Williams Earl of Southampton.

William Fitzwilliam, Earl of Southampton, the man responsible for questioning Margaret and her sons throughout the Exeter Conspiracy.

Left: Thomas Goodrich, Bishop of Ely, who would join Southampton in questioning those involved in the Exeter Conspiracy.

Below: The Tower of London, where Margaret Pole, her brother, and her eldest son would all lose their lives.

ROBERT CARDINAL DE LENONCOVRT
EVESQVE DE METZ LAN·15 0·

Cardinal Reginald Pole, resplendent in the red robes of his office.

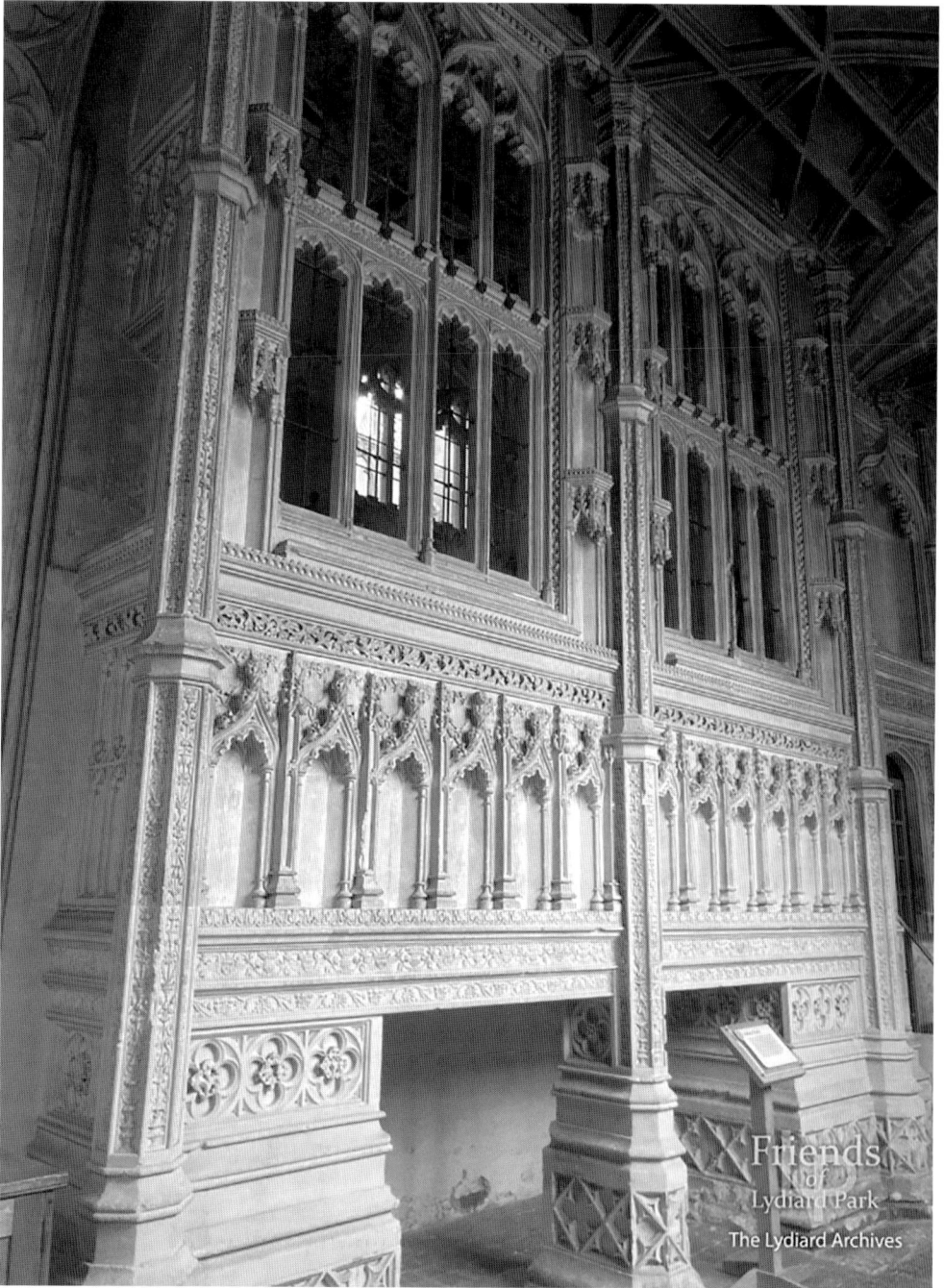

Margaret's Chapel, Priory Church, Christchurch. The space Margaret Pole intended to be buried in, but remains vacant to this day.

Above: The sole surviving tower of Margaret's once grand home, Warblington Castle.

Right: Queen Mary I.

'Portrait of a Lady' from The Courtauld Gallery in London. It is possible that this depicts Ursula Pole, Baroness Stafford. The clothing is correct for a noblewoman of the era, the ciborium indicates religious conservatism and the white rose is the eponymous symbol of the House of York.

Henry Hastings, Earl of Huntingdon, Margaret's great-grandson who served at the court of Elizabeth I.

Edward Courtenay, 1st Earl of Devon, the son of the Marquess of Exeter who rose and then fell under the reign of Queen Mary.

Queen Elizabeth I.

The Vaughan Porch at Leicester Cathedral. The third figure in from the right is Henry Hastings, Earl of Huntingdon.

Chapel Royal of St Peter ad Vincula, Tower of London, the final resting place of Margaret Pole and Henry, Baron Montagu.

Monument to Lady Dorothy Stafford at Westminster Abbey. The plaque which sits below provides a fitting epitaph to her grandmother.

points. Moreover, Cromwell, to whom all England is in subjection, as it was during the lifetime of the late queen, sent me a letter to the same effect. Without circumlocution or apology, I declined to return home until the king should have returned to his home, namely, the Church.'[21]

His actions were viewed with outrage by loyalists to the king, with Edward Hall decrying 'that arch-traitor Reynold Pole, enemy to God's word and his natural country, had moved and stirred divers great princes and potentates of Christendom to invade the realm of England'.[22] This was nothing new. Letters inviting the Emperor to invade England were a regular occurrence and pre-date *De Unitate,* but feature the Pole family in their content, nonetheless. As early as 1534, Chapuys had written to his master the Emperor, telling him:

'Should your majesty send the smallest possible force, all the people would at once declare in your favour, especially if the sade Seigneur Reynald (Reginald) were in the country. The latter's younger brother is with me, and would visit me almost every day, had I not dissuaded him from doing so, on account of the danger he might run. He, however, ceases not, like many others, to importune and beg me to write to your Majesty, and explain how very easy the conquest of this kingdom would be, and that the inhabitants are only waiting for a signal. I have never spoken to him about his brother, except warning him that the latter had much better remain where he is now, and beg his daily bread in the streets, than attempt returning here in these troubled times, for fear he should be treated as the poor bishop of Rochester, or worse still. This he assures me he has done, having written to him many a time, and made his mother also write and warn him not to come here.'[23]

With what came next, it certainly seemed that Reginald and Chapuys' hopes for England may come true.

In October 1536, what became known as the Pilgrimage of Grace broke out. It began in Lincolnshire, with protests directed against the ongoing closure of monasteries. It cannot be overstated enough just how devastating the closures were for many of the common people of England. Religion dictated practically all facets of life in the sixteenth century, and whilst there were undoubtedly some religious houses where extortion and general bad practice was afoot, this was not endemic across the board. Many of the monasteries carried out a great deal of good works, including feeding the poor and destitute. With their closure, the streets soon filled with vagrants, many of them former monks and nuns. As Seward points out, for members of the nobility such as the Poles and Exeters, the destruction of these houses was also personal, for some contained their ancestors' remains. The loss of the monasteries removed a sense of order and structure from daily life, for mass was greatly discouraged, feast days were cancelled, and shrines, many of them attracting large numbers of pilgrims, were destroyed. This robbed not only the common people of everything they knew and held dear, but also wiped monumentally significant historic sites from being seen to this day, most notably the shrine of Saint Thomas Becket. After Lincolnshire, the rebellion soon extended to large swathes of the north, with another key complaint being the ever-increasing tax burdens. It is worth remembering that much of the dislike directed towards King Henry VII at the end of his reign was tied to his parsimony. All these years later, it would appear that his son was following suit. Like the Peasants' Revolt of 1381, at its core the Pilgrimage was at the instigation of the common people. Separated as they were from the centre of action in London, the movement would also find support in members of the landed gentry in the north, most notably Thomas, 1st Baron Darcy. As with most political movements, the uprising, like a flame to gunpowder, exploded into mass protest, which at its heart was attempting to do good, but under a reign as tyrannical as Henry VIII's, was viewed as nothing more than treason. Although the rebels profusely asserted loyalty to the king, making it clear that their complaint was mostly directed at Cromwell, this did not alter the fact that they were rebelling against the king's authority. Simply put, to question policies brought in by Cromwell, was to question the king. The rebels would adopt a banner: a gold shield bearing the five wounds of Christ, against the traditionally Catholic background colour of red. This banner, like other sigils, came to embody the pilgrims' cause and was carried at all notable meetings and skirmishes. When it became clear just how large the uprising had become, with some historians suggesting as many as 50,000 took up arms[24], the king realised his own standing army was insufficient to quash the rebellion. Such vast numbers acts as a salutary reminder that the people of England remained loyal to the traditional Catholic faith; the faith adhered to by the Pole family, their kin, and most symbolically, the Lady Mary. The introduction of heretical books into England may have been given credence by Anne Boleyn and her ilk, but with their sponsor now an executed traitor, those in agreement with reformist theology ran the risk of falling prey to accusations of heresy. Despite his break from the church in Rome, and contrary to popular belief, King Henry VIII remained a Catholic throughout his life, and would die very much in that faith, albeit one of his own creation. There were undoubtedly ardent reformists living in England, but they remained very much in the shadows, usually confined to London and the south-east, which perhaps goes some way to explaining why religious dissent never broke out in that particular corner of England. The king would lean on the considerable might of the Dukes of Norfolk and Suffolk to retaliate against the northern uprising, as well as the Marquess of Exeter, sending them forthwith to the areas most openly in revolt. Uncharacteristically, the king gave strict instructions to reach a peace treaty without excessive bloodshed, something which no doubt pleased Queen Jane, who had earned her husband's displeasure when she fell to her knees before him requesting he restore the abbeys. A meeting between the rebel leaders and Norfolk took place in December 1536, during which the duke accepted the requests put forward. The king gave every appearance of standing by his word, even going to the steps of inviting the rebel leaders, including its most famous member, a one-eyed Yorkshireman, Robert Aske, to spend Christmas with the royal family.

As this very parlay was taking place, Pope Paul III elevated Reginald Pole to the rank of cardinal. A bold but nonetheless deliberate move, Reginald's new position was the precursor to a plan in which he would return to England in support of the Pilgrimage of Grace. The decision to endow Reginald with such honours may have been accelerated by Chapuys, who had written to Rome with repeated requests to send Reginald back to England bearing all the 'weapons of the Church'. Although beyond the clutches of the king, intelligence soon reached England that the cardinalship had been offered to Reginald. Thomas Starkey, now an employee of Cromwell's, wrote imploring him to not accept the Pope's offer, explaining that to do so would make

Reginald an enemy of the king. Unsurprisingly, Starkey's request fell on deaf ears. Made papal legate to England not long after, this rank made Reginald both a prince of the Church and the Pope's official representative. Like the safe conduct meted out to ambassadors, such as Chapuys, who regularly and openly rallied against Henry VIII but could not be touched by him, Pole now technically benefited from a degree of protection that, on paper, should see him safe were he to journey back to his homeland. It was at this time in Reginald's life that the man himself developed into a rather impressive, albeit truculent figure. Unlike his brothers, for whom no likenesses exist, we are blessed with several portraits of Reginald, many of them contemporary. He is perpetually presented in the red and white robes of his office, an impressively dense beard hanging low, with high cheekbones, piercing blue-grey eyes and an aquiline nose. His visage, beard aside, bears a passing resemblance to the portrait often believed to be his mother. A Spanish envoy of the time reported 'Here in Rome lives an English gentleman of the name of Reginald Pole. His Holiness honours him much and has given him lodgings within his own palace, and over his own apartments. Though he dresses as an ecclesiastic, he is not yet in holy orders'.[25] A reminder again that Reginald, whilst undoubtedly rising through Church ranks, was still free to marry, should he wish, something Chapuys would have known when he said of the Lady Mary 'I am sure she will never consent to marry anyone in this country, save perhaps Master Reginald Pole'.[26] Such commendations from the Pope point to a strong bond between the two men, and so it's probable, to the point of certainty, that the actions of Henry VIII, and what to do about them, would have been a regular topic of conversation. The Pope would have been well aware of the notoriety of Reginald's ancestry; could he represent a powerful alternative to, as they saw it, the monstrous rule of King Henry? With little tact and consideration for the symbolism of his actions, Reginald would travel to France, entering Paris, which as papal legate came with much pomp and pageantry. Given the ever turbulent relationship between Henry VIII and Francis I of France, that Reginald made it to the French capital in one piece suggests he had been given some degree of safe passage. Unfortunately, his journey was ultimately fruitless, for King Francis refused to receive Reginald at his court, perhaps knowing all too well how explosive such an action would be perceived across the channel. However, much to Henry VIII's annoyance, Francis would also not simply hand Reginald over. As an enemy of Henry's, and one with royal blood, it isn't too difficult to imagine that Reginald appearing in Paris would have amused the French king, a carrot to dangle before his old adversary. Shortly after, the Pope would issue a formal papal bull in support of the Pilgrimage of Grace, instructing the rebels 'to persevere until the King returns to the way of truth'.[27] This was an open declaration to the people of England to rise up against their monarch, with full papal support. Unfortunately, it was too little too late, for by this time the Pilgrimage of Grace had been sufficiently quashed, Reginald's journey to Paris and his elevation by the pope were thus largely pointless. Pope Paul III was canny enough to recognise this, accepting that the driving force of the Pilgrimage was now dead. To support the uprising was, to use modern day parlance, akin to flogging a dead horse. Understandably though, the situation was still of grave concern to the king and Cromwell. They had managed to subdue the Pilgrimage, but knew only too well that Reginald represented a Pope-approved standard around which other dissidents could rally. The situation was made all the more inflammatory when the king entirely reneged on his promises to the rebel leaders. Although the Christmas of 1536 is often portrayed as the king acting out a sociopathic period of revelry, whilst secretly knowing he would entirely destroy Aske and his supporters, this isn't quite accurate. Evidence suggests that the king intended to uphold his end of the bargain, but the outbreak of another revolt, and the threat of Reginald overseas, both influenced and impacted the eventual outcome meted out on the northern rebels. Robert Aske, already the de-facto leader of the Pilgrimage, would become the rebellion's most famous victim. Although spared the horror of a traitor's death, he was made to suffer, nonetheless. Aske would be hung in chains outside of York Castle. Lord Darcy was put on trial on a charge of depriving the king of his title, supreme head of the church. Overseeing the trial was the Marquess of Exeter, who had taken on the role as the Dukes of Norfolk and Suffolk remained busy in the north, with Exeter the next highest in rank among the nobility. Like his close friend Montagu, and despite helping to subdue the rebellion, Exeter maintained well known conservative political leanings, and fierce loyalty towards the king's elder daughter, Lady Mary. Helen Miller asserts that Exeter was chosen for the role, precisely because of his political beliefs, for it would apply greater pressure on him to maintain loyalty to the king.

As winter gave way to spring in 1537, the king did at least have one major thing to feel happy about; Queen Jane was pregnant. As the couple had been wed for approximately eight months by the time Jane conceived, there is some suggestion that they had experienced difficulties, which may well have lain with the king himself. By now, Henry VIII was 46 years old, over middle-aged by the standards of the time, and his once trim figure had given way to a much bulkier frame. For the king, his third wife's pregnancy must surely have felt like the last roll of the dice. Mercifully, the pregnancy progressed well, and of course, everyone hoped and prayed that it would be the much desired male heir. After a long and difficult labour, on 12 October 1537 Queen Jane gave birth to a son, Edward. The king had reigned for twenty-eight years, and it had been twenty-six years since the death of his and Katherine of Aragon's short lived prince, Henry, Duke of Cornwall. To say that Henry VIII reacted to the news with jubilation would be a gross understatement. Hugh Latimer summed up the general feelings of the populace, acknowledging the birth of the infant prince as one 'we hungered for so long'.[28] Just three days later, the tiny infant was christened with much splendour in the Chapel Royal of Hampton Court Palace. Henry, Baron Montagu was given a starring role in the proceedings, carrying a pair of covered basins alongside the Earl of Sussex. They were followed, in what must have been unbelievably challenging circumstances, by none other than Thomas Boleyn, Earl of Wiltshire, father to the late Queen Anne, who carried a wax taper. Montagu's involvement suggests that, at this stage at least, the Pole family had retained their standing at court, and were not tarred by association to Reginald. This isn't to suggest the day went off without a hitch for the family, for Geoffrey Pole caused considerable embarrassment for Montagu through his general lack of wisdom. As was increasingly customary for Geoffrey, the issue came down to money. Earlier in the year he had written to Sir Thomas Audley, who had been made Lord Chancellor following the reduction of Sir Thomas More back in 1532.[29] By now, Cromwell was as good as master of everything, very little business done in England did not cross his desk, including invitations to appear at court. It was to this point that Geoffrey sought out Audley, asking his advice on how to solicit Cromwell's approval. That such action needed to be taken highlights a clear breakdown in the relationship between Cromwell and Geoffrey, the former of whom we must remember had once paid off some of Geoffrey's debts. By now however, Cromwell could not be moved, and Geoffrey's requests went unanswered – he was not welcome at court. A wiser man would have read the room, but not Geoffrey. On the very day that Prince Edward was being christened, Geoffrey reappeared, only to be denied entry. Sir Thomas Palmer, a courtier who would eventually fall from grace under Queen Mary I, sent word to Lord Lisle that 'my lord Montague's brother came to court to do service, but the King would not suffer him to come in'.[30] Geoffrey was fast showing himself to be a rash and imprudent character, unappealing characteristics in anyone, let alone the brother of a cardinal in open revolt against the king. The jubilation King Henry felt at the birth of his long desired male heir was short lived, for within days of Prince Edward's birth it became clear that Queen Jane was dangerously ill. Twelve days after delivering her triumph, the queen died, aged approximately 29. The reason for her death is still a topic of debate, with both puerperal fever and infected retained placenta put forward as the likely cause. Since her death, Jane has been perpetually viewed as the great love of Henry VIII's life, a fact seemingly compounded by the king's decision to be buried alongside her. Whilst this latter fact is undoubtedly true, for the king does indeed rest beside Jane in a vault in St George's Chapel, Windsor, whether she was truly the love of his life is something I question. The more plausible assessment is that Jane was viewed with such reverence by the king because she gave him the much desired male heir, and died before the marriage had the scope of turning sour. Her character or successes outside of her progeny were, to the king's mind, negligible. She succeeded in the one thing her predecessors did not, and ultimately for Henry VIII, that's what mattered. Moreover, the king was never going to be buried alongside a woman he had divorced or had executed. Jane, as the mother of his son and heir, was the only possible choice for such an honour.

As Henry mourned the death of his third wife, the Pole family continued to walk the ever challenging tightrope between loyal service to the crown, whilst attempting to try and protect Reginald, and thus their own interests. Only Montagu was unequivocally welcome at court, for Margaret, although not outwardly barred, by not having a role within Lady Mary's household, in effect had no role to play at court, and as referenced, the actions of her two younger sons had tainted her own standing amongst loyalists to the king. Geoffrey had been denied access, and Reginald was public enemy number one as far as Henry VIII was concerned. Ursula Pole's whereabouts at this time are difficult to pin down. She is not mentioned in the court sources, which suggests she remained out of sight, living the life of a quiet country noblewoman. Her father-in-law's attainder had robbed her husband of the Buckingham dukedom, and so she carried no noble title. Ursula would thus not have been considered a senior member of the nobility, for whom a role at court was customary. She had given her husband three children, a son Henry, who died in infancy, a daughter Dorothy, born in 1526, and a second son, also given the name Henry, born around 1527. As infant mortality was commonplace at this time, it was not unusual for children to be given the name of a deceased sibling. During the reign of Anne Boleyn, Ursula gave birth to two more sons, Thomas in 1533 and Edward in 1535. Edward was born at Stafford Castle, which would indicate that this is where Ursula and her husband spent much of their time. Three more sons would follow, Richard, Walter and William. Unfortunately we have little to no information to pinpoint when they were born, save an estimated year of birth for Walter of 1539, which would place Richard's birth between 1536 and 1538. One insight into Ursula's life that we do have available, is in her apparent close friendship with the Duchess of Norfolk, Elizabeth Stafford. As the eldest daughter of the Duke of Buckingham, Elizabeth was Ursula's sister-in-law. The duchess had famously acted against the rise of Anne Boleyn as queen, which given the Pole family's politics was likely a cause of bonding between the two women. That a warm relationship existed between Ursula and her sister-in-law is evident from the bequests given after the duchess died. In her will she affectionately refers to Ursula as 'sister stafford', leaving all her jewellery and apparel, as well as a French hood and velvet covered riding saddle to Ursula.[31]

As Lord Privy Seal, Cromwell kept an increasingly watchful eye on Reginald's movements. He was able to achieve this through covertly installing an employee on his payroll within the cardinal's household. The man in question was Michael Throckmorton, who had been given the unenviable task of delivering *De Unitate* to Henry's court. Upon arrival, Throckmorton was arrested for his would-be association to Reginald, concern at his loyalties no doubt exacerbated by the fact that his brother, George, was lodged in the Tower for spreading

Robert Aske's manifesto.[32] However, Michael Throckmorton was clearly a good talker, for he sufficiently convinced the council that he could act as a spy, with the main goal of encouraging Reginald to return to England. Having a man on the inside was par for the course for Cromwell, providing as close to real time intelligence as it was possible to achieve in the sixteenth century. Throckmorton was assiduous in his reports, becoming, if not fond, at least impressed by Reginald. He informed Cromwell that the cardinal appears to have been a decent and honest man, but was also naive and easily swayed by his Roman peers. Throckmorton was clearly a man with either an innate ability to fly under the radar, or was simply very lucky, for he travelled between the court in London and Reginald's establishment in Italy without ever raising suspicion from the latter. The continually shifting relations between Henry and his European rivals, King Francis, and Emperor Charles, made it an all too believable reality that aid could be granted from either party, should Reginald make a bid to return to his homeland. The king would have also known about possible trouble coming from Ireland, when letters from the noble Fitzgerald family bound for Reginald were intercepted. In short, it was becoming increasingly clear to Henry that he had enemies, both real and imagined, facing him on all sides. His hatred for Reginald, a man he had sponsored, a man with whom he shared blood, now became all consuming. Reginald needed to be silenced. Taking up arms against Reginald's network of overseas supporters would be too difficult, and so assassination was the cleanest course of action decided upon by the king. Sir Francis Bryan would be tasked with journeying to France to carry out the deed. Bryan was a notorious one-eyed philanderer, known to history as 'the vicar of hell'[33] for his hard partying, bad boy image; upon arrival into Calais for example, he demanded 'a soft bed then a hard harlot'.[34] A cousin of Anne Boleyn, and her successors Jane Seymour and Katheryn Howard, Bryan managed to never fall out of favour with the king, achieved in no small part by his lack of scruples around changing his views to always suit Henry VIII's. Bryan would be joined in France by an accomplice, Peter Mewtas, husband of Jane Mewtas who had served in the household of the late Queen Jane. Their aim was to kill Reginald, or better still, capture and convey him to Calais, which as an English territory, would allow Reginald to stand trial for high treason. Unfortunately, Reginald would remain ever two steps ahead of his would-be captors. Geoffrey Pole had taken to writing to his brother, informing him that assassins were 'sent from England daily to destroy him'.[35] Cromwell, for now, remained unconcerned, publicly announcing that Reginald was likely to destroy himself before being caught. Reginald for his part would clap back, denigrating Cromwell's powers, saying 'And would my Lord Privy Seal so fain kill me? Well, I trust it shall not lie in his power. The King is not content to bear me malice himself, but provoketh others against me'.[36] Reginald's words suggest he treated Henry's actions as lacking originality, almost as if the king's decision to send assassins was a disappointment to Reginald, as though it were beneath the king's dignity. No doubt to Henry's chagrin, King Francis was one of those who sent word to Reginald to warn him of the impending danger. Upon arriving on the continent, Sir Francis Bryan made contact with the porter of Calais, Sir Thomas Palmer, who having realised Reginald had escaped, quickly gave orders for three of his men to chase after him, Palmer himself also joining. Alas, they were too late. Reginald was able to reach an imperially protected bishopric in Cambrai, from where he was safe. Bryan and Mewtas could not touch him, they had failed. Reginald became aware that the king had sent letters to the French court demanding they expel him from Cambrai, the letters stating 'We would be very glad to have the said Pole by some means trussed up and conveyed to Calais, we desire and pray you to consult and devise thereupon.'[37] Henry VIII's wishes would go unanswered.

Now secure from immediate danger, Reginald maintained regular correspondence with a fellow cardinal, Rodolfo Pio da Carpi. In his letters, Reginald likened the state of England as one suffering infection, with the disease caused solely by the king. He explained that the only means to save England would be through 'surgery or diet'. Reginald's choice of words was merely symbolic, with surgery as a cover for invasion, and diet in place of diplomatic resolution. Outwardly peace-making, it was Reginald's hope that diplomacy would lead to the king's destruction.[38] Reginald would have to remain vigilant though, for Bryan and Mewtas' failed assassination attempts on his life did not extinguish the overall plan. By now, Bishop Gardiner had also been brought in to work alongside Bryan. They struck up a relationship with John Hutton, who served as the English ambassador in Brussels. In a bid to curry favour with Henry VIII,

Hutton claimed he would be able to ensure Reginald's assassination came to pass. At this stage, Cromwell's spy, Throckmorton, had his own retinue of retainers, so gaining a place in his household would be a solid way of having potential access to the cardinal. Hutton worked with a Welshman, William Vaughan, who had fled his native country to try and escape a charge of manslaughter. Vaughan claimed that he knew someone, Henry Phillips, who could secure a place as a servant to Throckmorton. Upon arrival at Reginald's home, Throckmorton surveyed Vaughan, and did not like what he saw. Nonetheless, Throckmorton agreed to present Vaughan to the cardinal, who had clearly been brought up to speed on Vaughan's backstory, telling him 'I am informed you be banished out of your native country as well as I'. After being let down gently that Reginald had all the servants he required whilst on the road, Vaughan was advised that he should journey to Italy, and that once Reginald was back at the centre of things in Rome, employment could more realistically be offered. Reginald did, however, provide Vaughan with some money, and advised him rather ambiguously to 'gather news'.[39] Vaughan soon became aware that Throckmorton was planning a journey to England, supposedly to convey secret letters to Reginald's supporters. Vaughan informed Hutton of what he had heard, who promptly advised that he should travel alongside Throckmorton in a bid to uncover a spy against the king. Hutton even went to the steps of providing payment, blithely unaware that the man he hoped to uncover as a spy, was indeed one, but for the other side. Throckmorton was clearly adept in his duties.

By 1538 the Pole family were moving increasingly closer to danger, caused unsurprisingly by the assistance they had given to Reginald. What truly kickstarted their descent started, somewhat expectedly, with Geoffrey. Letters and communication channels had been set up between Geoffrey and Reginald, facilitated by a man in the former's employ, Hugh Holland. Holland had built a career shipping goods to the continent, and even dabbled in a period of piracy for a time. He had been contacted by Geoffrey as early as Easter 1537, and asked to convey what, at this point, were purely verbal messages to Reginald. When the Pole family fell, Holland was the very first person to be questioned and he provided extensive information which greatly implicated Geoffrey Pole as having committed treason. Rather like *De Unitate*, as will be examined, Geoffrey made his feelings on England, and by extension the policies of the king, abundantly clear. He also expressed a desire to leave England and join his brother, asking Reginald's permission to do so. Geoffrey's desire to leave the country was likely twofold, driven by his distaste for Henry VIII's policy, and his own ever burgeoning mountain of debt. It was at this juncture that another figure who would fall with the Pole family appeared in the story, George Croftes. Croftes was Chancellor of Chichester Cathedral, and like the Pole family was deeply committed to the traditional Catholic faith. He had considered fleeing England in 1534 when the Act of Supremacy was passed, before being convinced by a friend to remain and conform to the king's wishes.[40] Geoffrey now turned to Croftes, expressing his determination to depart England at the earliest opportunity. The churchman lent Geoffrey some money to aid his travels, and wished him well. Just a day later, however, Geoffrey received a letter from Croftes imploring him to remain in England. Croftes claims to have had a dream in which the Virgin Mary 'appeared unto him and she pledged him that it should be the destruction of the said Sir Geoffrey and all of his kin if he departed the realm'.[41] Geoffrey was sufficiently convinced, for he abandoned his plans, and despite no doubt needing the money, returned it to Croftes.

It would be later revealed that someone else Holland carried letters to was John Helyar, Margaret's ex-chaplain, whose departure from England had caused Stephen Gardiner disquiet. Holland arrived at the cardinal's place of residence, which at this stage was the Palace of Liège in Flanders. Reginald was kept in great splendour as a guest of Érard de la Marck, the Cardinal of Liège, commenting that he was treated as befitting his rank as papal legate. Holland was examined carefully by Throckmorton, ostensibly to ensure he wasn't one of the potential assassins, although his concerns were likely superficial. The more accurate justification, at this stage at least, is that Throckmorton quizzed Holland so rigorously hoping he would capture information of interest to his actual master, Cromwell. During Reginald's time at Liège, officials for the city became aware of the planned assassination attempts against his life. They managed to intercept letters from John Hutton, who as ever was keen to ingratiate himself with the king, whilst maintaining clear personal interest. He had written that 'If he (Reginald) can be killed, as we earlier discussed among ourselves, it would certainly be the gateway to being looked into the highest favour with the King, and earn us a valuable reward'.[42] Reginald himself appears to have been well briefed on the identity of the would be assassin, explaining that he was an Englishman who had attempted to secure a place in his household, before getting cold feet and ducking out of the appointment. As Vaughan was Welsh, it's possible that the assassin Reginald speaks of was not Vaughan himself, but a professionally hired hitman. Equally, his assessment that the assassin had attempted to gain employment in his household and was on the run, is conveniently coincidental. Without knowing how strong Vaughan's Welsh accent was, it's entirely reasonable to conclude that Reginald simply didn't know he was Welsh, and that he took him for an Englishman. Thus the assassin was either Vaughan, or someone unknown to history.

Not long after returning to England, Holland was arrested. Just weeks later, on 29 August 1538, the first significant arrest in what became known as the Exeter Conspiracy took place; Geoffrey Pole was conveyed to the Tower of London as a prisoner, entering on a charge of high treason. The downfall of the Pole family had begun.

Chapter 8

The Exeter Conspiracy

'The Folly of one brainsick Pole'
                                    Thomas Cromwell

The Exeter Conspiracy remains precisely that, conspiracy. A mere title for something which would ultimately become much more serious. Ever since the publication of *De Unitate* in 1536, the Pole family had been consistently watched. It has been argued that Cromwell, eternally vigilant for an opportunity to destabilise the remaining scions of the Plantagenet dynasty, now used Henry VIII's naturally suspicious personality to drive home the theory that his life and thus the throne were in danger. Like the downfall of Anne Boleyn, Cromwell's hand in uncovering the supposed Exeter Conspiracy is certainly there, but other arguments as to the root cause remain at play. The first thing to say is that no irrefutable proof has ever been uncovered which would implicate those who would eventually lose their lives. Like other notable falls from grace from Henry VIII's reign, offhand and entirely natural responses between family members and close groups of friends, could, and would, be turned into treason. This isn't to suggest that there is no evidence full stop. As will be discussed, there is considerably more to the story than is often believed, and when one breaks down the 'evidence', such as it is, it becomes clear that Henry VIII had at least some justification in acting the way he did to certain individuals. As outlined in the preceding chapter, the Exeter Conspiracy's origins started with the Pilgrimage of Grace, but general mistrust of the White Rose families had been ever present, and so when Reginald Pole came out in such fervent support of its mission, aided covertly by his family, it naturally inflamed tensions considerably. The politics and loyalties of the Pole family were well known, as was their close relationship to the Marquess and Marchioness of Exeter, from whom the conspiracy gets its name. While these families remained outwardly loyal to the king, their beliefs would be largely tolerated. As Reginald continued to remain at liberty however, protected by powerful friends in Europe, Henry VIII grew more and more incensed. His inability to get to Reginald had dire consequences for the Poles. Some have thus suggested that Margaret and her family became, in effect, a scapegoat for Reginald. If the king couldn't reach him, then he would go for the next best thing. Soon, the Pole family, their servants and members of their kin would find themselves at the centre of one of the most explosive periods of Henry VIII's reign. Some of the king's oldest friends would be swept up in the drama, which led to a total of thirteen arrests, and would eventually conclude with the execution of Lady Margaret Pole herself. Just as Anne Boleyn had been brought low in a matter of weeks, now, two years later, some of the people who had been her fiercest critics would suffer the same fate. In only three months, several members of England's pre-eminent families, the remnants of the great Plantagenet dynasty, were all but destroyed. This chapter will tell the story of how this came to be.

As best we can tell, Hugh Holland's arrest took place in the summer of 1538. He was likely with Baron Montagu and his master, Geoffrey Pole, at Montagu's residence, Bockmer House. A contrary story suggests that Geoffrey Pole came upon Holland after his arrest, as he was being conveyed to London. Holland sat atop a horse, his arms tied behind his back and his legs tied beneath the saddle. Geoffrey, noted for his use of puns, supposedly asked Holland where he was 'bound' to go, the latter retorting ominously that Geoffrey should 'keep on his way, for he should not be long after'.[1] Whilst this makes for an amusing little exchange, it is likely apocryphal, stemming, as Hazel Pierce notes, from idle gossip. According to more accurate sources, Holland did not respond well to his arrest, which led to a fight between himself and those sent to apprehend him. Pinpointing exactly when Holland was arrested is difficult, for as a commoner, rather than a member of the nobility, such facts were not committed to posterity. That the arrest took place in the summer of 1538 also comes from Pierce, who has examined the evidence extensively. Reactions by the Pole family to Holland's arrest were mixed; Montagu was not especially worried at this stage at least, remarking that he always burned the letters he received. Geoffrey was less circumspect, and grew anxious. He instructed John Collins, Chaplain to Montagu, to travel to Lordington, the chief residence of Geoffrey and his family, to burn letters apparently held there. It is believed that this took place on 21 June 1538.[2] This burning of letters would become central to the case brought forward against the Pole family. When examined on 11 November 1538, Constance, Geoffrey's wife, confirmed that Collins did arrive at her home, bearing her husband's signet ring as a token. During the visit he burned five to six letters, the contents of which Constance claimed she knew not. She also stated that Collins had arrived between the holidays of Whitsun and Midsummer.[3] Collins would later state that he had been sent during Corpus Christi and that his arrival at Lordington had been on a Friday. Pierce notes that Corpus Christi 1538 took place on Thursday 20 June, which through a process of elimination, allows us to conclude that Holland was arrested no later than 21 June 1538. As to why he was arrested is a murkier story still.

It is at this point that one Gervase Tyndall arrived on the scene. Tyndall, not to be confused with his infinitely more famous distant relative, William Tyndall, was a failed schoolmaster who was deeply committed to religious reform. Tyndall had a working relationship with Thomas Cromwell that went back at least as far as 1535, when showing his adherence to the king's reform, he made the lord privy seal aware of a sermon he had witnessed arguing against the act of royal supremacy.[4] Tyndall's primary residence was Deene Park in Northamptonshire, which makes his sudden appearance in Hampshire intriguing. Claiming sickness, he sought lodgings at a surgeon's house, a sort of small hospital, within the lands of Warblington Castle, which as we know, belonged to Lady Margaret Pole. It is probable, however, that the real reason for his arrival in Hampshire was on the orders of Cromwell, the latter hoping intelligence could be gathered on the dealings of the Pole family. Tyndall's illness was thus likely feigned. The chief surgeon of the property was a man called Richard Ayer, who naturally maintained regular contact with Margaret Pole and her family. What became clear, was that Ayer, rather like Geoffrey Pole, had minimal prudence, and was soon openly discussing the activities of the Pole family with Tyndall – precisely what Cromwell had been hoping for. Tyndall soon discovered that Ayer had reason to feel aggrieved at Margaret's influence over the county, and so he played on Ayer's already flimsy loyalties. He told Ayer that he would be able to organise a meeting directly with Cromwell, if Ayer were happy to reveal information, even telling the gullible man 'my lord [Cromwell] would give him great thanks in that behalf, and do more for him than ever my lady would'.[5] The offer clearly worked, for Ayer provided more salacious news, specifically on the activities of Holland, and the significance of the intelligence he was supposedly carrying over the channel and into Europe. He claimed Holland 'conveyed letters to Master Pole the Cardinal, and all the secrets of the realm of England are known to the bishop of Rome as well as though he were here'.[6] This accusation was explosive in the extreme, for letters to Reginald was one thing, but accusations of leaking state secrets to one of the king's great enemies was something else entirely. Ayer's testimony made it clear that contact between the Pole family and Reginald remained as strong as ever, and that the person who facilitated it, was Hugh Holland. Soon, Tyndall had come into contact with practically every priest in the area surrounding Warblington, picking fights along the way with the men he deemed as acting against the true word of God, and crucially, the desires of the king. This latter fact must be kept in mind because it solidified for Cromwell his growing suspicions that the Pole family remained hostile to the king's new policies, and that for all their lip service, their true adherence to the traditions of the Catholic faith, and by extension the Pope, remained as strong as ever. Of course an alternative reading on this could be that Cromwell twisted the information presented to him, in order to displace conservatives at court hostile to his plans for England. News of Tyndall's activities across Hampshire soon reached Geoffrey Pole's ear, causing him significant distress. He journeyed to meet with Cromwell, taking Ayer and Holland along for good measure, hoping that getting the two men in front of Cromwell would assuage his concerns. Geoffrey admitted to Cromwell that letters had been exchanged between himself and John Helyar, but stopped short of telling the full story, instead suggesting he was simply keeping his mother's former chaplain abreast of news from his old parish. Geoffrey was clearly unaware of just how much Tyndall now knew. Cromwell accepted Geoffrey's word, and he, Ayer and Holland left the lord privy seal as they had found him. However, shortly after, Tyndall delivered his full report to Cromwell. The report provided all the evidence Cromwell needed to put in motion the first round of arrests, which started, as covered, with Hugh Holland. Upon entering the dread fortress, Holland began to speak openly of the activities of Geoffrey Pole. As Holland was not noble, it is possible that he was tortured for information, but given the extent of his confessions, and the details therein, it is clear that he was more than willing to incriminate his master, likely being told that to do so would see him granted mercy.

What he said was more than enough for the king's council to then order Geoffrey's own arrest. Although from the report Geoffrey Pole was now seriously implicated, the rest of the Pole family remained reasonably safe at this stage. The king's guard came for Geoffrey, quite suddenly, on the last Monday of August 1538. Chapuys, ever au fait with the machinations of Henry VIII's court, correctly surmised that Geoffrey's arrest had been caused by his writing to Reginald, but moreover for his having not disclosed the information to the king[7], an act of misprision.

How Margaret herself came to be involved in Tyndall's story ties back to her own conservative religious beliefs. Like Tyndall, Ayer was keen to promote religious reform, which likely acted as a bond between the two men. If Ayer is to be believed, Margaret's power over the operational running of religion in Hampshire was verging on dictatorial. He claimed that priests in Margaret's employ, from across the county, regularly broke the rules of confession, revealing to Margaret what their parishioners had disclosed.[8] The inference here being that Margaret and her senior chaplains wished to know if members of the Pole households, and their retainers, harboured reformist sympathies. When, for example, at Easter 1537 members of Montagu's household journeyed to Chichester to give confession, Margaret was said to be 'not a little discontent'[9], for it was in lands outside of her control and would thus rob her of knowing what they had confessed. If true, this was a gross misuse by Margaret of the power she wielded, although probably fairly common practice with other great nobles of the court. The issue was that Margaret's commitment to the traditions of the Catholic Church now had the very real capacity to cause her and the Pole family irreparable damage, for it became clear that her approach to religion, the way she chose to pray, and by extension the way she expected her servants, tenants and family to pray, was contrary to the policies of Henry VIII. Just how devout Margaret Pole was, is made clear from Tyndall's testimonies. He explains that once Margaret was made aware of his reformist leanings, she banished him from her lands, ordering Ayer to oversee his departure. Tyndall would use his supposed illness as a means to remain, causing Margaret to in turn order all other patients within the surgeon's house to move on, not wishing them to be open to potential religious conversion. A more damning fact against Margaret was that her council had also blocked access for her many tenants to the newly created English language bible. As having the ability to read God's word in the English vernacular was a central component to the king's church reform, by blocking it Margaret was displaying once again her obdurate nature, and frankly, lack of common sense. She knew well that her actions were contrary to the wishes of the king, and yet she chose to act anyway. Given the magnitude of what her youngest son was accused of however, these slights were, for now, overlooked. To use modern parlance, Cromwell had bigger fish to fry.

The final examination of Hugh Holland took place on 3 November 1538. As he had been imprisoned since the summer, and questioned repeatedly, Holland's testimony is extensive and filled with considerable information. It paints a clear picture of how Geoffrey Pole had been working with his brother Reginald, which by very definition makes the youngest Pole brother unequivocally guilty of treason, under the laws of the time. Holland's statements also prove beyond doubt that Bishop Gardiner had been correct when raising his concerns around Helyar's flight from England. Holland recalled that Helyar's escape had been entirely facilitated with Geoffrey's approval, and assistance, the latter instructing Holland to organise a ship that would take the priest across the channel. In the records from Holland's examination, it is stated:

'At the end of the summer the examined [Holland] hired a French ship, and at Portsmouth shipped the said vicar [Helyar] with his servant, Henry Pyning, two horses, and 36 pounds in money, besides goods of his own, and landed at Newhaven. Then went in company with the vicar to Paris, and there left him in company of two English scholars named Reynolds and Bucklar. Being asked what communication he had with the vicar by the way, he says the vicar told him he was glad he was overseas, for if he had tarried in England he feared he should have been put to death; for he considered the ordinances of England were against God's law. He said he had departed secretly, partly because my lady of Salisbury would not give him leave.'[10]

Whether Margaret not giving Helyar leave was due to her own need for his continued services, or that she was concerned about how it would be perceived, is difficult to say. Her son's direct involvement, however, confirms Helyar's departure was by no means a midnight flit. When Geoffrey was made aware that Helyar had made it to Paris safely, he thanked Holland, saying he 'would not lack as long as I live'.[11] According to Holland, roughly two years after his return to England he was called on by Geoffrey once again, after hearing that he was planning to visit Flanders to sell some wheat. Geoffrey requested Holland convey a message to Reginald, a message which would become central in the case against him. Holland was instructed to tell Reginald that 'in England waxeth all crooked, god's law is turned upside down, abbeys and churches overthrown and he [Reginald] is taken for a traitor; and I think they will cast down parish churches and all at the last'.[12] According to Holland, it was in this same message that Geoffrey gave the warning to Reginald about Sir Francis Bryan and Peter Mewtas's mission to assassinate him. Reginald also had a message for his mother, asking Holland to tell Lady Margaret 'that she and I looking upon a wall together read this, *Spea mea in deo est* [My hope is in God], and desire her blessing for me. I trust she will be glad of mine also'. His wheat duly sold, and messages to Reginald conveyed, Holland told his examiners that he once more journeyed back to England, and in turn delivered all the messages given to him by the cardinal, directly to Geoffrey Pole. He showed nothing to either Maragret Pole or Baron Montagu, apparently on the orders of Geoffrey, who feared his eldest brother 'was out of his mind and would show all to the lord Privy Seal'.[13] It would seem that the previously cautious Montagu was developing a reputation for carelessness in his speech. This is backed up by a statement given by Baron Stafford, the husband of Ursula Pole, who said 'I like him not, he dare speak so largely'.[14]

Geoffrey Pole would spend two whole months in the Tower of London before being examined for the first time, on 26 October 1538, a week before Holland's final round of questioning. Already troubled by his financial woes, the act of leaving him to stew was likely deliberate. No doubt terrified, and by this point starving both literally and for want of human interaction, his captors perhaps hoped that a downtrodden Geoffrey Pole would be a more forthcoming figure than one well looked after. A key piece of evidence that had been ascribed to Geoffrey was supposed conversations based around 'a change in the world', with the most explosive take on this being a desired change in sovereign. Questioning Geoffrey was William Fitzwilliam, Earl of Southampton, an imposing figure, who had been one of the key enforcers in both the downfall of Anne Boleyn and in the suppression of the Pilgrimage of Grace. The first round of questions related entirely to Geoffrey's relationship with Reginald; how often the brothers had spoken, had letters been passed to other members of the family by Geoffrey, did Geoffrey agree with any of the slanders made by Reginald against the king, and so on. John Helyar was also the subject of many questions, again all based around Geoffrey and Reginald's interactions with him. Given the nature of the accusation, the aforementioned 'change in the world' was of particular interest to the government, and became central to the examinations against Geoffrey Pole. Although it is unlikely that Geoffrey, as a member of the nobility, would have been tortured, he may well have endured terrifying threats, which combined with his already fragile state of mind would be akin to torture none the less. Under such pressure, he soon told Southampton that his brother Montagu had been part of the group who had discussed the desired change. Hoping to lessen Montagu's culpability, Geoffrey caveated his confession by saying that Montagu had only meant a change in relation to religious policy, and not in the person of the king directly. Geoffrey's desire to join his brother Reginald in Europe may also have extended to Montagu, for in Holland's testimony it is recorded that Geoffrey had said Montagu 'would as fayne be over as he'.[15] Unfortunately, these facts alone would prove inflammatory, because in Holland's third examination, Baron Montagu was discussed in greater detail. When Holland's evidence was coupled with Geoffrey's words, it created major suspicion around the eldest Pole son. Holland was able to recall with clarity that Montagu had several interactions with Cromwell's old informant, Michael Throckmorton. Whilst at one time this would have been deemed safe, the situation had changed entirely, for Cromwell had uncovered proof that Throckmorton had been playing double agent all along. So taken aback was Cromwell that he threatened his former spy, saying in a letter 'I must, I think, do what I can to see you punished'.[16] Any association to Throckmorton thus had the scope to become deeply problematic. For the Poles, a family whose members were already under investigation, such association wasn't problematic, it was catastrophic. As Holland tells it, Throckmorton requested he remind Montagu 'Of their communication at his last being in England, and say that when he would come overseas, Throckmorton would come himself and fetch him'.[17] If Holland is to be believed, it was also to him that Montagu would utter one of the most well documented pieces of evidence brought forward against him. Montagu, we are told, said that those who flocked to Henry VIII's court were mere flatterers, and that 'none served the king but knaves'.[18] At Holland's home, Montagu supposedly went further, expressing his desire that 'they were both over sea with the bishop of Liege, for this world would one day come to stripes'.[19] At a distance of nearly 500 years, it is difficult to say exactly what Montagu meant by 'coming to stripes'. He could have meant a general breakdown of social norms, or, yet more radical shifts in the king's policies. There is some suggestion also that stripes were associated with outlaws and vagabonds, particularly in reference to clothing, so perhaps Montagu was suggesting outlaws would have the run of England. Either way, his words were naturally viewed in a negative light.

Geoffrey Pole would undergo two further rounds of questioning, which took place on 2 and 3 November. The situation was becoming graver with every passing day, and understandably, Geoffrey began to crack. Coddled as he was from a lifetime of being part of the nobility, and the baby of the family, the scenario Geoffrey was now in was one he was hopelessly ill equipped for. His family name was not enough; if anything, it made matters worse. His powerful mother could no more demand his release than she could lead armies in the field. Geoffrey had begun to talk freely to his captors, and even took the step of writing to the king directly, begging for a pardon. In a letter to Henry VIII, Geoffrey hoped 'he may have good keeping and cherishing, and thereby somewhat comfort himself and have better stay of himself, and he said he would truly and fully open all that he did know or may remember whomsoever it touch, whether it be mother, brother, uncle or any other whatsoever he be'.[20] Geoffrey was making it clear that he would talk, and that no degree of familial loyalty would unsteady his hand. With no response from the king forthcoming, the horror of realising what was happening finally set in. Geoffrey, frantic with fear, suffered a complete mental collapse. Geoffrey's wife, Constance, had also been questioned at length and was permitted a visit to her husband when she was briefly held in the Tower. She was so distressed by her husband's behaviour that upon leaving the fortress she wrote to her brother-in-law, Montagu, warning him that Geoffrey was 'in a frenzy and might utter rash things'.[21] Exactly what these 'rash things' were is impossible to say, but is certainly enlightening, for it shows that Constance was aware of the conversations her husband had with his brothers, and adds more weight to the argument that the Pole family were, at the very least, talking of matters that would be deemed traitorous. By now, entirely wretched and deeply troubled by having provided evidence against his own family, Geoffrey did the unthinkable; he attempted to commit suicide. He stabbed himself in the chest, but the attempt failed. This should not, however, downplay the severity of such an action. Suicide was considered to be one of the gravest of sins in the sixteenth century. It was contrary to God's law, something Geoffrey, as a member of a family so entrenched in the traditions of the Catholic faith, would have known all too well. That he would thus attempt such an act speaks volumes about his state of mind. On hearing the news, John Husee wrote to his masters, the Lisles, informing them that 'he [Geoffrey] was so in despair that he should have murdered himself and has hurt himself sore'.[22] It was in Geoffrey's third examination that he more dangerously implicated Gertrude, Marchioness of Exeter, and another lady of the court, Elizabeth Darrell. The daughter of Sir Edward Darrell, she was a long time mistress of Sir Thomas Wyatt, and was even rumoured to have had a brief dalliance with the king. Montagu had known Darrell for a few years, having provided her with legal counsel, as well as acting as an intermediary between her and Sir Anthony Hungerford who owed Elizabeth Darrell money.[23] Geoffrey gave evidence to suggest that it was Darrell who had been responsible for leaking the information to him about the planned assassination of Reginald.[24] As Geoffrey tells it, on hearing the news he rushed to Montagu's residence, finding his brother in the garden. He told Montagu 'I hear our brother beyond the sea shall be slain', to which Montagu replied 'No, he is escaped, I have letters'.[25] The evidence Geoffrey provided which placed Gertrude Courtenay in danger was in relation to a letter the marchioness had sent Montagu. When news of the Pole family coming under suspicion reached the king's council, the Marquess of Exeter had supposedly said aloud that he would be 'bound body for body for him [Montagu]'.[26] If true, this was a dangerous and brave move by Henry Courtenay. The reputation of the Pole family was sinking fast, so to place his lot in with Montagu shows clear evidence of the two men's continued close relationship. Unfortunately for the marquess his name had also been brought up by Geoffrey in his interrogations at the Tower. Geoffrey told his captors that 'He has not spoken with him [Courtenay] for nearly two years; but by his communications with lord Montagu during these two years he knows that the Marquess and his said brother were of one opinion'.[27] Naturally, this 'one opinion' was viewed with considerable suspicion.

The very day after Geoffrey's final examination, the largest number of arrests took place. The Marquess of Exeter was the most senior arrestee. Shortly after arriving at the Tower of London, his wife and their young son, Edward, were also arrested and joined him. Sir Edward Neville, a brother of Montagu's father-in-law, George, Baron Bergavenny, was also taken. The final major arrest was Montagu himself. According to Charles Wriothesley, he was conveyed by boat to the Tower early in the morning alongside his wife Jane, and their son Henry. Lady Margaret Pole now had two of her sons in prison, and the third constantly on the run from paid assassins. Only Ursula Pole remained safe and free from suspicion, largely helped by the wisely quiet life she and her husband had adopted. Completing the arrests were John Collins, Montagu's chaplain and George Croftes, the chancellor of Chichester Cathedral whom Geoffrey had befriended. Holland and Geoffrey's testimonies had led to this, nine arrests in total. Later that month, in a letter to Sir Thomas Wyatt, Cromwell defended the arrests of Montagu and Exeter, stating they had committed 'sundry great crimes'[28], and that the arrests were justified owing to the significant evidence and confessions collected.

The situation looked bleak for all concerned, with the intended outcome all but a foregone conclusion. Just as the expert executioner from Calais was on his way to England before Anne Boleyn had even stood trial, now the king authorised inventories to be drawn up of the goods within the Courtenays residencies, with the marquess described as 'the late Marquis', making it clear how Henry VIII intended the situation to play out.[29] Indeed Robert Ratcliffe, Earl of Sussex had received word from Robert Warner, an MP, that 'My lady Marquess is in the tower, and my lady of Salisbury is in hold, as I heard my lord say, but where I cannot tell, but there is like to be a foul work among them'.[30] If the Courtenays could suffer this humiliation, the Pole family were surely on the same downward trajectory. Although only French Ambassador to Henry VIII's court for just over a year, Louis de Perreau, Sieur de Castillon, provides some of the greatest insight available from the period of the Exeter Conspiracy. He states quite plainly that 'the king told me a long time ago he wants to exterminate the House of Montague that belongs to the White Rose, the Pole family, of which the cardinal is a member'.[31] The inclusion of Reginald in the statement is telling, for it suggests that he was viewed as the chief cause of his family's misfortune, indeed Cromwell had as good as said as much, observing that 'the folly of one brainsick Pole, or to say better, of one witless fool, should be the ruin of so great a family'.[32] And yet, as we know, the conspiracy stretched beyond purely the Pole family, so the root cause for all of the arrests cannot be solely laid at Reginald's feet. What then, was the evidence produced which justified the arrests of the three noblemen and their families now lodged in the Tower.

The earliest piece of intelligence brought forward against Exeter was in relation to a comment he had apparently made in 1536 from his home in West Horsley, Surrey. According to the report, he said he 'liked well the proceedings of the Cardinal Pole'[33], and shortly after told Montagu 'I trust to have a fair day upon these knaves which rule about the king; and I trust to see a merry world one day'. The notion of 'a merry world' was all too similar in tone to the 'change in the world' story which had imprisoned the Pole brothers. The evidence, such as it was, had clear correlation between the two families and became increasingly difficult to refute. Geoffrey Pole had also told his examiners that he overheard his brother Montagu say he would rather live in the West Country, for 'in the West the lord Marquess of Exeter is strong'.[34] Were this the case, it implied Montagu felt Exeter's strength was something that could be used against the crown. One of the more serious allegations made against Exeter was that he had been leaking secrets to Montagu from meetings of the Privy Council. Although Montagu was a member of the nobility, he was not so high as to reach the hallowed position of a privy councillor. That was the reserve of the very highest of the male aristocracy, to which the Marquess of Exeter belonged. According to Geoffrey, Montagu 'knew all that was done in the council when the lord Marquess was there'.[35] If true, this was both very dangerous and highly foolish. We must not forget that the government had evidence from Gervase Tyndall that Hugh Holland had conveyed letters to Reginald which may have contained within them important state secrets. If Exeter was indeed revealing the inner workings of the council to Montagu, then how much further would these secrets travel? Could they make their way to Reginald and the Pope? The two scenarios shared all too much similarity to be overlooked.

Where the evidence against Exeter was open to some interpretation, the comments made by Sir Edward Neville were clearer cut. Like Edward Stafford, Duke of Buckingham before him, Neville appears to have been a man of intense pride and little sense. He was open in his dislike of Cromwell, and would regularly alter the lyrics of songs to disparage the lord privy seal. However, unlike Montagu, for whom a close relationship with the king was never apparent, Sir Edward Neville and the king were at one time genuinely close, having known each other since childhood and fought in the tiltyard on several occasions. He was part of the conservative court faction, but had generally maintained a prominent role within Henry VIII's household and was in the king's considerable favour as late as 1535.[36] As evidence of Henry VIII's low opinion of Montagu, he had taken the liberty of personally warning Neville against mixing with him and the Marquess of Exeter.[37] It was therefore a shock to the king when he heard of Neville's own remarks about the men who sat on the Privy Council. According to Geoffrey Pole, Neville had said 'I am made a fool amongst them, but I laugh and make merry to drive forth the time. The King keepeth a sort of knaves here, that we dare neither look nor speak, and I were able, I would rather live my life in the world than tarry in the Privy Chamber'.[38] It was this statement that sufficiently convinced the king that he could no longer consider Neville as loyal, the association to Geoffrey no doubt exacerbating the situation further. Indeed during Geoffrey Pole's seventh examination on 12 November, he claimed to have overheard Neville 'many times deprave the King, saying that his Highness was a beast and worse than a beast'.[39]

Of the three noblemen arrested, the evidence against Montagu was the most extensive, and as with the other arrestees, the bulk of the information against him was produced through his own brother's statements. One of the most damning pieces of evidence against Montagu is that in response to his father-in-law's death. Montagu is said to have expressed his sadness at the death of Baron Bergavenny, not for the personal loss, but for the ten thousand men Bergavenny had at his disposal.[40] Whilst much of the evidence brought forward against those arrested is open to significant conjecture, if Montagu did truly express sadness at the loss of such considerable numbers, who we are to assume would have done Bergavenny's bidding, then this suggests rebellion was something they were seriously weighing up. Montagu had also made his feelings known about the treatment of the rebels from the Pilgrimage of Grace. He said 'time hath been when nothing was surer to reckon upon than the promise of a prince, but now they count it no promise, but a policy to blind the people, wherefore if the commons do rise again they will trust to no fair promise nor words'.[41] According to Geoffrey, his eldest brother had also told him 'Lord Darcy played the fool; he went about to pluck away the council. He should have first have begun with the head, but I beshrew them for leaving off so soon'.[42] The 'head' Montagu references was likely Cromwell, rather than the king himself, but it was a dangerous thing to say regardless. One of the most explosive pieces of evidence used to justify Montagu's arrest was a statement in which he mentioned the king's potential death. He is said to have exclaimed 'the King gloried with the title to be Supreme Head next to God, yet he had a sore leg that no poor man would be glad of, and that he should not live long for all his authority next gods'.[43] To think of, let alone outwardly speak of the king's death, was now a treasonous act. It was this, we must keep in mind, that justified the death sentence passed against Anne Boleyn in the spring of 1536. If such a course of action had been used against the wife of the king, it did not bode well for a man who himself had royal blood, and whose wider family were already viewed with such damning suspicion. A servant of Montagu's, Jerome Ragland, also gave evidence against his master and seemed to corroborate what Geoffrey had revealed about Montagu. According to Ragland, when the king, in a fit of rage, threatened to leave England altogether, Montagu had quipped that the people of England would be pleased to see the king go. John Collins, Montagu's chaplain, also provided some evidence against his master, unequivocally incriminating himself in the process. He admitted that he had told a friend to burn his sermons should he be taken to the Tower[44], an act which caused natural suspicion, and also confessed to telling the Pole brothers that 'both the King and Lord Privy Seal would hang in hell'.[45] By admitting to such statement, Collins was a dead man. He was also able to corroborate what Ragland and Geoffrey had told their examiners, re-referencing Montagu's famous line of the world coming to stripes, and mirroring the words of Gertrude Courtenay by stressing how close Montagu and the Marquess of Exeter remained. It is in Collins' testimony that we also see for the first time a reference to Montagu's son, which perhaps explains why the government felt his arrest, even though a child, was justified. When asked if the younger Henry Pole had access to the letters exchanged between the Pole brothers and their kin, Collins replied that he could 'not tell, saving that he did know at that time the examinent [the younger Henry Pole] went to the said Sir Geoffrey's house'.[46] A child visiting his uncle is hardly evidence of treasonous doings, but, it would seem the government twisted this to suggest the younger Henry had gone to Geoffrey's residence in the capacity of conveying letters.

An apparent tension between Montagu and Geoffrey also comes out in the evidence listed from Geoffrey's seventh examination. Although Margaret Pole is viewed as the head of the Pole family, her position, at this stage at least, was more de-facto, working alongside Montagu, who, as the family's representative at court, ultimately held the most sway. Geoffrey told his examiners that despite wanting to serve in the king's household, Montagu had rallied against it, informing his brother he 'should serve the lady Dowager'.[47] No further explanation as to whom this 'lady dowager' was is recorded, but given the Pole family's adherence to the interests of Katherine of Aragon, and the fact that after Henry VIII's marriage to Anne Boleyn took place, 'Dowager Princess of Wales' became Katherine's official title, it seems reasonable to assume that this was who Montagu felt Geoffrey should serve. If true, Montagu was essentially saying that service to Katherine of Aragon was a more desirable post than serving the king. As Geoffrey tells it, his appointment to the king's household was thus of his own volition, and was contrary to Montagu's wishes, the latter of whom saying 'the king would go so far that all the world would mislike him'[48], before confessing his own dislike of the king, that he had supposedly held since childhood. All of this evidence, on face value, points to unadulterated contempt for Henry VIII by Montagu, but we should also remain cognisant of the fact that Geoffrey had told the king that he would be willing to say whatever was asked of him, whether it incriminated his mother or brothers or otherwise. His recent attempt at suicide points to a man both deeply troubled and desperate. That he was speaking the truth is entirely possible, but it's equally reasonable to assume that Geoffrey entered a mode of pure self-preservation, saying whatever he thought his captors wished to hear. Some of Montagu's statements were certainly inflammatory, as were those made by Neville and the Exeters, but these may have also been mere banter between friends, as opposed to a premeditated and detailed conspiracy. An assessment of the evidence, taken one way, certainly points towards planned treason, but viewed through a different lens, it could be argued that those involved in the Exeter Conspiracy scandal were less a political party, than a gang of friends, made up of people who longed for a return to the traditions of the Catholic faith, without the prudence to keep these thoughts to themselves. Thoughts and words were now treason though, and so even if it was mere talk, that was enough. Crucially, we must also remember that hatred for Cromwell and everything he stood for united those arrested. This fact is germane when considering the evidence at large. If we accept the significance of Cromwell's role in the downfall of Anne Boleyn, then his hand in the downfall of the Pole family and those who fell with them must be considered. As referenced earlier, the distaste which Cromwell felt for members of the high nobility was reciprocated in spades. His plans for England and changes to the king's policies would be harder to achieve with dissidents of such power and influence remaining at full strength. Taking some out of the picture would certainly create a smoother path for the future. He had ousted a queen, so courtiers with a claim to the throne who opposed his policies were naturally a significant threat, could it be that this was how it was communicated to the king?

Once inside the Tower, examinations of the prisoners would begin. Unlike Geoffrey Pole, Baron Montagu maintained a steady hand. Stoic, clear and concise, he would be questioned only once. Montagu denied everything, save admitting to the burning of letters. Such an action could mean everything and nothing, and it was in those grey areas that so often interpretation could be viewed with the most damning of conclusions. Perhaps, in a twist of irony, Montagu's sangfroid aided his undoing. Where Geoffrey was emotionally demonstrative, putting it all out there for his captors to see, Montagu remained guarded and calm. Whilst one assessment could be that this was purely down to Montagu being genuinely innocent, to his captors it conveyed, at best, impertinence, and at worst, hidden treason. During George Croftes' examination on 12 November, he described having had several conversations with Geoffrey Pole, some of which were fresh from Geoffrey's times sitting in parliament. According to Croftes, Geoffrey expressed his distaste with how the government was managing business, as well as the actions taken against the abolition of the monasteries and in dispelling papal authority from England.[49] Geoffrey, in turn, had been questioned about Croftes, recalling a conversation in which Croftes had said of Reginald 'It is he that shall restore the Church again'.[50] As the situation continued to unfold, Lady Margaret Pole remained in the country at her favoured residence of Warblington. Naturally, news soon reached Margaret about Geoffrey's attempt at suicide. A concerned steward in her household told Margaret directly that 'I pray god, Madame, he do you no hurt one day', to which Margaret, in a moment of inspired public relations shot back 'I trust he is not so unhappy that he will hurt his mother, and yet I care neither for him, nor for any other, for I am true to my Prince'.[51] It was during this time that

Margaret likely penned a letter to her eldest son, again expressing clear loyalty to the king and desiring him to do the same:

> 'Son Montague, I sent you heartily God's blessing and mine. This is the greatest gift that I can send you, for to desire god of his help which I perceive is great, needs to pray for, and as to the case as I am informed that you stand in, my advice is to refer you to god principally and upon that ground so to order you both in word and deed to serve your prince, not disobeying god's commandment as far as your power and life will serve you to do above all. Remember who hath brought you up and maintained you, but his highness who, if you will, with your learning serve to the content of his mind as your bounden duty is that you may so serve his highness, daily pray to god, or else to take you to his mercy.'[52]

This letter is entirely in keeping with Margaret's stance on commitment to both the Church and, outwardly at least, the king, but is also a mass of contradictions. She makes it clear to Montagu that there was nothing greater than maintaining God's blessing, but directs this through the prism of loyalty to the king, only to somewhat contradict this in the next sentence when saying 'as far as your power and life will serve you'.[53] Such a statement is rather reminiscent of Sir Thomas More's famous quote from the scaffold that he would 'die the king's good servant, but god's first'.[54] By the time Baron Montagu received his mother's missive, he was already imprisoned in the Tower, from where little could be done to act in accordance with Margaret's wishes. The countess retained her liberty for now, but must surely have known that her freedom was on borrowed time. Margaret and Montagu had been responsible for the elevation of the Pole family to the zenith of Tudor England, but if her sons were under such intense suspicion, it was natural that Margaret herself would be tarred with the same brush. As her letters and comments attest, she had continued to project unflinching loyalty to the king, but this was not to be enough. And so, Margaret herself would finally be visited by the king's enforcers. Although not immediately conveyed to the Tower, as her sons had been, she would endure a barrage of questioning, all with the end goal of bringing down one of the country's most important and illustrious figures. The destruction of Lady Margaret Pole, Countess of Salisbury had begun.

Chapter 9

A Fallen Countess

'We may call her rather a strong and constant
man, than a woman'
Sir William Fitzwilliam, Earl of Southampton

On 12 November 1538 Sir William Fitzwillian, Earl of Southampton and
Thomas Goodrich, Bishop of Ely, arrived at Warblington Castle. The
men who had questioned Geoffrey Pole to breaking point, now turned
their sights on the family matriarch. They journeyed to Hampshire to
begin the process of questioning Lady Margaret Pole in relation to the
accusations which had imprisoned her sons. As Pierce notes, at this stage
Margaret Pole was in the least danger of any of the arrestees; the actions
of her contemporary, Gertrude Courtenay, for example, were far more
serious, and despite his assurances to divulge any intelligence deemed
worthwhile, Geoffrey Pole had said nothing to seriously implicate his
mother, nor had Montagu or the other men of her kin now lodged in
the Tower. All that Southampton and Goodrich had to go on, for now,
was the information given to Cromwell by Gervase Tyndall and Richard
Ayer, and the belief that if her sons had been acting treasonously, that
Margaret was either party to it, or actively involved herself. Margaret
would be examined at length for two days, before being transferred
to Cowdray House, Southampton's property, in neighbouring Sussex.
Much to the chagrin of Margaret's examiners, she would answer
all questions put to her with poise and clarity, defending herself and
her sons with aplomb, despite what were clearly increasingly trying
circumstances. The Earl of Southampton described the approach he took
in his dealings with Margaret, stating he used 'sometimes mild words,
now roughly and asperly (sharply), by traitoring her and her sons to the
ninth degree, yet will she nothing utter, but maketh herself clear, and
as unspotted, utterly denying all that is objected unto her; and that with
most stiff and earnest words'.[1] And yet, Margaret did not back down, she

held firm, her proud and sometimes haughty nature now deployed as a means of protection. The earl was clearly a man for whom women had hitherto acted in accordance with the expected social norms of the time. His surprise therefore at finding Margaret Pole both formidable, and impressive, was something he struggled to countenance. After extended rounds of questioning, Southampton wrote in exasperation that 'As we wrote we would do, we travailed with the Lady of Salisbury all day, both before and after noon till almost night; but for all we could do she would confess nothing more than the first day'. They went on, telling the lord privy seal that 'we may call her rather a strong constant man than a woman. For in all behaviour, however we have used her, she hath showed herself so earnest, vehement and precise that more could not be'.[2] The two men were forced to conclude that 'either her sons have not made her privy nor participant of the bottom and pit of their stomachs, or else she is the most errant traitorress that ever lived'.[3] With so little to go on, further 'evidence' against Margaret Pole started to appear, evidence that was either genuine, or more likely, twisted or fabricated to put together a compelling case against her. This chapter will examine the downfall of Margaret Pole, and the court cases against her family, which would lead to their convictions of high treason.

The questions asked of Margaret, and her responses to them, provide some of the most detailed pieces of information from the entire Exeter Conspiracy affair. We have in-depth accounts of what she was asked, which allow for a clearer picture to be pieced together than say the examination of her son Montagu. The records open with Margaret being questioned about her relationship and contact with Reginald. When asked whether Reginald had confided his distaste for the changes occurring in England before his escape to the continent, Margaret told her examiners that 'he never opened his mind to her touching any statutes or proceedings of the King, and it was sore against her mind that ever he went abroad'.[4] She also played a trump card, reminding Southampton and Goodrich that the king himself had sponsored, and thus approved of, Reginald's education in Europe. When pushed as to the significance of the tokens left to her containing the words *'spes mea'* (Latin for 'I hope'), Margaret retorted that it was a common phrase used by those of faith, and that it could be found throughout her home in windows and other locations. Margaret was asked whether Throckmorton had delivered any letters to her from Reginald, to which she vehemently confirmed he had not, going further to say the only letter she had received concerning Reginald was the one sent to her by the king, for which she had a copy.[5] Margaret was also questioned as to whether John Helyar had told her of his views on England before his escape across the channel. Margaret was able to confirm that he had not, and furthermore explained her rejection of Helyar's request to leave the country. When asked whether Margaret was aware of, and thus supported, Hugh Holland's escape from England, she confirmed he had done so without her knowledge or consent. The next question put to Margaret concerned the assassination attempts made on Reginald's life, and whether she was aware of any moves made by Baron Montagu and Geoffrey Pole to join their brother. On the first point, Margaret's response was entirely natural, but also surprising in its bravery. When asked if Geoffrey Pole had told his mother that the king had authorised assassins to go after Reginald, Margaret confirmed that he had, and that she had in turn 'prayed god heartily to change the king's mind'.[6] She went further, explaining that when news reached her of Reginald's escape, that 'for motherly pity she could not but rejoice'.[7] Her relief at Reginald's continued liberty is, as I have said above, the perfectly reasonable response you would expect from any concerned parent, however, we must also keep in mind that this is the same woman who until very recently had told a member of her household that loyalty to the king came before anything, even her family. And yet, here she was, telling Southampton and Goodrich that her son remaining alive and well, despite his treasonous activities, gave her great joy. Such a frank admission of how she truly felt suggests that Margaret Pole spoke the truth throughout her examinations. Her open admission of responding positively to something deemed controversial tells us that Margaret was clearly a woman unafraid of saying something she knew could be contentious, which gives her other responses a strong measure of believability. When asked if Margaret was aware that her sons had expressed a wish to leave England, she responded passionately, telling Southampton and Goodrich 'she may be torn in pieces if ever she heard such a thing of her sons'.[8] Margaret also confirmed that she had never heard Montagu mention knaves ruling about the king, that the world had turned upside down, and that under Henry VIII's rule all would come to stripes.[9] When asked if she had heard Montagu express regret at the death of his father-in-law because of the numbers of men Bergavenny commanded, Margaret confirmed she had not. She was then asked if the Pole family had openly commended the activities of Reginald, and whether they had said he would one day return to England as Pope. In another moment of inspired personal self-preservation, Margaret denied ever having had such conversations, save that she wished Reginald could return to England with the king's favour, before adding that her son was ultimately a mere parish priest, and thus his word and deeds were not of consequence.[10] Margaret was deliberately trying to play Reginald down, as if his words and being were inconsequential. The countess was playing a good game.

When weighing up if Margaret was indeed telling the truth, her own personal faith is something we should also factor in. Throughout her examinations, Margaret repeatedly leaned into her belief in the almighty, using religious prose to both defend and add weight to the truth of the answers she gave. In this, Margaret was acting in complete accordance with the conventions of the time. The overwhelming majority of Tudor England believed that all of their actions were both viewed, and latterly judged, by God. Heaven and hell, and one's admission to the former, rested heavily on actions committed whilst living. These were very real, very clear, concerns. Margaret lived and breathed the traditions of the Catholic Church, and whilst I do not make a habit out of psychoanalysing people from the sixteenth century, I think in Margaret Pole's case that we can accurately surmise that she always strived to act in line with God's teachings, or at the very least as she perceived their meaning. To Margaret, to do the opposite would hinder her soul's admission to heaven, and in an age of such fervent religious belief I struggle to see why she would have taken such a risk by outwardly lying. Church law was to many a higher authority than common law, which explains why so many people executed throughout the Tudor period died on account of their faith. Take for example the execution of Anne Boleyn. As the queen awaited her death, she requested Thomas Cranmer, Archbishop of Canterbury, be present whilst she gave her last confession. A confession in which she swore, both before and after taking the eucharist, that she was completely innocent of all charges laid against her. Given the nature of religious conviction from the time, Anne Boleyn's confession acts to many as categorical proof that she was indeed innocent. Margaret Pole makes similar statements throughout her interrogations, and so if we accept that Anne Boleyn, a notable reformist, provided proof of her innocence through the words she spoke in God's name, then the same courtesy should be extended to Lady Margaret Pole. If we look at the question put to Margaret about whether she was aware of Baron Montagu 'beshrewing the lord Darcy, saying he played the fool', Margaret 'answers upon the damnation of her soul that she never heard such words spoken'.[11] When asked again about Montagu and Geoffrey Pole wishing they could be overseas with Reginald, Margaret 'denieth utterly on her baptism and prayeth that she never see God in the face if ever she heard any such words'.[12] Margaret repeatedly defending her answers by calling upon the word of God made her responses all the more compelling.

As we know, Margaret Pole held little to no love for those responsible for the dissolution of the monasteries. She was an unquestioned member of the old guard, who apart from believing in the sanctity of these great religious houses, as a major magnate also benefited from the large incomes such establishments within her lands provided. Margaret's opinion on the monasteries destruction was thus naturally of interest to her questioners, and so unsurprisingly, questions around the dissolution soon cropped up. Margaret was asked if she had openly lamented the actions taken by the crown; accusations that Margaret flatly denied. Furthermore, she had already formed a solid response as to why the closure of the monasteries was such a personal concern. When asked for her opinion, Margaret cleverly responded that her issue was for the remains of her ancestors who had been laid to rest in the religious houses now destroyed.[13] In reality, Margaret was horrified at the dissolution of the monasteries, and so it seems plausible to conclude that her words were driven by a desire to deflect any suggestion that she was acting against the will of the king. Instead, she would place her lot in with a group of people for whom no response could be garnered – the dead. Margaret Pole's well known conservatism was thus under greater pressure to refute, but by suggesting that her sole distress of the taking down of churches related to those in their grave, it provided her examiners with a more personal but largely non-treasonous viewpoint. It would be difficult to spin Margaret's response into anything too sinister. However, although Margaret wasn't speaking openly against the king, what she said brought home the reality that his and Cromwell's actions had a broader negative impact on the lives of both the nobility and commons. The issue was that this alone was problematic, for Cromwell's actions were the king's actions, and to contradict one was to offend the other. And so, whilst Margaret's real feelings about the dissolution were kept quiet, she drew attention to one of its negative outcomes, without finding a positive to balance her story out. We must also remain cognisant of the fact that sixteenth-century England was one built on deep and unflinching dedication to God. Although strange for many in the twenty-first century, religion almost entirely structured how the Tudors would spend their days. The Church informed how, when and where one should pray and all public holidays were entrenched in religion; the Church and God were all consuming facets of existence. Just because the king had overturned the process of how religion should be practised in England did not mean that this received universal assent across the country, as rebellions such as the Pilgrimage of Grace attest. By not openly championing the dissolution, it could be argued that Margaret inadvertently made her feelings known.

Given the prominence of letter burning in the evidence brought forward against the Pole sons, it was inevitable that Margaret would herself be questioned about this very same act. Margaret was asked if she had received and later burned letters from Reginald Pole, the Marquess and Marchioness of Exeter, and Hugh Holland. Margaret freely admitted to burning letters that were of no consequence, and also confirmed that any missive she had received from the Exeters had not been prejudicial to the king's wishes.[14] My assessment of Margaret's response to the idea of burning letters is further proof that she told the truth to her examiners. She could have outright denied burning letters at all. This would have been an easy response to make and would have probably not warranted further discussion, but instead, she confirmed what Southampton and Goodrich had been hoping for. Although Margaret assured the two men that any letters she had burned were not suspicious, it could be spun that the very nature of burning any letter was cause for concern. It was a grey area which could be neatly filled with the most damning of conclusions. It is of course entirely possible that Margaret was lying, and that she had received and burnt letters that contained treason within. The letters of Gertrude Courtenay, for example, carry flashes of treason, and so it's entirely possible that Margaret had also committed disloyalty to the king to pen and paper, but, unlike the marchioness, had the sense to cover her tracks. Ultimately though, this seems unlikely. My belief is that Margaret did indeed only burn letters she deemed inconsequential. Her willingness to admit to burning letters reiterates the point that Margaret was unafraid to make statements which had an air of controversy attached. At the conclusion of Margaret's interrogations, she brought up the conversation she had with Henry VIII after *De Unitate* had made its way into his hands. Parts of the transcript are illegible, but the overall gist of her statement can be gleaned from what remains, telling Southampton and Goodrich:

> 'When she spoke with the King his Grace he showed her how her son had written against him. Alas, what grief is this to me to see him whom […] set up to be so ungracious and unhappy, and upon this when her son Montagu came home to her she said to him "what hath the King shown me of my son? Alas, son said she, what a child have I in him". And then my lord Montagu counselled her to declare him as a traitor to their servants, that they might so report him when they came in to their countries. And so she called her servants and declared unto them accordingly. She took her said son for a traitor and for no son, and that she would never take him otherwise.'[15]

That Margaret chose at this stage to resurrect this conversation with Montagu is certainly telling. We do not know if it was in answer to a question put to her, or if she simply believed retelling it would reiterate her innocence and loyalty to the king. The problem, as covered earlier, is that she had also told Southampton and Goodrich of her joy in Reginald not being killed by the king's assassins, which undeniably dilutes the strength of her statement that 'she took her son for a traitor and for no son'. In reality, the most accurate assessment is that Margaret was simply being contrary, a perfectly natural human response, but in sixteenth-century England this was a problem. When under such intense suspicion, one could not hope to rest in the grey areas of life; it was black or white, true or false, and this was more acute still when the king himself was so central to the investigations. Declaring this story to Southampton and Goodrich thus rings somewhat hollow, as if Margaret felt she had insufficiently convinced them of her loyalties and felt more was needed. Her questioning now over, Margaret dutifully signed her name at the bottom of each page of the transcript. Despite their best efforts, basically nothing came out of the extended rounds of questioning that made Lady Margaret Pole unequivocally guilty of treason. The juiciest parts of Margaret's responses had been around

Reginald's assassination and the burning of letters, but as she had reasonable and sound responses to both elements of the interrogation, it would be difficult to build a solid case against her. Southampton and Goodrich were clutching at straws.

Growing wearisome at finding nothing to implicate Margaret, her examiners had to resort to other means. They hoped that what would eventually turn the tide in their favour would not be Margaret Pole's own words, but those of others, who were happy to be more verbose in the countess' activities. As such, on 14 November Southampton and Goodrich called all the male servants within Margaret's household before them for questioning, which concluded with their arresting a clerk of the kitchens, Thomas Standish. Mirroring his mistress' equanimity, Standish confessed to nothing[16], save that Hugh Holland had confided to him the visit he had made to Reginald, which suggests that it was via Standish that Margaret learned of it. Shortly after, Margaret was informed that she would be moved and her goods seized. Unsurprisingly, she was greatly displeased. Southampton wrote that Margaret 'seemeth to be somewhat appalled, and therefore we deem that if it may be so, she will then utter somewhat when she is removed, which we intend shall be tomorrow'.[17] Southampton and Goodrich soon gave orders to gentlemen in the neighbouring towns and villages that they should 'have vigilant eyes to repress any stirring that may arise'[18]. Clearly the two men felt Margaret's popularity and loyalty from her retainers and neighbours had the capacity to cause problems if they were seen to be treating Margaret poorly. As it was, this was not to be the case, for the fallout of the Exeter Conspiracy was more widely discussed in the inner court circles than among the populace of England. Southampton and Goodrich saw a slight upturn in their hopes of pinning something against Margaret Pole when a letter was uncovered within Standish's quarters at Warblington Castle, sent from Margaret to Baron Montagu. According to Margaret, who freely admitted the letter was indeed hers, it was sent in the period between Geoffrey's arrest and Montagu's own incarceration. The letter contained a conversation she had had with the comptroller of her household, Oliver Frankelyn, in which concern had been raised that Geoffrey might 'slip away'[19], that is to say would die, no doubt in response to the news of Geoffrey's failed attempt at suicide. Frankelyn had predicted that Geoffrey would 'one day do you a displeasure' to which Margaret retorted 'Nay, he will not be so unhappy' – Margaret clearly felt that no matter how low her son might reach, that he would never truly turn his back on the woman who had raised him.

The next inevitable stage in the Pole family's destruction was when news broke that there was sufficient evidence to move to trial for Baron Montagu, which was to take place on 2 December 1538, with the Marquess of Exeter's call to the bar scheduled for the following day. As befitting their rank, both men would be judged by a jury of their peers. The day after that, the two remaining noblemen, Geoffrey Pole and Sir Edward Neville would be tried alongside the three commoners, George Croftes, John Collins and Hugh Holland before a commission of oyer and terminer. With dates set, summons went out to noblemen across the country requesting they sit in judgement on men they had known for decades. A total of twenty-eight would be called forward. Demands to sit on juries was a commonplace part of being a member of the English nobility, indeed both Montagu and Exeter had served in this capacity on several occasions, most famously sitting amongst those convened to judge Anne Boleyn and her brother George in 1536.[20] In addition to fresh demands to make up the jury, the inevitable outcome of the trials created space for 'new men' to ascend into the English peerage through acquiring available titles. As is the case now, there are only so many noble titles available within the British peerage system. With Montagu and the Marquess of Exeter brought low, ennoblements of courtiers could take place. One such elevation was given to the king's lord chancellor, Sir Thomas Audley. Although as chancellor he had the scope to preside over much of the activity within the House of Lords, under ancient courtly protocol by his lacking a peerage title he was barred from acting as lord high steward. The king's desire for Audley to play an active role in the trials of Montagu and the others accused alongside him was thus the impetus behind Audley's rise to the parliamentary barony of Walden. Once the title was conferred, the king appointed him lord high steward for the trials.[21] Audley was a smart choice. Much like Cromwell, he was a self-made man with an exemplary understanding of the law. His appointment to this role highlights once again the continued disaffection the king felt for the role of old members of the nobility. Just as Cromwell and Richard Rich had brought down countless nobles before, now Audley would take up the post and oversee the destruction of further noblemen of royal blood.

The charges read out against Montagu were that he had spoken out against the king, had envisioned the king's death, and remained in contact with and thus approved of the activities of his brother Reginald. When asked how he would plead, Montagu declared not guilty. This small detail is all the information we have from the trial, save for that it appears to have been relatively fair, with no hint of rigging among the judges. There is more colour available from Exeter's trial the following day, for according to a contemporary source, albeit one who was not an eye-witness, a scene broke out during the trial which saw Geoffrey Pole and the marquess come to blows. Some reference is also made to Montagu and Edward Neville. Unfortunately we do not have a name for whomever wrote the report, but in it, is recorded:

> 'All the time of their [Montagu, Exeter and Neville] arraignment they stood stiff, with a casting up of eyes and hands, as though those things had been never heard of before that then were laid to their charge. The Marquess of all the rest stuck hardest, and made as though he had been very clear in many points, yet in some he staggered, and was very sorry so to do, now challenging the King's pardon, now taking benefit of the act, and when all would not serve he began to charge Geoffrey Pole with frenzy, folly and madness. It is much to be noted what answer Geoffrey made to the Marquess in this point. Some men, saith Geoffrey "lay to my charge that I should be out of my wit and in a frenzy. Truth it is, I was out of my wit, and in a great frenzy when I fell with them in conference to be a traitor, disobedient to God, false to my prince, and enemy to my native country. I was also out of my wit and stricken with a sore kind of madness when I chose rather to kill myself than to charge them with such treasons, as I knew would cost them their lives, if I did utter them. But our lord be thanked, God wrought better with me than I thought to have done with myself. He hath saved my soul at the last, the knife went not so far as I would have had it gone. His goodness it is that I have not slain myself, his work that I have declared myself, my brother, the Marquess, with the rest to be traitors".'[22]

The letter concludes by mentioning for a second time the Marquess of Exeter's 'stiff' posture, and that he remained firm in denials of all charges put to him. Despite the two men's protests, the sentence of guilty was passed, and with it the customary judgement of death. This was entirely expected. When Sir Edward Neville, Geoffrey Pole, Croftes, Collins and Holland appeared before their juries, only Neville pleaded not guilty, the others admitted to the charges. Again, all would be found guilty. The terrifying prospect of a traitor's death – being hung, cut down whilst alive, disembowelled, castrated, beheaded and quartered – was the standard method of execution for male traitors, and it was this dreaded method of execution that was initially to be the fate of all concerned. Because of the charges laid against the accused, particularly Montagu and Neville, there was zero hope of a reprieve. If the evidence presented was accurate, then by the laws of the time the two men had indeed committed treason. Following the revisions made to the Treasons Act of 1534, it was stated clearly that 'if any person do maliciously wish, will or desire, by words or writing or by craft, imagine any bodily harm to be done or committed to the King's most royal person he is guilty of high treason'.[23] It was this legal technicality which had ultimately set the seal on Anne Boleyn's death two years earlier. As a reminder, this meant that even imagining the king's death was a treasonous offence, so openly speaking of it was a graver crime still. Even if the statement was made in general conversation, without spite or desire, it was enough, for the perpetrator had envisioned the king's death. Montagu's supposed pronouncement about Henry VIII's sore leg ensuring the king 'should not live long for all his authority next gods' had thus crossed a line. A line which when applied to the very specific structures of treason laws of the time rendered him guilty. Neville's statement about the king being 'a beast and worse than a beast', although denied by the man himself, was likely a key factor in his downfall. Always an incredibly proud man, and with age increasingly susceptible to criticism, such a statement would have been a personal blow to the king. Coddled from a lifetime of flattery, for Henry VIII insults towards his person were something he simply could not overlook. As precedence dictated, Montagu, Exeter and Neville were soon informed that their sentence had been commuted to the far swifter death by decapitation, which must have been a relief, albeit a dubious one.

On 9 December, a Monday, the first executions of the Exeter Conspiracy took place. George Croftes, Hugh Holland and John Collins were led from the Tower of London to Tyburn, where they would endure the torturous end meted out to those of low birth. Once dead, their heads were dipped in tar and placed on spikes at the south side of London Bridge. With the Tyburn executions complete, it was then the turn of the three noblemen. Montagu, Exeter and Neville took the short walk from their lodgings inside the Tower of London out onto Tower Hill, to meet their ends as so many had done before them. Against howling winds and torrential rain, the three men prepared themselves for death, with Exeter, as the highest in rank, dying first. Given his stout denials of guilt throughout the trial, there was some concern that the marquess would use his time on the scaffold to reassert his innocence. However, Exeter had accepted his fate, and gave the customary speech from the scaffold in which he admitted to being a sinner, worthy of death. Montagu would die afterwards and lastly, Neville. Despite the significance of the men on the scaffold and the overall scale and drama of the Exeter Conspiracy, there are no detailed accounts of their final moments. Only a cursory description was made by Richard Morisyne, who mentioned the men 'did all three acknowledge their offences towards the King, and desired all men that were there present, to pray God to forgive them'.[24] We have no description of what they actually said, or how the executions would unfold. Following their deaths, all three men were buried within the walls of the Chapel of St Peter ad Vincula where they remain to this day. Their remains were not unearthed during restoration work in the Victorian era, nor do we have a definitive location of their burial sites within the chapel. Years later, Reginald sent a letter to Exeter's son in which he told of the steadfast bond between Montagu and the marquess, telling him 'they had been so linked by God in sincere affection during their lives that he would not at the last hour let them be separated, both dying together in the cause of god'.[25] By saying their deaths were 'in the cause of god', Reginald was clearly suggesting that they had died as martyrs for the Catholic faith. Upon hearing of the deaths, the Pope reissued the bull of excommunication against Henry VIII from 1534. This was an open invitation to anyone brave enough to try and displace the king, placing yet more pressure on the remaining members of the Pole family and the wider White Rose network. The king plainly believed the conspiracy was a real and genuine threat, but arguably nothing more; nothing more than a possibility. This comes across in his strident attempts after the executions of Montagu and Exeter to defend his actions. Although at times indecisive, a trait inherited by his daughter Elizabeth, the king seldom expressed regret at the deaths of people he held dear, or felt he had to justify his deeds. This wasn't the case with Montagu and Exeter. Feeling further rationales were needed, Henry instructed Sir Thomas Wyatt, whilst on a diplomatic trip to Spain, to report directly to Charles V that under Reginald Pole's instruction, Montagu and Exeter planned to assassinate the king and his family, going further to say that Exeter had attempted to secure the throne for himself for over a decade.[26] As Desmond Seward points out, the king also informed the French ambassador to his court, Louis de Perreau, Sieur de Castillon, that new documents had been uncovered which proved beyond doubt that Reginald had plotted treason with Montagu and Exeter. Castillon later retorted, no doubt behind the king's back, that he and Cromwell wished to put the dead men on trial after they had been executed.[27] This unusual behaviour by the king belies his lack of conviction and security in the decisions he made – it smacks wildly of the line from Hamlet 'the lady doth protest too much'.

We have no record of when or how Lady Margaret Pole was informed that her eldest son was now dead. When the news reached her, the shock and complete heartbreak must have been overwhelming. Her father, executed, her brother, executed, now her first born child, executed. We must remember that Montagu was also Lady Margaret Pole's heir apparent, the future Earl of Salisbury, the future of her once great house. That future was now destroyed. Geoffrey was imprisoned, having already made an attempt on his own life, and looked set to follow his brother to the scaffold. Arthur Pole was long dead, and Reginald was unlikely to ever have children, and in any case, whilst Henry VIII lived, Reginald was also a dead man walking. Margaret's male-line grandsons were also imprisoned or had predeceased her. As a daughter, Ursula Pole could no more pass on the Pole name than Margaret could Plantagenet. She must have known, at that moment, that the future of her branch of this great dynasty was now likely to become extinct. It is unsurprising, therefore, that Margaret had taken steps to protect her remaining family members, and hopefully provide for their future, should the worst happen. This is evidenced through her decision to create a new will in the autumn of 1538. Southampton had located the document when rifling through Margaret's coffers shortly after Montagu's execution. A second will was also uncovered, which had been cut in half. Margaret herself told Southampton that 'when she made her new will, she cut her name from the old to utterly damn it'.[28] Yet again, Margaret was being open in her admission that the goods seized were indeed hers. As with all other intelligence gathered, Margaret's wills were sent on to Cromwell.

Ultimately, the Pope doubling down on his excommunication of Henry VIII was perfunctory, for the real threat, even if largely imagined, had now passed with the deaths of Exeter and Montagu. As the capital became more entrenched in the reformist leanings of the Protestant faith, so diminished the popularity of those viewed as blockers to its success, ergo Exeter and Montagu. Indeed a close knit group of Protestants residing in London conveyed news to friends overseas that 'the principal supporters of Popery among us have been cut off'.[29] Even so, the knowledge that Reginald remained safely ensconced in Rome, and that the old enemies of France and Spain were always looking for an excuse to cause trouble remained intact. It was this that accelerated the king's decision to consider the proposition put to him by Cromwell about aligning England in marriage to the Protestant duchy of Cleves[30], and yet despite the ongoing concerns of the Henrician court, one nobleman miraculously survived – Geoffrey Pole. On 2 January 1539 news reached the Tower that he had been pardoned. Ever close to the latest scandal, Chapuys wrote 'I am told his life is granted to him, but he must remain in perpetual prison'.[31] Exactly why Geoffrey did not follow his brother and the other noblemen to the block is open to debate. The factor which most likely contributed to his remaining alive was the willingness he had shown in providing evidence against the men now dead. This, coupled with his complete mental breakdown, perhaps saved him from an appointment with the executioner's axe. The latter point in particular is worth discussion, because at this time it was illegal to execute those judged insane. At a distance of half a millennia, it is difficult to accurately diagnose exactly what level of sanity Geoffrey maintained, but to his contemporaries, the attempts at suicide and the general breakdown of his wits may well have been viewed as enough evidence to provide a reprieve. Indeed, on 28 December, just a couple of weeks after the executions, Geoffrey had made a second suicide attempt, unsuccessfully trying to smother himself with a pillow.[32] As would later become clear, the king was not above changing the law around the ability to execute the insane when it suited him. In 1542 for example, Henry VIII overturned this law to condemn Jane Boleyn, Viscountess Rochford. The viscountess had suffered a complete nervous collapse in the fallout from her involvement in Queen Katheryn Howard's extramarital affairs. This would normally have seen her life spared, but the king had decided her guilt was plain, and that her descent into madness did not change that fact. A change in the law was duly passed, and so Jane Boleyn suffered the same fate as her husband and sister-in-law had done some years earlier. Three days after Geoffrey tried to kill himself for the second time, the final notable figure entered the Tower on suspicion of playing a role in the Exeter Conspiracy – Sir Nicholas Carew. Carew was the king's master of horse and was once an extremely close friend, despite his well-known conservative leanings and the difficult relationship he had held with Anne Boleyn. Despite being viewed as a bad influence on the king in his youth by Cardinal Wolsey, Carew became a central part of the king's council and was entrusted with several diplomatic embassies to France from where a close relationship with the French king was born. He had largely avoided association to the Exeter Conspiracy and the fallout caused, which made his sudden arrest all the more strange. The evidence against Carew was particularly lacking, and appears to have been driven mostly from suspicion arising from his fondness for the Lady Mary and thus the memory of her late mother. According to Chapuys, what linked Carew to the broader Exeter Conspiracy was a letter found in the coffers of Gertrude Courtenay which proved that he belonged to the 'White Rose' network. However, this 'belonging' seems highly improbable, for Carew was a man whose entire career and position in life was owed to the good graces of the king. Carew may have been popular, he may have been an excellent courtier, but his ancestry was far from noble. Simply put, he was not an equal in pedigree to the Pole and Exeter families, and thus carried absolutely zero claim to the English throne. Without their shared adherence to the interests of Lady Mary, practically nothing united Carew with the others brought down. That isn't to suggest that Carew did not know the families, indeed it was claimed he had been in regular correspondence with Montagu and Exeter, but it's quite a leap to twist a friendship into dynastic kinship. As further evidence of the lack of close ties between the men, Carew soon spoke out against Exeter, perhaps inspired by Geoffrey Pole's willingness to divulge information. In doing so, he was actively attempting to distance himself from association to the men central to the Exeter Conspiracy. Carew claimed that Exeter had been disappointed by the birth of Prince Edward, for it removed the chances of Lady Mary ascending to the throne and further displaced his own chances of one day becoming king. Carew went further still, by conspicuously reading the bible in English during his imprisonment in the Tower, markedly distancing himself from the well-known traditional Catholicism of the Poles and Exeters. His hopes were in vain, and shortly after his trial, Carew was beheaded on Tower Hill on 3 March 1539. Montagu's one time comment to his brother Geoffrey that 'the King never made man but he destroyed him again, either with displeasure or the sword' felt particularly apt.

As winter gave way to spring, Margaret Pole's position remained unchanged. She had been held at Cowdray House for four months, isolated from her loved ones, in the household of a man openly trying to find evidence which would implicate her in the treasons that had seen her eldest son executed. Southampton's wife, Mabel, had also made her distaste for Margaret's presence well known. Margaret knew that at any time word could reach Cowdray House, ordering her to make the all-too-likely one-way trip to the Tower. It is amazing therefore that despite increasingly trying circumstances, Margaret maintained her composure and continued to outwit Southampton and Goodrich. The former, in a letter to Cromwell dated 14 March 1539, briefed his master on how challenging a houseguest Margaret was proving to be, stating:

'Because my wife since her coming hither has not seen my lady of Salisbury, nor I, since my first coming, repaired to her, she takes it grievously, inasmuch that a gentleman of mine, who does nothing but attend on her, told me she besought me to speak with her. I went this afternoon and showed her I and my wife could not find it in our hearts to see her when that arrant whoreson traitor, her son the Cardinal, went about from prince to prince to work trouble to the King and realm. She replied with a wonderful sorrowful countenance that though he were an ill man to behave so to the King who had been so good to him, yet was he no whoreson, for she was both a good woman and true. She wished he were in Heaven or that she could bring him to the

King's presence, and she hoped the king would not impute his heinous offence to her. I had no further talk with her, nor will while I am here. I beg you to rid me of her company, for she is both chargeable and troubles my mind.'[33]

A sharp and intelligent politician, Margaret's life had been dominated by court intrigue, which no doubt helped her navigate the position she was now in, but even so, living under the roof of two people so clearly irritated by her presence must have been galling in the extreme. We must keep in mind that Lady Margaret Pole was a countess of royal blood, the daughter of a royal duke, niece of two of England's kings. She owned vast amounts of land, oversaw a huge household, and was the one-time most senior member of a royal princesses' household. Ordinarily, she would have been a highly coveted guest for any household, and yet here she was, an unwelcome house guest, taking up room, viewed as nothing more than an irksome nuisance. One hopes that the reality of her situation must have been both parts frustrating and in some respects amusing. You can almost picture Margaret getting a kick out of repeatedly besting her inquisitors, giving them nothing, whilst putting a drain on their resources, for despite her house arrest she would continue to be treated as befitted her rank, which ensured a certain level of day-to-day grandeur, particularly in the food presented to her. Upon receiving Southampton's letter, Cromwell took steps to remove Margaret Pole from Cowdray House, much to the earl and his wife's relief. This took place towards the end of March 1539. Sadly it is not clear if she was lodged in another house straight afterwards, or if she made the dreaded journey towards the capital, bound for the Tower. What we do know for certain however, is that in May 1539, after months of uncertainty, parliament formally moved against Lady Margaret Pole, Countess of Salisbury. She was attainted for high treason, a process which removed the need for a trial to condemn her. Joining Margaret in the attainder was Hugh Vaughan, steward of her Welsh estates. Why Margaret was denied her chance to stand in court and face her accusers is unknown. Attainders were usually as a result of there being such irrefutable evidence that a trial seemed unnecessary, but in Margaret's case it smacks more of a government not wishing to give voice to a woman who could produce such a sturdy response that acquittal could have been possible. It feels almost as if Henry VIII's council and parliament wished simply to hush Margaret up, to remove her entirely from conscious being. Gertrude Courtenay would suffer the same indignity, and is also referenced in the attainder, which read:

> 'Where also Margaret Pole, Countess of Salisbury, and Hugh Vaughan, late of Beckener, in the County of Monmouth, yeoman, by instigation of the devil, putting apart the dread of Almighty God, their duty of allegiance, and the excellent benefit received of his Highness, have not only traitorously confederated themselves with the false and abominable traitors Henry Pole, Lord Montagu, and Reginald Pole, sons to the said Countess, knowing them to be false traitors, but also have maliciously aided, abetted, maintained, and comforted them in their said false and abominable treason, to the most fearful peril of his highness, the commonwealth of this realm, the said marchioness and the said countess be declared attainted, and shall suffer the pains and penalties of high treason.'[34]

The attainder was particularly personal in its language. By referencing Margaret's sons as being so crucial to the cause of her situation, it drove home the reality that this was a family viewed as inherently depraved. Reginald Pole was also included within the attainder in his own right. Referred to simply as the 'late dean of the Cathedral Church of Exeter' the crime which condemned him was having 'taken and pursued worldly promotions from the bishop of Rome'.[35] In a no doubt stage-managed drama, once the attainder had been read out before parliament, Cromwell produced a tunic which he had supposedly seized from amongst Margaret's goods. Although lost to time, the tunic itself has become one of the great showpieces in the condemnation of Margaret Pole, for it was used as 'evidence' of the countesses' grand designs for both the throne of England, and an intended marriage between Reginald and Lady Mary. The discovery of this tunic was certainly convenient, and only cropped up six months after Margaret's households were searched following her arrest. If the item was genuine, surely it would have been spotted earlier, particularly as the royal arms had been woven into it. We have details of how the tunic was designed, and its intended meaning, thanks to a letter sent to Margaret's cousin, Arthur, Viscount Lisle, which explained:

'There was a coat-armour found in the Countesses of Salisbury's coffer, and by the one side of the coat there was the King's Grace his arms of England, that is, the lions without the fleur de lys, and about the whole arms was made pansies for Pole, and marigolds for my Lady Mary. This was about the coat armour. And betwixt the marigold and the pansy was made a tree to rise in the midst; and on the tree a coat of purple hanging on a bough, in tokening of the coat of Christ; and on the other side of the coat all the Passion of Christ. Pole intended to have married my Lady Mary, and betwixt them both should again arise the old doctrine of Christ. This was the intent that the coast was made, as it is openly known in the Parliamentary house, as Master Sir George Speke showed me. And this my Lady Marquess, my Lady Salisbury, with divers others are attainted today by act of Parliament.'[36]

The authenticity of the tunic is impossible to prove, and thus we cannot conclusively say whether it was created with intended malice in mind. If the item was real then it's possible it was made years earlier when discussions had taken place between Katherine of Aragon and Margaret Pole on a potential match between Mary and Reginald. With such a massive household and countless properties, one tunic could be easily forgotten about. Indeed in Froude's account of the scene from parliament, he mentions that the item was 'concealed amidst the countesses linen'.[37] The reference to the passions of Christ, e.g. the five wounds, was an extremely common image at the time, and therefore cannot be defined as one used solely during the Pilgrimage of Grace and its aftermath. Such considerations did not matter however, for the imagery within the tunic was viewed with the most damning of conclusions possible – depose the king, install Lady Mary as queen, with Reginald Pole as her consort. This was precisely the piece of evidence that Cromwell was desperate for, which does make its discovery all the more suspicious. Again, nothing can be proved, but it is my belief that the item was a forgery, created by Cromwell and his cronies as a means of having something to pin against Margaret Pole. We must keep in mind that essentially nothing had been gleaned from her many interrogations that convincingly alluded to treason. We know from the downfall of Anne

Boleyn that Thomas Cromwell was not above fabricating evidence, and on balance, the saga of the tunic feels all too neat and convenient to seem genuine.

Margaret's life and her goods were now forfeit. She was stripped of the title the king had reinstated to her twenty-seven years earlier – no longer Margaret, Countess of Salisbury, she was back to being known simply as Margaret Pole. She could be executed at the king's pleasure. As referenced earlier, Margaret's immediate location following the attainder is unknown. She crops up as a prisoner in the Tower of London's list of inmates in November 1539, but she was likely held there way before that date; those who suffered the indignity of attainder were not given the luxury of house arrest! Unusually however, no date for her execution was set. Practically all members of the nobility had died within days of being judged guilty of treason; Baron Montagu for example had died seven days after his trial, George Boleyn had died just forty-eight hours after his own trial in 1536, but Margaret Pole was left to linger. The question is why? Reticence and sympathy were not qualities in abundance with Henry VIII, but he did on occasion display flashes of conscience. In not ordering Margaret's death, is it possible that Henry VIII held scruples around her downfall? For all Henry VIII's laissez-faire attitude to destroying political enemies, Margaret did in many respects represent something quite different; this was no ordinary death sentence. She was now sixty-five years old, elderly by the standards of the time, and this mattered. In the natural course of life, she would probably have died of natural causes within a few years. Born of the highest birth, Margaret also shared a close blood bond to the king via the mother he famously idolised. It seems probable that Elizabeth of York's memory was evoked when having to agree to Margaret's destruction, for Elizabeth and Margaret were first cousins; surely the king considered how his mother would have felt, knowing he was condemning her? Could the king truly consign Margaret Pole to such an ignominious death?

Chapter 10

To Death

'For traitors on the block should die; I am no
traitor, no, not I!'

Although unable to be proven beyond doubt, this line and its further
content is said to have been carved into the wall of Lady Margaret Pole's
cell at the Tower of London. As she languished in prison, living in a
constant state of limbo, much time must surely have been given over to
wondering how she had come to this. Her life was one of extraordinary
highs and monumental lows, but could she have truly expected that this
is how it would end? Sure, Margaret had seen her father and brother
executed, the former being one of the few examples where guilt is
highly probable, but she herself had always been a loyal and dedicated
courtier, hadn't she? Had she not gone out of her way to please the
king? Was she not willing to bend her will to his? Had she not raised
her children to be consummate courtiers, to play down their claims to
the crown of England and remain loyal to their sovereign? Undoubtedly,
she had, across the board, but like the Duke of Buckingham years
earlier, and the more recently dispatched Marquis of Exeter, Margaret's
bloodline was something she could neither control nor gloss over. She
was a Plantagenet, and for a king as distrustful as Henry VIII, that was
reason enough to justify his actions. Margaret was not the only person
who remained alive from among those initially arrested. Montagu's
son, Henry, was still held in the Tower, as were Gertude Courtenay,
Marchioness of Exeter and her son, Edward. Although the two young
boys suffered under the acts of attainder passed against their parents,
there was no indication that they would be sentenced to death – even
in the sixteenth century the execution of children, particularly those of
noble blood, would have been met with significant outrage.

The one man who had the possible scope to defuse the situation,
particularly for Margaret and her grandson, remained safely under the

protection of powerful friends on the continent – Reginald. Naturally he would not return to English shores, but even a humble letter to the king showing obedience and remorse may have softened Henry VIII's resolve. Such a letter was never written, instead, Reginald doubled down in his efforts to undermine the English sovereign. When news reached his ear of the attainder against Margaret having passed, he wrote to a confidante saying 'You have heard, I believe, of my mother being condemned to death by public council, or rather, to eternal life. Not only has he who condemned her, condemned a woman of seventy, than whom he has no near relation except his daughter, and of whom he used to say there was no holier woman in his kingdom; but, at the same time, her grandson, son of my brother, a child, the remaining hope of our race'.[1] With every action taken, it pushed his mother closer to destruction, so where was Reginald, and what was he doing? With assassins still crawling across Europe seeking him out, Reginald was required to travel in secret and would often have to resort to disguises. At the end of December 1538 he was found crossing the Apennine mountains of Italy, trudging through deep snow dressed, not in the red robes of his office, but as a regular member of the public. To drive the ruse home further, he rode a horse, as opposed to the mule normally used by cardinals. Reginald's intended destination was Spain, with a mission so crucial that he braved such perilous elements. Earlier in the month Pope Paul III had created a new cardinal, the Scottish David Beaton. The Pope's reasoning behind creating this new cardinal is seen almost at once when he ordered Beaton to widely circulate the excommunication of Henry VIII. Seeing an opportunity to resurrect his plans of removing Henry VIII from the throne, Reginald implored the Pope to support the mission, which was granted. It was for this reason that Reginald was trying to make his way to Spain, to parley with Charles V, with hopes of securing the Emperor's assistance, which if successful, would have given Reginald's cause such much needed impetus. An audience with the Emperor was granted in February 1539, despite protests from Sir Thomas Wyatt, who was still serving the king at the Spanish court. As with his earlier attempts at overthrowing Henry, this new mission was to be in vain, but was treated with no less concern in England. Reginald admonished Henry VIII in detail, recounting the executions of the Carthusian monks, of Bishop Fisher and Thomas More. Naturally he referenced the death of his eldest brother and their kin, Exeter and Neville, using this as evidence that the king had also turned on his own people. Signs of an increasingly inflated ego also come across in a letter written by Reginald to Nicolas Perrenot de Granvelle, Chancellor to the Emperor. He openly states that the people of England regard the Pole family as those best suited to displacing the king, inadvertently inflaming Henry's suspicions and Cromwell's resolve further:

'If they did not choose me, then every decent man in England would choose someone else from my family to ask the Emperor for help because no family has endured more of his kindred. Queen Katherine used to say that all the trouble dated from the time when she heard that my mother was no longer the Princesses governess. She had been so anxious for my mother to become the child's governess that she had gone to visit her with the King, in order to persuade her to take the post. The Queen's physician, who is now at the Imperial court, can testify to this. My family suffered a very great deal for her, and the Queen often declared how deeply she was obliged to us. I am saying all this to demonstrate just how much our Island deserves the Emperor's help when it is asked for by the English family best qualified to do so.'[2]

The reference to Queen Katherine and the suffering of the Pole family on her behalf must surely point to the execution of Reginald's uncle, the Earl of Warwick, which Katherine of Aragon did famously believe acted as something of a curse in the success of her marriage to Henry VIII. Rumour soon spread that Reginald had asked for 12,000 men from the Emperor, caveating his request, and tying in the words of his earlier letter, by saying 'the wounded minds of England (those who prescribed to the old doctrine) would join them'.[3] Reginald's appeal to the Emperor fell flat, and no support was granted. Granvelle soon informed a mortified Reginald that he should get back to Rome as quickly as possible. In a moment of inspired public relations, Henry VIII played on any monarch's fears; that of their people assuming powers above their station. Although he and Charles V were at odds more than they were at peace, they did at least respect the dignity of their shared office. Henry VIII's clever depiction of Reginald as a man trying to overthrow their role of ruler, as one disrupting the natural order, sufficiently weakened the way he was viewed by the Emperor. Once safely back in Rome, Reginald was gifted large sums of money by the Pope, and given the comforting assurance that whilst his mission may have failed, that the Pope himself was satisfied. In England, despite the danger passing, the king continued to treat an alliance between Reginald and European rulers as a potential threat. Such was his concern that he made the arduous journey of visiting all major ports along southern coastlines to check they were suitably ready for invasion. By now, given way to obesity and regularly troubled by ulcerated legs, that the king felt it prudent to make such a trip highlights how seriously he treated the matter. Furthermore, although the chief suspects of the Exeter Conspiracy were now either dead, imprisoned or banished from court, the continued presence of Reginald Pole would see yet more members of the White Rose faction suffer by their association to him, even if only tenuous. For example, on 19 May 1540, Lord Lisle was arrested on suspicion of traitorous dealings with the cardinal, with several of his household also arrested when it was believed they plotted to hand Calais over to the French.[4] As Calais was one of the very last pieces of overseas territory held by the English, such a threat was treated very seriously. Lisle, we must remember, was a Plantagenet, a cousin of Margaret Pole. Brought over from Calais to be lodged in the Tower, he did not suffer the indignity of a trial or attainder but remained imprisoned for just under two years, despite being by this stage in his late 70s. When told in March 1542 that he was to be released, Lisle was so shocked that he suffered a heart attack and died two days later.

Although held in prison with no apparent hope of a reprieve, Margaret Pole was at least generally well cared for under instructions from the king. He paid £13 6s 8d per month to cover the food provided to Margaret, her grandson and young Edward Courtenay, and also paid 18d per week to the servant attending Margaret Pole at all times.[5] It would appear, however, that over time, the king's willingness to ensure a degree of comfort for Margaret began to wane. She and Gertrude Courtenay were finally forced to complain to one of the Tower's keepers, Thomas Philips, that further clothing was needed for both themselves and their serving women. Philips reported to Thomas Cromwell that 'the Lady Salisbury maketh great moan for that she wanteth necessary apparel both for to change and also to keep her warm'.[6] As Margaret was now of an advanced age, and the Tower a cold and draughty place, it isn't a surprise that her general health would have begun to suffer. At the end of 1539, Gertrude Courtenay's name was included in a general pardon from the king. This pardon saw

Gertrude released from the Tower, although her son would remain. Such an action must have been galling beyond measure for Margaret to accept. As Pierce notes, there was significantly more evidence implicating Gertrude Courtenay in having committed treason than there ever had been against Margaret, and yet she was given back her liberty, while Margaret remained a prisoner. Such actions from the king highlight how clearly he saw a difference in the positions of the two women. Where Gertrude was now merely the widow of a traitor, with all power and revenues returned to the crown, Margaret was not only royal by birth, but had a son causing havoc for the king in territories beyond his grasp. Simply put, Margaret was suffering because Reginald remained free.

Very little is known of Margaret's time in the Tower throughout 1540. There is evidence to point to a planned rescue attempt by Reginald's accomplices, for at some point during that year he wrote to a bishop in France explaining that plans were underway to release Margaret from the Tower, but that they had been scuppered when the person orchestrating the coup was imprisoned, although released shortly after. Exactly who this person was remains unclear, although it may have been Gregory Botolph, a chaplain of Lord Lisle's.[7] Whether intelligence of such a plot ever reached Margaret's ears is unknown, indeed even the king may have been ignorant of it. It was also during 1540 that we have one of the very few fleeting references to the state of Margaret's grandson, the younger Henry Pole. Sadly, it appears he was suffering far more than the other young man lodged inside the Tower's walls, Edward Courtenay. In the summer of 1540 the French Ambassador, Charles de Marillac, reported that the young Courtenay remained healthy and had been assigned a tutor; Henry Pole by contrast was described as 'poorly and strictly kept and not desired to know anything'. Marillac gets to the crux of the issue by referring to Henry as 'the little nephew of Cardinal Pole'.[8] The idea that young Henry Pole was being denied an education feels particularly cruel, for it was history repeating itself. His existence was almost entirely reenacting the fate of his great-uncle, Edward, Earl of Warwick. It was also at this time that the king brought down his one-time chief minister, Thomas Cromwell. Beheaded on Tower Hill in July 1540, the fall of Cromwell was largely orchestrated through religiously conservative members of the high nobility, most notably the Duke of Norfolk. As Cromwell's hand in uncovering 'the Exeter Conspiracy' is well documented, his fall could have been a positive sign for Margaret's chances of release, and yet there is no evidence to suggest that it altered her circumstances in the slightest. This acts as further proof of the king's continued desire to punish those closest to Reginald Pole.

With every passing day, the king became more and more suspicious of anyone with ties, however tenuous, to Reginald. As this accelerated, Margaret Pole moved closer, inch by inch, to her destruction. What eventually set the seal on her fate is perhaps best understood by taking a macro view on a series of events beginning in early 1541. All reason seems to have now vanished from Henry VIII, no doubt exacerbated by the loss of Cromwell, who for all his machinations did not act rashly. In January, Sir Thomas Wyatt, now back in England after concluding his period as ambassador to the Spanish court, was arrested on a charge of 'having had intelligence with the King's traitor Pole'. The absurdity of Wyatt's arrest is clear, for this was the man who had hitherto attempted to block Reginald from gaining access to the Emperor, and had gone to great lengths to try and get the cardinal killed. Another ambassador, Sir John Wallop joined Wyatt in the Tower shortly after, suspected of writing letters to Richard Pate, English ambassador at the Imperial Court, who broke away from adherence to the king, becoming part of the Pope's retinue. At the intercession of the king's teenage fifth queen, Katheryn Howard, both men were released, but the simple fact that their arrest was connected to both Reginald and the Pope, was naturally detrimental to Margaret's plight. There were further issues when John Babham, a former steward of Margaret's was examined by the king's Privy Council, although on what charge is unknown. Jerome Regland and his wife Anne, a gentlewoman who had been in Margaret's employ, were also questioned on 23 February over suspected letter burning in the wake of Henry, Baron Montagu's arrest. That such stories were being raked over again, two years after Montagu's death, points to renewed hopes of finding more information that would unequivocally condemn Margaret Pole. It is this that makes the king's next course of action against Margaret all the more difficult to make sense of. Just weeks later, a sizable order of new clothing arrived at Margaret's quarters, traditionally believed to have been sent by Queen Katheryn Howard. A niece of the Duke of Norfolk and a first cousin of Anne Boleyn, Queen Katheryn's scandalous downfall has resulted in her being perpetually, and rather unfairly, consigned to history as an air-head harlot, and yet if she did orchestrate the delivery of clothing to Margaret, then she clearly held enough sympathy and presence of mind to keep the elderly woman in her thoughts. The items listed were a nightgown trimmed in fur, a fur-lined petticoat, a satin-lined nightgown and four pairs of shoes.[9] As Pierce notes, the inclusion of multiple pairs of shoes perhaps indicates that at this time, Margaret was still permitted some ability to walk around the Tower complex, and not confined to a single cell. As Conor Byrne points out in his biography of the doomed queen, if Katheryn sent these items of her own volition, then she would have been required to seek her husband's permission. Were this the case, then clearly Henry VIII accepted, for Margaret did indeed receive the goods. If the queen did orchestrate the order, then such an action highlights a note of caring charity, in direct contrast to the flighty and trivial young woman so often portrayed in film and television. The delivery of these items makes for a stark realisation that Margaret Pole's life was not yet entirely lost, but as we know, displays of support or loyalty could be fleeting in the king. In April 1541, a small but consequential conspiracy arose in the ever volatile north of England. Marketed as a planned revival of the Pilgrimage of Grace, the uprising was quashed before it even truly began, but devastatingly for Margaret one of the suspected leaders was Sir John Neville of Chevet, who had acted as high sheriff of Yorkshire on three occasions. Although unable to be proven, it is possible that Sir John was a distant relative of Margaret's, for we must remember that on her mother's side Margaret was a Neville, a granddaughter of the great Earl of Warwick who had placed Edward IV on the throne. Henry VIII would have known all too well that Margaret carried Neville blood, highlighting again the complexity and illustrious nature of her pedigree. Responding to the repeated threats from the north of his country, and hoping to parley with the Scottish king, James V, Henry VIII was finally convinced into a northern progress. Before setting off, however, the king gave instructions that the Tower was to be cleared of all prisoners. According to Marillac, the king 'Before his departure has given order for the Tower to be cleared of prisoners, either by condemnation or absolution'.[10] In other words, the prisoners awaiting execution would either see their verdict carried out, or they would be pardoned and released.

On the morning of 27 May 1541, at 7 am, Margaret was visited in her chambers and told that the hour of her death was imminent. After over two years' incarceration, it had finally come to this. She would follow in the footsteps of her brother, Edward, Earl of Warwick, her son, Montagu, her kin, Exeter. As a woman of devout faith, the speed at which she was required to prepare herself to meet her God must have been greatly distressing. To reference the very start of this book, 'mors improvisa', a sudden death, was one all God-fearing Christians tried to avoid, but one hopes the fervency with which Margaret adhered to the Catholic faith acted as a crutch in her final moments. Stripped of her lands and titles, her sons either dead or neutralised, her spirit broken, Margaret posed no real threat to the king, and yet here it was, this final humiliation. Margaret left her lodgings, accompanied by the constable of the Tower; it is unclear if she was joined by the servant who had been with her throughout her imprisonment. Although considered a private execution, a crowd of approximately 150 were present to see Margaret die, including the Lord Mayor of London. Exactly where Margaret was escorted to die is not known. The space commemorated as the execution spot with a glass installation on Tower Green has been convincingly proven as misplaced. Records of Anne Boleyn's execution for example point to the scaffold being placed in front of what is now the entrance to the Crown Jewels.[11] Exactly what happened when Margaret reached the executioner's block is also debated. Whilst it is generally accepted that Margaret's death was not swift or clean, the accounts suggest a total of eleven blows of the axe were required before she was dead, there are different versions which describe the overall way in which her execution played out. The most famous, and least plausible, comes from Lord Herbert of Cherbury, who quotes from an unknown source years after Margaret's death. According to this account, upon mounting a scaffold, Margaret was asked to kneel before the block and lay her head down, at which point she refused, stating 'So should traitors do, and I am none' and that if the executioner 'would have her head, to get it as he could'.[12] She was then supposedly forced down, with the executioner striking a blow into her shoulder, at which point Margaret sprang up and ran around the scaffold being, quite literally, hacked to bits. Whilst an undoubtedly dramatic story, this seems an unlikely end to Margaret Pole's life, for a couple of reasons. Firstly, her age and frailty, no doubt exacerbated by her long imprisonment, would not have been conducive to running around a scaffold, especially if she was already injured from an ill-placed blow of the axe. More importantly however is to consider Margaret's own identity. As low as the king had brought her, she was, and always had been, a life-long member of the high nobility. She was witness to countless numbers sent to their deaths in this same manner. Margaret knew what was required of her, she knew even though she was (in all probability) innocent, that it didn't really matter. The law had found her guilty, and thus, she was guilty. To not behave in a way commensurate to her rank thus seems highly improbable. She would have wanted to end her life with dignity, not by creating further chaos which could have ramifications for the few members of her family who remained alive. An element of this account of the execution, dramatics aside, is also unique in that it mentions a scaffold. The other accounts suggest that no scaffold had been prepared, and that Margaret was required to basically lie on the ground, her head resting atop a low wooden block. This would be different to the more traditional taller block, with a large section cut out for the victim to place their head into. If the records are correct, then it may go some way towards understanding why Margaret's execution was not achieved with one strike. The lower a victim would be to the ground, the further the axe had to fall, distorting both accuracy and positioning relative to the victim's neck. It is this, no doubt compounded by the fact that the regular Tower headsman was away carrying out executions of northern rebels, that resulted in the protracted end Margaret would face. The two extant accounts of Margaret's death come from Charles de Marillac and Eustace Chapuys. Both men age Margaret incorrectly, stating she was much older than she actually was. This may have been genuinely misplaced information, or possibly done to make her death seem even more horrific. According to Marillac, Margaret was 'beheaded in a corner of the Tower, in presence of so few people that until evening the truth was still doubted. It was more difficult to believe as she had been a long prisoner, was of noble lineage, above 80 years old, had been punished by the loss of one son and banishment of the other, and the total ruin of her house'.[13] Although he was not present at the execution, it was Chapuys who provided the more detailed accounts of Margaret's death. Inclined to dramatics, Chapuys' words should be treated with some degree of caution, but, he states:

> 'When the sentence of death was made known to her, she found the thing very strange, not knowing of what crime she was accused, nor how she had been sentenced; but at last perceiving that there was no remedy, and that die she must,

she went out of the dungeon where she was detained and walked towards the midst of the space in front of the Tower, where there was no scaffold erected nor anything except a small block. Arriving there, after commending her soul to her creator, she asked those present to pray for the King, the Queen, the Prince and Princess, to all of whom she wished to be particularly commended, and more especially to the latter, whose godmother she had been. She sent her blessing to her, and begged also for hers. After which words she was told to make haste and place her neck on the block which she did. As the ordinary executor of justice was absent doing his work in the North, a wretched and blundering youth was chosen, who literally hacked her head and shoulders to pieces in the most pitiful manner. May god in his High grace pardon her soul, for certainly she was a most virtuous and honourable lady, and there was no need or haste to bring to ignominious a death upon her, considering that as she was then nearly 90 years old.'[14]

If Chapuys' account is accurate, and these were indeed the actions of Margaret Pole, then her decision to omit Princess Elizabeth in her commendations was a deliberate attack on the daughter of Anne Boleyn. That he made no mention of Margaret supposedly running around the scaffold tells us that this part of the legend is likely apocryphal. Margaret's body was then buried below the altar inside the Chapel of St Peter ad Vincula. Although this was entirely expected, as the chapel was the final resting place of most people deemed traitors to the crown, in authorising her burial there Henry VIII delivered one final insult to Margaret's memory. Where his father had allowed her brother to be buried at Bisham Abbey, resting beside his York forebears, Margaret would remain at the Tower. The spectacular 'Salisbury Chapel' structure Margaret had commissioned in Christchurch Priory as her planned final resting place, was instead defaced, the Pole family coat of arms removed. Although empty, thankfully the chapel can still be seen to this day.

In 1886, 345 years after her death, Margaret Pole, Countess of Salisbury was beatified as a martyr of the faith by Pope Leo XIII. Becoming known as Blessed Margaret Pole, each year on 27 May, the anniversary of her execution, she is commemorated in Catholic churches across the United

Kingdom. During the reign of Queen Victoria, the Chapel of St Peter ad Vincula required desperate repair work to its foundations. Initially it had been hoped that the remains of those buried within the chapel would not need to be disturbed, but this wasn't to be. Although hundreds of people are buried within the church, burials of the nobility, even those executed for treason, were still treated with some degree of reverence, hence there being information available as to where the remains of notable figures from the Tudor period were kept. Queen Victoria took a distinct interest in the proceedings, and instructed one of her own surgeons, Dr Frederic Mouat, to undertake an examination of the bones uncovered. The remains thought to be of the Tower's most infamous victim, Anne Boleyn, were unearthed and examined at length. The description said that the bones belonged 'To a female of between twenty-five and thirty years of age, of a delicate frame of body, and who had been of slender and perfect proportions; the forehead and lower jaw were small and especially well formed. The vertebrae were particularly small, especially one joint (the atlas), which was that next to the skull, bearing witness to the Queen's "little neck".' Beside Anne Boleyn's resting place were the bones thought to belong to Edward Seymour, Duke of Somerset and John Dudley, Duke of Northumberland. Beside them, where the remains of Katheryn Howard may once have rested, nothing was discovered. It is thought that the queen's youth at her death and the appearance of limestone in the ground, simply turned her bones to dust. Next to the space where Katheryn was supposedly buried, the remains of two further females were uncovered. The first belonging to a woman of approximately 40 years of age, and given the placement next door to where Katheryn Howard was supposedly interred, suggests that these were the remains of Jane Boleyn, Lady Rochford. The second female's bones belonged 'to a woman of considerably advanced years, who had been tall and certainly of above average height'. As the only member of the nobility buried in the chapel, who was both a woman and of advanced age, these bones are almost unequivocally those of Margaret Pole. After examination, all of the remains were placed into lead lined boxes, inscribed with the name of the person to whom the bones were believed to belong. They were then reinterred in front of the chapel's altar, with marble memorial plaques sat atop.

Lady Margaret Pole's marble plaque restores in death what she was stripped of in life; she is buried as Countess of Salisbury.

Her remains are still there to this day.

Chapter 11

Life After Death

The Pole family figureheads, Margaret and Montagu, were now destroyed, Reginald continued to cause trouble in Rome, Geoffrey Pole was broken beyond repair, and Ursula Pole, although living in England and safely distanced from scandal, as a woman was unable to pass on the Pole name. It would have been easy to assume that the Pole family would be wiped from the pages of history, but this was not to be, not by a long shot. Reginald would remain a constant thorn in the side of the king for as long as he lived, and regain spectacular position and respect when Lady Mary finally, and shockingly, ascended the throne. Ursula Pole, the often overlooked daughter of Margaret would outlive them all, living to witness the first twelve years of the reign of the final Tudor, Elizabeth. This chapter will explore how the remaining members of the Pole family fared in the wake of Margaret's execution.

After his release from the Tower, Geoffrey Pole, a man who seemed incapable of staying out of trouble, got into a heated argument with a former colleague, John Gunter. Perhaps hoping to offload some of his own culpability in the destruction of his family, Geoffrey lambasted Gunter for having told the Earl of Southampton too much during the interrogations he had undergone. Overlooking the fact that Gunter had little choice in the matter, Geoffrey ferociously attacked him, leaving the bewildered Gunter with a severe head injury. Southampton chose to overlook the scandal, in part because he felt Geoffrey was mentally unstable; the king however was less forgiving. A stint in the Fleet prison followed before Constance Pole sufficiently begged for her husband's release. This was granted provided he remained away from the royal court. In a sign that Geoffrey did finally turn his life around, by 1543 he and his wife were gifted a property, Grandysomes, in Kent. Hazel Pierce suggests that the house may once have belonged to Margaret Pole.[1]

Just as there had been two princes in the Tower, now two young men of royal blood remained confined in its walls, Edward Courtenay

176

and Henry Pole. It was suspected the latter would eventually suffer execution, with Chapuys writing 'it is supposed that he will follow his father and grandmother'.[2] Last mentioned in 1542 under payments for meals, he did not suffer execution, but instead died without trace inside the Tower walls. How he died and when, and where he was buried, remains a complete mystery.

Exactly how and when Reginald became aware that his mother was now dead is difficult to determine. When he was told, he supposedly told his secretary that he was now the proud son of a martyr. We also have a fascinating account from Reginald's first biographer, Beccatelli, who likely spoke with Reginald's secretary, for he tells us that:

'One day when he had received a great number of letters from France and other places, and had requested me to answer them, I perceived, as I was gathering them up, that there was one among them in the English tongue, and suggested that to this I could not reply, because I knew absolutely nothing of the language. "I would that you could both read and understand it, for it brings me glad tidings." Inflamed with curiosity, I eagerly begged to be allowed to share his happiness, and this was his reply, "I have always been sensible of God's great goodness in having made me the son of a woman no less illustrious for her virtues than for her rank, but now he has granted me a yet more signal grace. My mother has received the crown of martyrdom, for because she held fast to our Catholic faith, and could by no means be shaken, she has been beheaded by Henry's orders. She was seventy years old, and this is her reward for all the care she had bestowed upon his daughter." I was completely overcome, but he continued firmly, "Let us be of good cheer, she has been added to the number of our patrons and advocates in heaven." He then withdrew into the little chapel where he always went to pray, and remained there some time, but when he rejoined us his face was as cheerful as usual.'[3]

Threats on Reginald's life were still commonplace. In 1541, whilst staying in Capranica, two Englishmen were arrested on suspicion that they were there to assassinate him. Under questioning, they confirmed that they were in Italy for that very reason. Reginald was, by this stage, Legate of Bologna, and thus sat in judgement of the men sent to kill him. They received the relatively mild punishment of being a galley slave (a rower) for a short time. Reginald's next appointment was when he was made Legate of the Patrimony of St Peter, taking up residence at Viterbo. He would spend four years there before receiving a summons to attend the Council of Trent. His time in Viterbo opened up yet more access to some of the shining lights of Renaissance Italy, and his friendship with Vittoria Colonna remained as strong as ever. Despite there only being an age gap of ten years, Reginald's relationship with Vittoria developed into something deeper in the wake of Margaret's execution. Although Reginald had spent the majority of his life apart from his mother, he evidently felt her loss at a deep level, for he asked Vittoria if she would, in effect, become his surrogate mother. Vittoria complied and thereafter referred to Reginald as her son in their communications. They remained close for the rest of Vittoria's life. She died in a nunnery at the age of 56 in 1547. Reginald's role as Patrimony was not without issues. He was undoubtedly conservative, but not cruel. He was accused of taking a too lenient approach in punishing heretics, but instead of taking offence he simply blessed God. He encouraged others to follow in his example, telling priests at Liege 'I have often been accused of a reluctance to chastise evil men, which amounts to cruelty toward the good; but I cannot do violence to my nature, least of all with those I love, and though it is undeniable that rebels must sometimes be punished by way of example, yet upon this one point I must ever insist that even when rebellious, they are still sons'.[4]

Back in England, the court of Henry VIII continued to break into ever more volatile factionalism. Religion was naturally the defining issue which split the court down the middle. On one side, the Duke of Norfolk led the traditionally conservative nobility, whilst the progressive evangelicals were led by Edward Seymour, uncle of the king's precious son, and Archbishop Cranmer. For a time, Norfolk was firmly in control, but when his niece, Queen Katheryn fell so spectacularly at the end of 1541, his own power began to significantly wane. The king was growing ever more obese, the ulcers in his legs which his doctors insisted on keeping open causing constant debilitating pain. In 1543 Henry VIII married for the sixth and final time. His bride was the twice widowed Catherine Parr. No one realistically expected children out of the marriage, and so in many respects Catherine assumed the role of a nurse to the ailing king, as well as a mother figure for his three children, the king's younger daughter Elizabeth becoming particularly fond of her final stepmother. Catherine was no pushover though, she was a shrewd and courageous woman, deeply committed to religious reform. In 1544, Geoffrey Pole resurfaced and was granted some of the lands back that had been taken in the wake of his mother's death, but the broken man never felt at ease whilst Henry VIII lived. As the king only had one son living, concern for what would happen at his death was naturally something Henry VIII mulled over constantly. Ever aware of the fact that his family had taken the throne by conquest, the king knew how vulnerable his son would be should he die whilst Edward was a minor. The presence of noblemen like Geoffrey Pole, those with royal blood in their veins, thus remained a source of disquiet. Although the king's daughters, Mary and Elizabeth, never regained their formal titles of princess, they were reinstated to the line of succession. Henry VIII solidified their position by having a bill pass through parliament which stated quite plainly that at his death, the throne would pass to his son Prince Edward, and from there to Lady Mary and then Lady Elizabeth. The descendants of the king's elder sister, Princess Margaret, would be entirely left out of his plans for the succession, and instead jump straight to the children of Lady Frances Grey, the elder daughter of the king's younger sister Princess Mary, these being Lady Jane, Lady Katherine and Lady Mary Grey. Prince Edward was the lone boy amongst a sea of female contenders to the throne. On 28 January 1547, aged 55, King Henry VIII died at the Palace of Whitehall. Virtually unrecognisable from the handsome and effervescent man of his youth, the king died a bloated and unpopular tyrant. Having achieved virtually no overseas successes, he left behind a greatly depleted treasury and major dissidence between the men who would need to run the country, for the dreaded reality of a minority rule had now come true, King Edward VI, as he now was, was a boy of just 9 years old. Under King Edward VI, Ursula Pole's life took a definite upturn, for in the first year of the boy king's reign, her husband Henry Stafford petitioned parliament for a restoration in blood, and in 1548 he was summoned to parliament on the orders of the king from where he was created Baron Stafford, making Ursula Baroness Stafford. It had taken twenty-six years, but finally the Staffords had a title back, albeit the most junior in the English peerage system. The title was given greater cache when it was recognised as being descended directly from the first creation of the Stafford Barony dating back to 1299.

The two living Pole brothers, Geoffrey and Reginald, did not fare so well under the young king Edward. In 1548 Geoffrey left England for Rome. When he arrived, he threw himself at the feet of his brother, begging for forgiveness for having caused the death of their eldest brother, Henry, Baron Montagu. Reginald took Geoffrey under his wing, introducing him directly to the Pope for absolution. Geoffrey left behind his wife and children, who remained at their home of Lordington. He was sent to Flanders by Reginald with an allowance of forty crowns per month. In 1549, Reginald made contact with Edward Seymour, Duke of Somerset, who had assumed the role of Protector of England whilst Edward VI remained a minor. Reginald had hoped that he could return to England in the capacity of a religious advisor, but as the court of Edward VI was openly Protestant, his hopes would be in vain. Reginald Pole was as unwelcome at the English court as he had ever been. The natural differences between Reginald and the man now running the country were clearly visible. Where Reginald was a member of the high nobility from birth, the Seymours, like the Boleyns, had achieved their positions at court through marriage. A natural superiority was thus embedded into Reginald's psyche, made stronger through his many illustrious achievements in Rome. As Mayer points out, 'Pole dealt with Somerset as one great noble to another who badly needed to be taught manners'.[5] A return to England not possible, Reginald instead continued in his service to the Catholic Church, and came close to achieving the highest office possible. When staying at his residence of Viterbo, news reached Reginald that the pontiff was dangerously ill, and all members of the Sacred College were thus summoned to journey to Rome. When Pope Paul III died, the conclave met and at the end of the first ballot it seemed inevitable that Reginald would be chosen, only for a sudden shift in voting which led to the appointment of Pope Julius III instead. Taking the news graciously, Reginald returned to Viterbo to continue in his role as governor. He held this position for the next three years, before resigning at the end of 1552. Thereafter, a hoped for return to England was resurrected, with Reginald beginning work on an updated version of his infamous tract, *De Unitate*. This new version would carry a preface addressed to the teenage Edward VI, supposedly in the hope of having the attainder which had been passed against Reginald lifted.[6] As it was, the young king was never to read the updated version of *De Unitate,* for he died, aged just 15, in the summer of 1553, following a long and painful bout of what is generally believed to be tuberculosis.[7] Just like that, the unbroken line of kings of England came to a grounding halt, for whoever took the crown next, was unquestionably going to be a woman. The will of Henry VIII made the line of succession crystal clear, but the precocious young Edward had decided before his death to completely overturn the work of his father, naming instead his cousin, Lady Jane Grey, as his choice of heir. The king had decided the bastardy of his sisters, and in particular the religion of his eldest sister, Lady Mary, made them unsuitable to follow in his footsteps. John Dudley, Duke of Northumberland, was instrumental in having Jane Grey's path to the throne solidified, self-interest apparent given Jane's marriage to his son Guildford. The rule of Queen Jane was fleeting, lasting just thirteen days.*

Lady Mary, having always been popular with the English people, soon rallied enough support to oust Jane from the throne that she rightfully saw as her own. Aged 37, Mary was a political animal through and through. She had stood firm in her religious conviction, refusing to not hear mass despite the demands of her young brother. She would not countenance her throne being taken away by what she saw as an upstart. This is the woman who had lived through the humiliation of her father's separation from her mother, and suffered at the hands of Anne Boleyn and her supporters. Now she had the wherewithal and scope to finally claim her right to rule, and she played it perfectly. Jane Grey, having entered the Tower of London as queen, was now lodged there as a prisoner. Mary's ascendancy was greeted with jubilation across the country, and she soon made good on her intentions to undo the work of her father and brother. This started with ordering the release of men who had suffered under

---

* Lady Jane Grey is perpetually referred to as the nine day queen, but this is technically inaccurate. The role of sovereign is constant, there is never not a monarch, and so the moment King Edward VI died, Lady Jane as his nominated heir became queen. This took place on July 6 1553, and she was then deposed on July 19, her reign thus lasting thirteen days.

the previous reigns, including most significantly, Edward Courtenay, the long imprisoned son of the Marquess and Marchioness of Exeter. Mary's feelings for Courtenay became plain, for within weeks of his release, she bestowed the title of Earl of Devon upon him. Mary was making a clear statement that members of the old guard, those of Plantagenet blood, would not suffer under her watch, quite the contrary, they would be celebrated and given positions of honour at her court. She put this into play almost at once, for the daughters of Henry, Baron Montagu were given back lands seized following their father's attainder.[8] The elder of the sisters, Catherine, Countess of Huntingdon, was also allowed to reinstate communication with her uncle Reginald, for whom, unsurprisingly, the news of Edward's death and Mary's ascendency was greeted with great enthusiasm. Reginald was made papal legate to England by the Pope, with Reginald writing to Mary to inform her of his appointment.[9] Naturally, a return to England was hoped for, as was a return of England into the papal fold, but neither would be as smooth nor as immediate as Reginald had expected. Reasons for the delay came from an unexpected source – Edward Courtenay, Earl of Devon. The scale of Devon's influence over Mary's court becomes clear, as does the perceived culpability of Reginald in the outcome of the Exeter Conspiracy, for the newly created earl blamed the Pole brothers for the death of his father. Indeed such was his distaste for the two men that he threatened to murder Geoffrey with his own hands, causing the queen to place armed guards around the earl's lodgings.[10] Reginald was delayed further owing to the queen's intention to marry Prince Philip, son of the king of Spain. Reginald saw no reason as to why England should not undergo an immediate return to the papal authority, but the Emperor blocked such movement until the royal marriage had taken place. In his frustration at what he saw as sacrilegious vacillation, Reginald stated that the queen's marriage was 'more universally odious than the cause of the religion'[11], and kept up a steady stream of letters imploring Mary to accelerate the restoration of Catholicism in England. He told her that 'what greater neglect can there be, than by setting aside the honour of God to attend to other things, leaving religion to the end'.[12] As we know, Queen Mary was a deeply devout Catholic, and a return to papal authority in her kingdom was one she would strive to achieve, but she also had the insight of having remained in England throughout her entire life and had thus witnessed the monumental shift in the way the English lived and worshipped, particularly in the capital. A whole generation of her people had grown up during the reformation, and so the prospect of returning to Rome was not universally desired. The country that Reginald so craved to return to was not the one he had left. Where he naively believed all could be overturned at once, Mary, despite the burnings that became so synonymous with her reign, was more circumspect and recognised that it would take time to achieve complete restoration of the true Catholic religion. The queen's intended marriage was also a source of great unrest, and led to Edward Courtenay's loss of favour, for it was believed that he was involved in the uprising known as Wyatt's Rebellion, which sought to block the marriage. Initially returned to the Tower, he was eventually sent overseas, where he died in 1556 aged just 29. Unfortunately, another extended member of the 'White Rose' network came out in support of Wyatt, highlighting the continued issue that Plantagenet blood and Plantagenet pride remained alive and well. It came from an unexpected source – Ursula Pole's family. She and her husband, Henry Stafford, had wisely stayed out of trouble, never coming close to any suspected inclusion in the Exeter Conspiracy or any other court dramas. This loyalty and general good behaviour clearly impressed the queen, for she rewarded the Staffords with the return of the fabulous Thornbury Castle, one of the key ancestral estates that had been taken by the crown following the Duke of Buckingham's attainder. Unfortunately, the behaviour of one of their sons, Thomas, placed a significant strain on the relationship between Ursula and the queen, for Thomas, thus a nephew to Reginald, also became involved in Wyatt's Rebellion. From the fleeting records of the man, Thomas Stafford comes across as having woefully misplaced judgement, seeing himself as a genuine contender for the English throne. In the wake of Wyatt's defeat, Thomas was imprisoned at the Fleet, before making an escape to France. He was soon captured, and subsequently beheaded for treason on 28 May 1557. Relations between the queen and Ursula Pole must surely have been difficult thereafter. With the rebellion crushed, Mary went ahead with her unpopular marriage, and after months of wrangling, Reginald's attainder was finally lifted by the English government. He could finally return to his motherland – safe, secure and most significantly, welcome.

Reginald set sail from Calais on 12 November 1554, landing at Dover eight days later. As he made his journey towards the capital, he built up an ever increasing train of councillors and noblemen in his wake. In scenes more akin to a returning prince or conqueror than a churchman, Reginald had 800 horsemen by his side by the time he reached Rochester. He then travelled into the centre of London in a state barge, bedecked with the emblems of his legatine authority. The city thronged with spectators, watching as the cardinal arrived at Whitehall, where he was met by Philip of Spain, now technically addressed as king of England, albeit in a limited capacity. Reginald was escorted to the queen's presence chamber, where he knelt before her, before the queen did 'receive him with great signs of respect and affection'.[13] It was said that both shed tears. It seems probable to assume that the emotion displayed at their reunion was driven in part by the memory of Margaret Pole, for she was a mother to both of them in one way or another. The sheer unlikelihood of such a reunion ever having been thought possible, particularly in such a setting, no doubt heightened emotion. Mary and Reginald had much in common. They had spent years living in isolation, separated from loved ones, in constant fear of their lives. Both had suffered for the faith which they so cherished, and yet, despite all the setbacks, despite the horrors of their past, here they were, reunited, with Mary uncontested queen, and Reginald papal legate to her kingdom. It must have felt like being reborn. With her husband by her side, and her cousin Reginald as legate to England, Mary authorised the latter to begin the reconciliation between England and the Holy See. Naturally the queen and her husband would be instrumental in setting out the process for aligning their kingdom once more with the Pope in Rome, as was Stephen Gardiner, who had been released from the Tower upon Mary's rise to the throne. On the morning of 29 November 1554, in a scene quite unlike anything seen before, England was officially received back by the Catholic Church. An attendant of Reginald's read aloud the papal bull which was followed by a short sermon from the cardinal. Setting the tone for all those watching, the queen and her husband knelt down to be absolved of sin. A witness to the proceedings states 'And while the legate pronounced the words the queen wept for joy and for devotion, and many of the members did the same. And after it was over they might be seen rapturously embracing one another and exclaiming, "today we have been born again"'.[14] The success of the occasion solidified Reginald's place in the day-to-day machinery of Queen Mary's kingdom, and ensured a member of the Pole family had constant and untrammelled access to the sovereign. His importance cannot be overstated, nor should it be overlooked that his ascendancy rehabilitated the Pole name to one of honour, rather than scorn. In his contemporary assessment of England under Mary's rule, John Elder stated:

'And thus England, and all we that dwell therein, account ourselves not only happy, yeah and most happy, which from so many outrageous storms of errors, cares, and calamities, are thus called home again to the sure haven and port of the most holy Catholic faith but also we do believe with our very hearts, and do confess with all our mouths, that almighty God of divine providence hath preserved and kept three persons as lodestars and chief guides for the defending, in bringing, and restoring of England thus to the unity of Christs church. The first is the queen's majesty, who being from her infancy a virgin, and immaculate from all spots of heresies; it hath pleased God to defend her, aide her, and save her from the hands, power and might of her enemies, and giving her the victory over them in the twinkling of an eye, which as roaring lions would have devoured her. The second is my lord Cardinal, who being an exile out of his native country England these 21 years, and in the mean season so abhorred, so hated, and so detested, as no man dust scarce one name him, whom the queen's majesty now have restored to his blood, and to the honour of his house.'[15]

This last line is particularly poignant, for it lifts the passage of time, it revokes the destruction caused by the Exeter Conspiracy, for Reginald now became the living embodiment of his once great house, resurrected, born again. And yet, whilst Margaret would no doubt applaud this characterisation, it should not be forgotten that it was also Reginald who arguably caused the most problems for his family. Despite the queen's advancing age, she was by now 38, reports were soon released that Mary had fallen pregnant. From a spiritual perspective, it seems that Mary believed Reginald had been instrumental in her 'happy condition', for he had greeted her by saying *'Benedictus frutus ventris tui'* –

'Blessed be the fruit of your womb'. The reports tell us that Reginald was informed of the queen's pregnancy by a 'Lord Montagu', which Higginbotham suggests was likely Geoffrey Pole. The youngest Pole brother had followed in his brother's footsteps and returned to England now that Mary was queen. According to this 'Lord Montagu', Mary had felt the baby kick when Reginald had greeted her.[16] Whether the early stages of the suspected stomach cancer that would eventually kill her, or a severe case of pseudocyesis, the growing belly which the queen so gleefully displayed to her court housed no child, dead or alive. Her marriage failing and the chances of a child ever being born to her fading by the day, the queen, always a sickly woman, recoiled and became dogmatic in her attempts to stamp out Protestantism in England. What became known as the Marian persecutions began at the start of 1555, and over the next three years around 300 men and women were put to the flames on the orders of the queen. The persecution's most famous victim, Archbishop Cranmer, had been stripped of his office before being consigned to the flames, and Reginald was duly made Archbishop of Canterbury. Reginald's hand in the atrocities appears lacking. He had shown a more conciliatory approach when dealing with accused heretics in the past, issuing acts of penance followed by absolution rather than sanctioning torture and execution.[17]

In early November 1558, Sir Geoffrey Pole died at the age of approximately 57. He was buried at Stoughton near Chichester. He left behind his wife, Constance, and their eleven children. Dogged by debt as he was throughout his life, very little was left to sustain his enormous family. As the man so central to much of the evidence which brought low his mother and brother, that he died of natural causes was nothing short of miraculous. Constance died twelve years after her husband, and is buried alongside him. Clearly the want of prudence which Geoffrey so painfully lacked extended to his children. In 1561 during the reign of Queen Elizabeth, Geoffrey's eldest son, Sir Arthur Pole, requested to serve the queen but was denied a post. In that same year he was briefly imprisoned for openly celebrating the mass. Arthur and two of his younger brothers, Edmund and Geoffrey, raised the ire of the queen further when they indelicately suggested Arthur's right to succeed Elizabeth was stronger than that of Mary, Queen of Scots. The three men were imprisoned in the Tower for their insolence, although the youngest, Geoffrey Pole, was released shortly afterwards and married a Catherine Dutton with whom he had nine children. To this day, visible graffiti within the Beauchamp Tower where Arthur Pole was housed can be seen. It reads *'Deo Servire, Penitentiam Inire, Fato Obedire, Regnare Est, A Poole, 1564, IHS'* ('To be subject to God, to enter upon penance, to be obedient to fate, is to reign, A Poole, 1564, Jesus').[18] In the same month that Sir Geoffrey Pole died, both Queen Mary and Reginald became dangerously ill. Both had succumbed to a fever at the end of the summer, which likely weakened their already poor constitutions. Mary was also afflicted with more personal matters, for she was by now old and unpopular, and knew her time was short. Her reign of just five years had been largely ineffectual and had cost England much of its treasury. This isn't to say it was a totally disastrous reign, indeed many of the initial pieces of governance adopted by her successor were inspired by Mary's policies, but what she desperately lacked was time. Despite repeated attempts to discredit her sister, which included a stint in the Tower for the latter, much of Mary's court now began to turn its attention to the youthful, elegant and charismatic Elizabeth. The sting in the tail – that she was the daughter of Anne Boleyn – would have been almost too much for Mary to bear. After finally acknowledging that Elizabeth would be named her successor, Mary slipped from a life marred by almost constant tragedy. She died, aged 42, on the morning of 16 November 1558 at St James's Palace. Even in death, Mary's final requests were ignored. Despite her wish to be buried alongside her mother, Katherine of Aragon, Mary was instead interred at Westminster Abbey. She is housed in the same tomb as her half-sister, Elizabeth, but unlike the latter has no grand effigy, but a simple memorial plaque signifying her final resting place. News of the queen's death was soon delivered to Lambeth Palace where Reginald was in residence. According to an Italian member of his household, Reginald took the news calmly, before addressing the Bishop of St Asaph and telling him:

> 'that in the whole course of his life nothing had ever yielded
> him greater pleasure and contentment than the contemplation
> of God's providence as displayed in his own person and in
> that of others, and that in the course of the queen's life and
> of his own he had ever remarked a great conformity, as she
> and himself had been harassed during so many years for one

and the same cause, and afterwards, when it pleased God to raise her to the throne, he had greatly participated in all the other troubles entailed by that elevation.'[19]

Whether Reginald was covering over his extreme grief, or a moment of pure coincidence, but just hours after the news had reached him of Mary's death, Reginald would follow his mistress to the grave. According to the same member of his household who wrote the above account, a great stroke came over the cardinal, followed by intense cold and profuse sweating. Although impossible to prove beyond doubt, Reginald's symptoms are commensurate with the sweating sickness, or some other influenza-type malady. Reginald breathed his last at around seven in the evening, just twelve hours after the death of Queen Mary I. Aged 58, he was the very last Catholic Archbishop of Canterbury in English history. Reginald was buried in 'The Corona' at Canterbury Cathedral, so named as it was built to contain the shrine of England's greatest martyr, Thomas Becket. His tomb can still be seen to this day.

All that now remained of the core Pole family was its quietest and least controversial figure, Ursula, Baroness Stafford. She and her husband would suffer the same ongoing financial issues that afflicted Geoffrey Pole, with neither able to sustain the lifestyle expected of those with royal blood in their veins. As I have covered, she would also lose a son to the headsman on Queen Mary's orders, and yet, Ursula, and her eldest daughter Dorothy, managed to become the Pole dynasty's great survivors. They were not completely alone, for another descendant of Margaret Pole's also found great favour at the court of the last Tudor sovereign. Henry Hastings, 3rd Earl of Huntingdon, became a highly trusted member of the court of Elizabeth I, serving as President of the Council of the North for twenty-three years. Huntingdon was the eldest son of Lady Catherine Pole, daughter of Montagu. This made him a great-grandson of Margaret's. Although he did not carry the Pole name, he remained a claimant to the throne, and was treated as such by ardent Protestants who feared the crown of England falling into the hands of Mary, Queen of Scots. As Lord Lieutenant of Leicestershire for a time, he is honoured with a statue in the Vaughan porch at Leicester Cathedral. He died, aged 60 on 14 December 1595 and is buried at St Helen's Church, Ashby-de-la-Zouch. It is a curious thing that figures such as Huntingdon and Dorothy Stafford, who are deemed forgettable or largely inconsequential, often, with hindsight, gain posthumous praise. This is most overt when assessing the impact of Anne of Cleves for example. Consigned unfairly, and inaccurately, to history as the 'ugly wife', she was Henry VIII's shortest reigning queen, their marriage lasting just six months, but who through wise capitulation to the king's demands lived a life of extraordinary privilege, surviving long enough to attend the coronation of Queen Mary I. Anne was given great prominence at the ceremony, sitting beside the queen's half-sister Elizabeth, and recognised as the third highest ranking woman in England. Mirroring this, albeit with less grandiosity, was Ursula Pole, and perhaps even more so, her daughter Dorothy. Ursula lived to witness the last Tudor monarch ascend to the throne, dying in 1570, twelve years into the reign of Queen Elizabeth I. She was 66 years old. Ursula had given her husband countless children, and lived long enough to become a grandmother several times. A portrait exists of what may well be Ursula Pole, although it cannot be identified with certainty. The sitter is in the right style of dress for the period, her clothing black with gold trim, rich red satin sleeves and the customary French hood also trimmed in red and gold. The clue which points to it being Ursula Pole is the clear presence of a rose, clasped in her right hand – a pure white rose, the symbol of the house of York. Ursula's eldest daughter, Dorothy, became a great favourite of Queen Elizabeth, serving as Mistress of the Robes. In a twist of irony considering her maternal grandmother's aversion to all things Boleyn, Dorothy's husband was none other than Sir William Stafford, the widower of Mary Boleyn. Furthermore, she and her family adhered so firmly to the new Protestant religion that during the reign of Queen Mary, they fled England, living in exile in Geneva before returning once Elizabeth had ascended to the throne. Despite being seven years older than her royal mistress, Dorothy outlived the queen by a year, dying at the grand old age of 78 on 22 September 1604. A clear mark of both the respect and importance that she represented is seen most overtly in her burial, for she rests in great splendour at St Margaret's Church, Westminster Abbey. The inscription on her tomb reads:

'Here lyeth the Lady Dorothy Stafford, Wife and Widow to Sir William Stafford, Knight, Daughter to Henry, Lord Stafford, the only son of Edward, the last Duke of Buckingham: Her mother was Ursula, Daughter to the

Countess of Salisbury, the only daughter to George, Duke of Clarence, brother to King Edward the Fourth. She continued a true widow from the age of 27 till her Death. She served Queen Elizabeth 40 years, lying in the bedchamber, esteemed of her, loved of all, doing good, all she could, to everybody, never hurt any; a continual remembrancer of the suits of the poor. As she lived a religious life, in great reputation of honour and virtue in the world, so she ended in continual fervent meditation, and hearty prayers to God. At which instant, as all her Life, so after her death, she gave liberally to the poor, and died aged 78, the 22 of September 1604. In whose remembrance, Sir Edward Stafford, her son, hath caused this memorial of her to be in the same form and place as she herself long since required him.'[20]

Although her grandmother would have likely disapproved of Dorothy's religion, and the fact that she served not Mary, but Elizabeth, Margaret Pole would surely have approved of, and taken great pride in, the sentiment seen in this inscription. It shows Dorothy as a good, noble and respected figure, with clear reference to her spectacularly grand ancestry. The perfect representation of what it meant to be a Pole, what it meant to descend from the great house of Plantagenet. History, we are told, is written by the victors. The Pole family is considerably lacking in victors. Yes, Reginald Pole avenged much of the lost pride and prestige that had been taken from his family by King Henry VIII, but his entire purpose, his being, rested on the continued success of the Catholic faith. When he and the queen he was so devoted to died, so died Catholicism as the dominant religion of England. Despite Margaret's three other sons and countless grandsons, the Pole name, like the family themselves, died out in ignominious fashion. The delicious irony is that like the 'great whore' Anne Boleyn, who gave birth to the monarch who ultimately supersedes her father as the most exceptional Tudor sovereign, it was in Margaret's often overlooked daughter's line that emerged the individual with the scope and authority to commemorate the hugely important Pole dynasty. The fact that this shrine rests at the most famous and historically significant abbey in the whole of the British Isles is perhaps the most fitting epitaph to a long forgotten family; a family who at one time all but ruled the kingdom.

At Margaret's attainder, her title, Countess of Salisbury was revoked. Then, as in now, titles were not reappropriated at once, but held in place, waiting for a suitable individual to either claim it, or have it bestowed on them, and so today, the current Marquess of Salisbury holds no links to the family for whom the title meant so much. The Salisbury earldom remained unused for the duration of the Tudor reign, and was eventually unearthed by King James I, who gave it to Robert Cecil, son of Queen Elizabeth I's great advisor, William Cecil, 1st Baron Burghley. In 1789 the title was elevated to a Marquessate, and nearly became a dukedom in the reign of Queen Victoria. The then Marquess of Salisbury, Robert Gascoyne-Cecil, who had also served as Prime Minister over three terms, declined the offer from the queen, citing the costs required to maintain a dukedom as prohibitive. The Salisbury earldom now sits as a subsidiary title to the Marquessate, and has passed in an unbroken line right through to the current occupant, another Robert Gascoyne-Cecil, 7th Marquess of Salisbury. He remains one of Great Britain's highest ranking nobles, and was in attendance alongside the Marchioness of Salisbury at the Coronation of King Charles III and Queen Camilla in 2023.

No link between the current Marquess of Salisbury and the Pole family exists.

Assessment

Like most people who have a passion for Tudor history, Lady Margaret Pole was, to me, the elderly lady senselessly beheaded for the crime of simply being who she was. The plucky old girl who refused to lay her head on the block and ran around a scaffold being hacked apart by a bewildered executioner. Indeed I still held that opinion when I began my research for this book, and I will continue to believe that her death was unnecessary. I will admit, however, that having spent so much time in the Pole family's company, albeit from a distance of half a millennia, that there is arguably some proof which implicates at least certain members of the family in having committed high treason, by the standards of the time, a technicality which must always be kept in mind.

A question that we must ask when trying to make sense of Margaret Pole's end is to also question why Gertrude Courtenay, Marchioness of Exeter, escaped the axeman. Why did she receive a pardon? Why did she, a woman ostensibly more guilty of actions against the king than Margaret Pole, get to walk out of the Tower to her future, whilst Margaret Pole's final walk was to her doom? Like much of the evidence brought forward against both women, it is circumstantial and certainly subject to conjecture, and yet one would be released without charge, whilst the other would suffer the horror of decapitation. We know that the king was far from concerned about the prospect of spilling noble female blood. This was the man who sent two of his wives to the scaffold, and may well have authorised his own daughter's execution had she not eventually succumbed to the pressure of his wishes. Anne Boleyn and Katheryn Howard had, to the king's mind, publicly belittled his sexual potency, and Jane Rochford had helped facilitate Katheryn Howard's affairs. Unlike these women however, Margaret Pole was the king's close kinswoman, of extraordinarily exalted birth, and yet, this would not save her. What then, set Margaret and Gertrude apart? To answer that, let's firstly review what they had in common. Both were senior female members of the nobility. Both had spent much of their adult lives in and out of service at the royal court. Both had sons who, at one time, were highly in favour with the king. Both had been ardent supporters of Katherine of Aragon, and remained committed to her daughter. Both disliked Anne Boleyn and showed no interest in her daughter, Elizabeth, despite Gertrude being the younger princess' godmother. Both were wealthy, with several homes, and large households that they oversaw. Both adhered to the traditional Catholic faith, and had several brushes with danger over the years for their beliefs. So what was their key difference, what set them apart? The answer could be a simple one – blood. Historical novelist, Philippa Gregory, believes that this was the distinction, this is what ultimately divided the gravity of these two women's roles. Margaret was a Plantagenet, Gertrude married one. Whilst the conclusions of novelists such as Gregory should be treated with caution, this assessment is one that feels more grounded in reality. Margaret was, in many ways, a living fossil. She was the very embodiment of the powerful Yorkist dynasty, an unequivocally noble link between the house of Plantagenet and Tudor. While her blood descended through a legitimate male line, Courtenay and the other White Rose houses were born through the female line. It is this fact which leads me to conclude that the Pole family held the most senior claim to the English throne at the time. Where Gertrude married into a noble family, and was, in the eyes of the law, subject to her husband's command, Margaret was both noble in her own right and more crucially, had acted as a femme-sole for decades. She commanded as much land, power and influence as her male counterparts, and was thus as every bit susceptible to the king's ever present suspicion. Factor in her bloodline and the actions of her sons, particularly Reginald, and there was a recipe for disaster. When taken at large, it is this that allows me to land at the following conclusions.

The biggest problem for the Pole family was indeed their blood, however, this should not be taken as the sole reason for their downfall. It is my belief that the responsibility for their fall can most convincingly land at Reginald and Geoffrey's feet, but, it is precisely because of the Pole family's blood that their actions were all the more problematic. It exacerbated their faults; it made them more open to suspicion. Having royal blood was by no means unique to the Pole family. As we have seen, the houses of Stafford and Exeter would all suffer for this same reason, but none would suffer quite so significantly as the Poles. At its crux, the Exeter Conspiracy is less a conspiracy, and more a series of events with two distinct stories to tell. On one side, you had the familial unity which brought together the remaining Plantagenets on the Yorkist side. They comprised a wide network of people who by virtue of their birth were either royal or highly noble; a giant spider's web of cousins, siblings and kin, stretching across the whole kingdom. To their supporters they represented the best of England, but to their detractors, they were a ready-made affront to the fledgling Tudor dynasty. Conversely, there was the ever-present uncertainty, which must have been acute for all Tudor monarchs to live with, that ultimately they had no right to the throne of England. The presence of so many Plantagenet dynasts was thus a constant reminder of what came before – a legitimate, unquestionably royal family, moreover one known for its fecundity, hence the 'White Rose' network being so vast. Where the Tudors could be counted on one hand, the Plantagenets were arguably endless. Despite this, fortune's wheel ultimately brought low England's longest reigning dynasty, and replaced it with a family with only cursory rights to lead. That family would, in time, turn on its kin, which led to the Exeter Conspiracy. Rather than being great, or just, it was uncertainty and fear that defined much of Tudor rule. This was the impetus behind the actions of Henry VIII, which drove him to sanction the execution of two members of the Pole family. It drove Geoffrey Pole all but insane, and another member of the family, the younger Henry Pole, disappeared in the Tower completely – history's seldom discussed third 'Prince in the Tower'. There are of course two sides to every story, and whilst it is still debatable as to whether the Pole family were a legitimate threat, what is clear is that the story did not have to end as it did. As Pierce notes, if King Henry VIII always treated the Pole family as a threat then why did he authorise the marriages which Margaret Pole negotiated? These marriages created greater bonds between the old families, particularly those of strong Yorkist blood, something which wouldn't have passed the king by, and yet he did not block them, indeed he celebrated them, which points to a clear ease, at the start of his reign at least, with the White Rose families. Their loyalty was thus not taken for granted. The mistrust the king eventually felt, was thus built over time; it was not there from the outset. Indeed

I believe there was a real chance that the whole Exeter Conspiracy would have gone nowhere, had the one person who had the capacity to quell the issues, but chose not to, acted, and that person, is Reginald Pole. As I have made clear, I believe firmly in not judging Tudor people by modern day codes of behaviour. We cannot get inside the head of a Tudor and say we can understand them; to do so is folly. These were people who lived and acted in a way that was entirely defined by their times, a period of intense religious conviction, of unwavering belief in the almighty, of unflinching patriarchy, of heaven and hell. Reginald acted in a way entirely appropriate to his time, and we must remain cognisant of that. It seems probable, however, that had he behaved differently, that the intense pressure in which his family was placed under would have been lifted, or at very least lessened. Had he chosen not to issue *De Unitate,* or stopped in his regular attempts to cajole the rulers of Europe into funding rebellions against Henry VIII, then I am sure the story would have had a different outcome, particularly where Margaret Pole is concerned. I say this with the virtue of hindsight of course. Had Reginald done as I say above, then he wouldn't have been Reginald Pole, he would have been a different man, with different morals and beliefs, and if his life tells us anything, it's that he always remained true to his beliefs, even to the detriment of his family.

But what of Henry, Baron Montagu or Geoffrey Pole? Were they guilty of treason, or at least, was there sufficient evidence to justify the king's actions? I am of the belief that they were indeed guilty of treason, but again, strictly under the interpretation of laws of the day, particularly the updated Treasons Act of 1534, which made both thoughts and speech against the monarch, not just deeds, treasonous. Looking at Geoffrey first, his guilt is plain, on a few counts. Firstly, his and Hugh Holland's testimonies confirm he leaked state secrets to known traitors, and secondly, he maintained continued contact with Reginald, despite knowing such action was treason. That he, via Holland, informed Reginald of the planned assassination attempts on his life was undoubtedly the most damning of his communications. He also kept up regular contact with Eustace Chapuys; in fact it appears even the wily ambassador felt Geoffrey was seen in his company too frequently, the latter instructing Geoffrey to come to him less. That Geoffrey Pole managed to escape execution is frankly one of the most bizarre decisions ever made by the king; in fact I would go on record as saying it was the single most surprising decision King Henry VIII ever made. As I have said, Geoffrey was unquestionably guilty of high treason. Countless men and women had met their deaths on charges one hundredth as assured as those levied against Geoffrey Pole, and yet he managed to walk out of the Tower as a free, albeit greatly damaged man. His willingness to cooperate with his captors, through admitting his own guilt and incriminating several others, must surely be the sole justification for any form of leniency granted to him, but even then his remaining alive is surprising. Geoffrey's relationship with Chapuys also played a large part in implicating Henry, Baron Montagu, for the eldest Pole brother maintained a steady stream of information into the ambassador's ear about the goings on at court, actions that were both foolish and treasonous. With Montagu, his personal feelings got in the way. It was clear he held no love for the king, and struggled to maintain a cordial relationship with the sovereign throughout his life. His statements such as the world coming to stripes or that he approved of Reginald's behaviour all point to a disgruntled man who no longer recognised the court in which he played a part. Perhaps the most damning piece of evidence against Montagu, and what makes him unequivocally guilty of treason, is his prediction of the king dying suddenly. That he thought, let alone spoke of this, fell sufficiently under the updated Treasons Act, providing justification for the actions taken against him. All of these points, contrary to popular belief, show that there was certainly more evidence to warrant the king's actions against Margaret Pole's sons than is often acknowledged. This is not to suggest that I think people having their heads cut off for what may have been idle gossip is justifiable, but, we must remain aware of the different world in which the Tudors inhabited. If Margaret's sons and the other men brought down, did plot against or even just bad mouth the king, however much it may have just been talk, they were guilty of treason, as the law of the time dictated. What is also clear, however, is that their crimes, and indeed the crimes for which Margaret was also killed, all featured Reginald in one way or another. If we think back to the statement made by Castillon, 'the king told me a long time ago he wants to exterminate the House of Montague that belongs to the White Rose, the Pole family, of which the cardinal is a member', it is clear how much Reginald was central to the king's actions against the Pole family. All things considered, the name 'the Exeter Conspiracy' should probably be rechristened 'Reginald – the problem Pole'.

As for Margaret herself, I believe that she was, in all probability, guilty purely by association. Had Reginald trodden a safer path, Margaret would likely have been pardoned. That said, given her extraordinary power and the scale of her household, if her sons were plotting against the king, or simply gossiping traitorous words, then I find it unlikely that she wouldn't have known anything. Even if she had suspicions, by not acting on them she would have been guilty of misprision of treason. This, I think, is as far as her guilt would have extended. Margaret's story as a whole is also rather unique. The blood of hundreds of noble courtiers was spilt over Henry VIII's thirty-eight-year reign. It was a period made famous for its tyranny and bloodshed, and yet, only four women would suffer decapitation on the king's orders, compared to hundreds of men. As we know, two of these four women were Henry's own wives, the third, Jane Boleyn, Lady Rochford, was executed for her involvement in Katheryn Howard's adultery, which leaves us with the fourth, Margaret Pole. This highlights just how unique Margaret Pole's end was. She was the sole female executed during the reign of Henry VIII for what we might call political intrigue. Anne Boleyn, Jane Boleyn and Katheryn Howard all died on account of their behaviour; it could be argued that Margaret Pole was executed simply for being who she was.

The Pole family and the circumstances of their downfall were unique to their time. Henry VIII remains, in popular imagination, a bloated blood-thirsty tyrant, the man who killed two wives and countless other innocents. The actions taken against Margaret Pole are often used to defend this assessment. Henry's reign is characterised as the transition between a medieval and Renaissance era, a period in which England underwent the biggest constitutional shift in its history, the sixteenth-century Brexit. And yet, throughout it all, Margaret Pole and her family remained strong, watching from the sidelines as the world their family built shifted beyond recognition. Trying to understand the Exeter Conspiracy and determine what actually happened is a complex story to try and break down, which I hope I have sufficiently conveyed. Assessing a story that is nearly 500 years old will always be a challenge; indeed we may never know exactly what happened, especially when one considers that the Pole family remains so elusive, and were, for want of a better word, Tudor B-list. Consider the fact that historians still fiercely debate why Anne Boleyn was executed, and she's a Tudor megastar, so attempting to understand the reasons for the Pole family's ruin is tougher still. What I stand by, is my overall assessment that Reginald Pole represented the most dangerous threat, and that the behaviours of his brothers and mother may have been overlooked, or simply unknown, had he not acted as he did. Safely ensconced in Europe under the protection of the Pope, he could decry the king with impunity, whilst his family were left having to handle the fall out. His actions, which would today be regarded as both deeply selfish and irresponsible, need to be viewed through a sixteenth-century lens, where conscience would often outweigh familial loyalty, which given his separation from them by both time and space, may have also been compromised. Had he remained in the bosom of his family, might his scruples have been something he could live with? It's certainly possible, if not probable. The irony that Margaret Pole's son, who she had given over to the Church as a means of alleviating financial strain, ultimately posed the greatest threat to his family was surely not lost on the countess. Had the king managed to capture Reginald, it would have undoubtedly lifted pressure against the wider family, but this doesn't excuse that they themselves acted according to their beliefs, which became ever more removed from the king and the policy of his regime. Those to my mind who do not bear the mark of guilt are Edward Courtenay, Marquess of Exeter and Sir Nicholas Carew; the latter being particularly blameless. The entire 'Exeter Conspiracy' takes its name from the marquess being the highest in rank among the accused, but when one breaks down the 'evidence' it is clear that Exeter himself was not involved, or at very least, like Margaret Pole, was guilty merely by association. Gertrude Courtenay, as I have outlined earlier, most certainly acted against the king, but her position as a wife, and one without royal blood, neutralised her as a threat. However the evidence is interpreted, what cannot be ignored is that several people lost their lives, and among them was an elderly lady, born all but a princess. She was born to the second most senior man in the kingdom, to a mother who was England's richest heiress, two of her uncles were kings of England, her cousin was queen of England, and yet, Margaret Pole died a traitor to the crown. Her life was one of complete extremes, of major highs and crushing lows, but in the end, the thing that destroyed her was the very blood in her veins, and the actions of those she loved most.

Sources

Abbreviations

CSP, Spain	Calendar of State Papers, Spain
CSP, Venice	Calendar of State Papers, Venice
LL	Lisle Letters
LP	Letters and Papers, Foreign and Domestic, of the Reign of Henry VIII
HMC	Historical Manuscripts Commission
ODNB	Oxford Dictionary of National Biography
PRO	Public Records Office
TNA	The National Archives

Preface

1. Russell, p. 1.

Chapter 1: A Niece of Kings

1. Borman, p. 6.
2. Rickard, J. (19 February 2014), *Angers Agreement, July 1470.*
3. Gristwood, p. 106.
4. Nicoll, A. and J., *Holinshed's Chronicle as used in Shakespeare's Plays* (London, 1927, 1955).
5. National Archives document E 404/77/3/66.
6. Higginbotham, p. 6.
7. LP, E 404/77/3/66.
8. Alexander, Heather, *Recreating Richard III: The Power of Tudor Propaganda.* (Digital Commons, East Tennessee State University, 2016).
9. Buck, p. 162.

10. Buck, p. 198.
11. Higginbotham, p. 9.
12. *Coronation of King Richard III: Westminster Abbey.*
13. Galdieri, pp. 316–17.
14. *Croyland Chronicle.*
15. L&P.

Chapter 2: A Changing of the Guard

1. Galdieri 1993, pp. 316–17.
2. Henry VIII, C12. L&P.
3. Borman, p. 40.
4. TNA L&P Henry VIII E175/6.
5. Pierce, p. 11.
6. BL, Add. MSS 6113, f.77b; Hearne, *Johanis Lelandi Antiquarii,* Vol. 4, p. 206.
7. Williamson, p. 25.
8. Vergil, chapter 26, paragraph 7.
9. BL, Egerton MS 2219; BL, Yarnold, C., *A Collection for Buck's History of Richard III*, ff. 137-137b; Pollard, A. F., *The Reign of Henry VII from Contemporary Sources* (3 vols, London 1913), Vol. 1, p. 152.
10. Pierce, p. 16.
11. Hearne, *Johanis Lelandi Antiquarii,* Vol. 4, p. 225; BL Egerton MS 985, f. 19.
12. Pierce, p. 12.
13. PRO, E36/247, f.35.
14. Pierce, p. 14.
15. Pierce, p. 18.
16. Hall, p. 490.
17. Vergil, recorded by Pierce, p. 24.
18. Dormer, *The Life of Jane Dormer, Duchess of Feria.*

Chapter 3: The Princess of Spain

1. CSP, Spain, Vol. 1, no. 210.
2. Ibid.
3. LP, Vol. 1, p. 1442.

4. LP, Vol. 1, no. 158 (19).

5. Statutes of the Realm, p. 100.

6. TNA, Court of Augmentation, 305.

7. LP, Henry VIII, Vol. 1, p. 873 (1924).

8. LP, Henry VIII, Vol. 1, p. 58 (167).

9. LP, Henry VIII, Vol. 4. E 179/69/12.

10. TNA E 179/69/12.

11. LP, Henry VIII, Vol. 1, p. 1331 (2972).

12. TNA, Exchequer: Treasury of Receipt: Ancient Deeds, Series A, E40/13349.

13. TNA, L&P, Henry VIII, Vol. 2, p. 547 (1893).

14. Weir, p. 28.

15. Longcroft pp. 117–118.

16. LP, Henry VIII, Vol. 2, no. 3694.

17. LP, Henry VIII, Vol. 4, p. 2023 (4654).

18. Pierce, p. 93.

19. Jones and Underwood, *The King's Mother*, p. 102.

20. PRO, E.314/79, no. 305.

21. Borman, p. 140.

22. LP, Henry VIII, Vol. 3., p. 153 (429).

23. LP, Henry VIII, Vol. 3., p. 153 (429).

24. Pierce, p. 43.

25. Ives, Eric. *Anne Boleyn* (Blackwell, 1986).

26. LP, Henry VIII, Vol. 2., p. 435 (1573).

27. Weir, *Henry VIII, King and Court*, 2001, p. 202.

28. Harris, Barbara, *Privy Purse Expenses of the Princess Mary*, xli, p. 27.

29. LP, Henry VIII, no. 263.

30. Emerson, K, *A Who's Who of Tudor Women*.

31. LP, Henry VIII, Vol. 3., 704/3.

32. LP, Henry VIII, Vol. 3., 870.

33. LP, Henry VIII, Vol. 3., p. 323 (896).

Chapter 4: The Pole Family at Court

1. LP, Henry VIII, Vol. 1, Item 2453.

2. LP, Henry VIII, Vol. 2, Item 2736.

3. LP, Henry VIII, Vol. 3, Item 152 SP.

4. Steel, A. B., *The Receipt of the Exchequer, 1377–1485* (Cambridge University Press, 1954) p. 421.
5. LP, Henry VIII, Vol. 3, Item 2636.
6. PRO, Prob. 11/22 (36 porch).
7. TNA, Court of Augmentations, Private and Confiscated Papers of Margaret Pole, Item 301.
8. TNA, Court of Augmentations, Private and Confiscated Papers of Margaret Pole, Item 250.
9. Pierce, HP, pp. 74–75; Beccadelli, p. 157.
10. LP, Henry VIII, Vol. 2, Item 1893.
11. LP, Henry VIII, Vol. 2, Item 1970.
12. Harris, p. 55.
13. LP, Henry VIII, Vol. 3, Item 1284.
14. *Hall's Chronicle*, pp. 623–4.
15. Ibid, p. 213.
16. *Hall's Chronicle*, p. 630.
17. LP, Henry VIII, Vol. 3, p. 498, Item 1285/3.
18. Cal. of State Papers Spain, H. VIII, iii. Nos. 1204, 1268.
19. LP, Henry VIII, Vol. 3, Item 1284.
20. Sneyd, pp. 125–31.
21. LP, III (ii) 3516.
22. Anglo, tournament roll, p. 71.
23. LP, Henry VIII, Vol. 3, Item 2554.
24. LP, Henry VIII, Vol. 4, Item 6234.
25. LP, Henry VIII, Vol. 4, Item 6234.
26. LP, Henry VIII, Vol. 4, p. 681, Item 1519.
27. CSP, Venice, Vol. 4, item 682.

Chapter 5: The Scandal of Christendom

1. Starkey, pp. 261–263.
2. Ives, p. XV (preface).
3. *Hall's Chronicle*, p. 631.
4. CSP, Spain, Vol. 3, pt 2, item 113.
5. CSP, Spain, Vol. 3, pt 2, item 113.
6. CSP, Spain, Vol. 3, pt 2, item 131.
7. LP, Henry VIII, Vol. 4, Item 2972.
8. LP, Henry VIII, Vol. 5, p. 430 (909/36).

9. Ibid.
10. LP, Foreign and Domestic, Henry VIII, Volume 13 Part 2, n.800.
11. LP, Vol. 4, item 2972.
12. ODNB 'Reginald Pole', Mayer 'Reginald Pole and the Parisian Theologians'; Mayer, Reginald Pole, pp. 54–55.
13. LP, Henry VIII, Vol. 5, p. 351, Item 731.
14. LP, Henry VIII, Foreign and Domestic, Henry VIII, Vol. 10, part 2, Item 1212.
15. LP, Foreign and Domestic, Henry VIII, Vol. 13 Part 2, n.800.
16. Weir, 1991, p. 231.
17. Ives pp. 160, 170.
18. Ibid, p. 416.
19. LP, Henry VIII, Vol. 5, p. 327, Item 686.
20. Ibid, p. 198.
21. LP, Henry VIII, Vol. 5 1531–1532, p. 351, no 737 Vienna Archives.
22. LP, Henry VIII, Vol. 5 1531–1532, p. 351, no 737 Vienna Archives.
23. LP, Foreign and Domestic, Henry VIII, Vol. 13, part 2, n.805 (6).
24. CPS, Spain, Vol. 5, Part 2.
25. TNA, King's Remembrancer: Accounts Various. Wardrobe and Household, E101/421/13.

Chapter 6: Ainsi Sera, Groigne qui Groigne

1. LP Kings Remembrancer: Accounts Various, Wardrobe and Household E101/421/13.
2. LP Kings Remembrancer: Accounts Various, Wardrobe and Household E101/421/13.
3. LP Henry VIII, Vol. 6 1533.
4. CSP, Spain, Vol. 3, pt 2, item 113.
5. Ibid., Part i, p. 84.
6. CSP, Spain, Vol. 4, (2), item 1161.
7. LP Vol. 8, item 263.
8. Hughes, p. 177 (1957).
9. LP, Henry VIII, Vol. 6, n.1466.
10. Bernard, G. W., *The King's Reformation*, p. 89.
11. LP, Foreign and Domestic, Henry VIII, Vol. 6, n.1419.
12. Ibid, p. 308.
13. LP, VI, no 1468.

14. Ibid, p. 139.
15. Ibid, p. 178.
16. Ibid, p. 304.
17. Ibid, n 1466.
18. CSP, Spain, 1531–1533, p. 863, no 1153.
19. Mattingly, p. 299.
20. Penn, *Winter King*, p. 101.
21. LL, Vol. 2, no. 126.
22. LL, Vol. 2, no. 136.
23. CSP, Spain, Vol. 4 (2), item 1130.
24. TNA, L&P, Vol XIII (ii), no. 702 (1).
25. Roper, p. 58.
26. CSP, Spain, Vol. 5 (1), item 218.
27. PRO, SP1/88, f 174; L&P, VII, Appendix 32.
28. Knighton and Mortimer, *Westminster Abbey Reformed: 1540–1640*, p. 136.
29. LP, XIII (ii), no. 827 (1).
30. Ibid, Vol. 2, p. 138, no. 174a.
31. Ibid, no. 841 (ii).
32. LP, Vol. 9, item 701.
33. LP, Henry VIII, Vol. 8.
34. Weir, *Henry VIII, King and Court,* p. 362.
35. Mattingly, *Catherine of Aragon*, pp. 344–6.
36. Neale, *Queen Elizabeth I.*
37. Sander, *Schism*, p. 132.
38. LP, Henry VIII, Vol. 10, p. 495.
39. Weir, *Henry VIII, King and Court*, p. 365.
40. CSP, Spain, 1536–38, p. 106.
41. LP, Vol. 10, items 876(6), 908.
42. Ibid, i38.
43. Norton, E, *Anne Boleyn In Her Own Words & the Words of Those Who Knew Her*, pp. 263, 267.
44. Hall, p. 818, LP, Vol. 10, 911.
45. Ives, E., *The Life and Death of Anne Boleyn*, p. 359.

Chapter 7: De Unitate

1. Ives, E., *The Life and Death of Anne Boleyn* p. 580 (2).

2. LP, Vol. 3, no. 706.

3. LP Vol 10, item 901, 908.

4. Ibid, no. 1110.

5. Ibid, 804 (p. 317).

6. TNA, L&P XI, 7, pp. 7–8.

7. Loades, *Mary Tudor*, pp. 105–106.

8. Ibid.

9. TNA, L&P, Vol. 10, item 212.

10. LL, 4:863.

11. LL, 4:896.

12. Ibid, 850, (p.2, p.109).

13. Preston and Dodge, 1894.

14. Higginbotham, p. 108.

15. Pole, *De Unitate*, pp. 181–185.

16. LP, Foreign and Domestic, Henry VIII, Vol. 13, part 2, n 1036.

17. Pierce, *Margaret Pole, Countess of Salisbury 1472 – 1541: Loyalty, Lineage and Leadership*, (University of Wales Press, 2003) p.109.

18. LP, Vol. 11, item 93.

19. TNA L&P Foreign and Domestic, Henry VIII, Vol. 13, Part 2, n. 800.

20. LP Vol. 11., no. 451.

21. Preston and Dodge, 1894.

22. Hall, op. cit, p. 828.

23. CSP, Spain, Vol. 5 (I), item 109.

24. Crowther, D, *The Pilgrimage of Grace II, The History of England Podcast.*

25. LP, Henry VIII, Vol. 5 (i), 131.

26. LP Hen VIII, op. cit., Vol. 5(ii), 72.

27. Ibid, no, 779.

28. Erickson, *Bloody Mary*, p. 181.

29. Pierce, p. 113.

30. Ibid, p. 921.

31. Harris, B. J., *Edward Stafford, Third Duke of Buckingham*, p. 73.

32. LP, XIII (ii), 753.

33. Weir, p. 379.

34. Borman, p. 98.

35. Pierce, p. 123.

36. LP, Henry VIII, Vol. XIII (ii), 797.

37. LP Hen VIII, op. cit., Vol. XII (i), 1032.

38. Mayer, *Correspondence of Reginald Pole*, Vol. 1, p. 174.
39. LP, Henry VIII, Vol. XII (ii), p. 128.
40. Ibid, 797.
41. Ibid, 829 (i).
42. Mayer, *Correspondence of Reginald Pole, op. cit.*, Vol. 1, p. 168.

Chapter 8: The Exeter Conspiracy

1. LP, XIII (ii), no. 392 (2, iii).
2. LP, Vol. XIII (ii), no. 796.
3. TNA, LP, Vol. XIII (ii), no. 796 p. 308.
4. LP, Vol. IX, no. 740.
5. LP, Vol. XIII, (ii), no. 817.
6. Ibid, f. 84.
7. CSP, Spain, Vol. 6 Part 1, n 7.
8. Ibid, f. 84.
9. Ibid, f. 83.
10. LP, Vol. XIII (ii), 797, 308i, a.
11. LP, Vol. XIII (ii), 753.
12. LP, Vol. XIII (ii), 797, 308i, b.
13. LP, Vol. XIII (ii), 797, 308i, c.
14. Ibid, 804 (319).
15. LP, Vol. XIII (ii), 797.
16. Merriman, *Thomas Cromwell*, Vol. II, pp. 87–90.
17. LP, Vol. XIII (ii), 804, p. 315.
18. Ibid.
19. Ibid.
20. LP, XIII (ii), no. 695 (2).
21. LP, XIII (ii), no. 796.
22. Lisle Letters.
23. LP, XIII, no. 804 (3).
24. LP., XIII (ii), 804. p. 315.
25. Ibid.
26. LP, XIII (ii), no. 772.
27. Ibid, 695, 2.
28. LP, Henry VIII, op. cit, Vol. XIII (ii), 924.
29. LP, Foreign and Domestic, Henry VIII, Vol. XIII, part 2, p. 754.

30. Bellamy, pp. 9–11, 31–32.
31. Ibid, Pro, SP1/138, f. 198b.
32. Froude, J A, *History of England,* p. 216, Longmans, London, 1870.
33. Miller, p. 65.
34. LP, Vol. XIII (ii), 804, p. 315.
35. PRO, SP1/140, f. 12.
36. Ives, *Anne Boleyn*, p. 261.
37. LP, Vol. XIII Reference SP 1/138/213-230.
38. Dodds, p. 290.
39. LP, Vol. XIII (ii), 804, p. 315.
40. Bernard, *The Kings Reformation*, op. cit., p. 431.
41. Ibid, 702, 876, 960.
42. Ibid, 804, p. 317.
43. Ibid, 800.
44. Ibid. 829, p. 339.
45. John Collins Examination. Pro, SP1/139, f. 14b; L&P, XIII (ii), no. 827 (1).
46. LP, XIII (ii), no. 829 (2).
47. LP, Vol. XIII (ii), 804, p. 315.
48. LP, Vol. XIII (ii), 804, p. 315.
49. Examination of George Croftes, TNA, L&P Vol. XIII (ii), Item 803, p. 314.
50. LP, Vol. XIII (ii), 804, p. 315.
51. LP, Vol. XIII (ii), 875 (1).
52. Ibid, 855 (2).
53. Higginbotham, p. 121.
54. LP, Foreign and Domestic, Henry VIII, Vol. 8.

Chapter 9: A Fallen Countess

1. Miller, p. 66.
2. LP, XIII (ii), no. 855.
3. Higginbotham, p. 124.
4. LP, Vol XIII (ii) 818, 326.
5. Ibid.
6. Ibid.
7. Ibid.

8. Ibid.
9. Ibid.
10. Ibid.
11. Ibid.
12. Ibid.
13. Ibid.
14. Ibid.
15. Ibid.
16. Ibid, 835, 838 (iii).
17. Ibid.
18. L&P, XIII (2) 835.
19. Ibid, 818, 19.
20. Miller, p. 45.
21. LP, XIII, (ii), 967, g52.
22. LP, XIII (ii), 979 (3).
23. Gee and Hardy, op. cit. no. lvii.
24. Richard Morisyne, op. cit.
25. CSP, Venice., op. cit., Vol. V, 806.
26. LP Hen VIII, op. cit., Vol. XIV (i), 280.
27. Seward, p. 309.
28. Donelson, p. 140.
29. Ibid, p. 1036.
30. Weir, p. 386.
31. LP, Vol. 14 (i), item 37.
32. LP, Henry VIII xiv (1), 37, p. 19.
33. Cole, pp. 96–100.
34. Froude, Vol. 3, p. 387.
35. Mayer, Vol 1, p. 228.
36. LL, Vol. 5, no. 1419.
37. Froude, op. cit chap xvi.

Chapter 10: To Death

1. Haile, p. 267; Mayer, *Correspondence*, Vol. 1, pp. 242–43.
2. Mayer, *Correspondence of Reginald Pole*, op. cit., Vol. 1, p. 228.
3. Ibid, p. 560.
4. LP, xv, 697.

5. BL, Arundel MS 97, f. 186.
6. LP, XIII (ii), no. 1176.
7. Pierce, p. 176.
8. LP, Henry VIII, op. cit., Vol. XVI, 1011.
9. LP, Henry VIII, XVI 581.
10. LP, Vol. 16, 941.
11. Ridgway, *Anne Boleyn Execution Site*, 2010.
12. LP, Vol, 16, item 868.
13. CSP, Spain, Vol. 6 (i), 166.
14. Herbert, p. 401.

Chapter 11: Life After Death

1. Pierce, p. 182.
2. LP, XVI, 897.
3. LP, XVII, 880.
4. *Reginald Pole in Two Parts, Harriet Waters Preston and Louise Dodge* (The Atlantic, 1894, Part 2).
5. Mayer, p. 172.
6. Higginbotham p. 138.
7. Loach, p. 161.
8. Cross, p. 15.
9. CSP, Venice, Vol. 5, item 766.
10. CSP, Spain, 9 Sept, 1553.
11. Whitelock, p. 268.
12. CSP, Spain XI, pp. 420–21.
13. CSP, Spain, XIII, III, p. 105.
14. Reginald Pole in Two Parts, *Harriet Waters Preston and Louise Dodge* (The Atlantic, 1894, Part 2).
15. Nichols, *Chronicles of Queen Jane*, pp. 164–65.
16. Mayer, Correspondence, Vol. 2, item 998.
17. Thurston, *Reginald Pole*, Vol. 12.
18. ODNB, Arthur Pole.
19. Reginald Pole in Two Parts. *Harriet Waters Preston and Louise Dodge* (The Atlantic, 1894, Part 2).
20. Strype, *A Survey of the City of London and Westminster.*

Bibliography

Online Sources

Calendar of State Papers, Spain (British History Online).

Calendar of State Papers, Venice (British History Online).

HistoryofWar.org: *http://www.historyofwar.org/articles/treaty_angers_agreement.html*.

Letters and Papers, Foreign and Domestic, Henry VIII (British History Online).

Preston and Dodge, *Reginald Pole in Two Parts. Part One, The Atlantic:* https://www.theatlantic.com/magazine/archive/1894/11/reginald-pole-in-two-parts-part-one/635568/

Preston and Dodge, *Reginald Pole in Two Parts. Part Two, The Atlantic:* https://www.theatlantic.com/magazine/archive/1894/12/reginald-pole-in-two-parts-part-two/635481/

Ridgway, Claire: https://www.theanneboleynfiles.com/anne-boleyns-execution-site/

Published Sources

Alexander, Heather, *Recreating Richard III: The Power of Tudor Propaganda* (East Tennessee State University, 2016).

Ashdown-Hill, John, *The Third Plantagenet – George, Duke of Clarence, Richard III's Brother* (Stroud, 2015).

Bell, Doyne C., *Notices of the History Persons Buried in the Chapel of St. Peter ad Vincula in the Tower of London* (London: John Murray, 1877).

Bernard, George W, *The King's Reformation: Henry VIII and the Remaking of the English Church* (Yale University Press, 2005).

Borman, Tracy, *The Private Lives of the Tudors* (Hodder Paperbacks, 2017).

Buck, John, *The History of King Richard The Third.* (Sutton Publishing Ltd, 1982).

Byrne, Conor, *Katherine Howard, Henry VIII's Slandered Queen* (The History Press, 2019).

Cavendish, George, *The Life and Death of Cardinal Wolsey* (Houghton Mifflin and Company, 1905).

TNA, Calendar of Patent Rolls. 1476-1485.

Cooper, John, *Courtenay, Henry, Marquess of Exeter (1498/9–1538), Oxford Dictionary of National Biography* (Oxford University Press, 2004).

Dodds, Madeleine Hope, and Dodds, Ruth, *The Pilgrimage of Grace 1536–1537 and the Exeter Conspiracy 1538* (Cambridge University Press, 1915).

Emerson, Kathy L., *A Who's Who of Tudor Women* (Kathy Lynn Emerson, 2020).

Erickson, Carolly, *Bloody Mary, The Life of Mary Tudor* (Robson Books Ltd, 2001).

Froude, James Anthony, History of England from the fall of Wolsey to the Defeat of the Spanish Armada, Reign of Elizabeth volume VI (Longmans, London, 1870).

Gilpin, William, *The Life of Thomas Cranmer, Archbishop of Canterbury* (R Blamire, 1784).

Gristwood, Sarah, *Blood Sisters, The Women Behind the Wars of the Roses* (Harper Press, 2013).

Harris, Barbara J., *Edward Stafford, Third Duke of Buckingham 1478–1521* (Stanford University Press, 1986).

Haile, Martin, *Life of Reginald Pole* (Sir Isaac Pitman and Sons Ltd, 1910).

Harris, Barbara J., *English Aristocratic Women 1450–1550* (Oxford University Press, 2002).

Hall, Edward, *Hall's Chronicle* (J. Johnson, 1809).

Hall, Edward, *The Union of the Two Noble and Illustre Famelies of Lancastre and Yorke* (1548) (London, Printed for J. Johnson, 1809).

Higginbotham, Susan, *Margaret Pole, The Countess in the Tower* (Amberley, 2016).

Hughes, Philip, *A Popular History of the Reformation* (Cluny, 1960).

Head, David M, *Thomas Howard, Second Duke of Norfolk* (Oxford Dictionary of National Biography, 2004).

Ives, Eric, *The Life and Death of Anne Boleyn* (Blackwell Publishing, 2004).

Jones, Michael K., Underwood, Malcolm G. (1993), *The King's Mother: Lady Margaret Beaufort, Countess of Richmond and Derby.* (Cambridge University Press, 1993).

Knighton, C. Mortimer, R., *Westminster Abbey Reformed: 1540-1640* (Routledge, 2003).

Lewis, Matthew, *The Wars of the Roses, The Key Players in the Struggle for Supremacy* (Amberley, 2016).

Lipscomb, Suzannah, *1536: The Year That Changed Henry VIII* (Oxford: Lion Hudson, 2009).

Loach, Jennifer, *Edward VI*, (Yale University Press, 2002).

Loades, David, *Henry VIII* (Stroud: Amberley Publishing, 2011).

Loades, David, *Mary Tudor: A Life* (Blackwell Publishing, 1994).

Loades, David, *The Tudor Court* (Headstart History, 1992).

Mattingly, Garrett, *Catherine of Aragon* (Ams Pr Inc, 2005).

Mayhew, Mickey, *House of Tudor, A Grisly History* (Pen and Sword, 2022).

Miller, Helen, *Henry VIII and the English Nobility* (Wiley-Blackwell, 1989).

Mosley, Charles, *Burke's Peerage and Baronetage*, 106th edition, 2 volumes (Crans, Switzerland: Burke's Peerage (Genealogical Books) Ltd, 1999), Vol. 1, pp. 16, 18.

Neale, John E, *Queen Elizabeth I* (Jonathan Cape Ltd, 1934).

Norton, Elizabeth, *Anne Boleyn In Her Own Words & the Words of Those Who Knew Her* (Amberley Publishing, 2012).

Penn, Thomas, *Winter King, The Dawn of Tudor England* (Penguin Books, 2012).

Philips, Thomas, *The History of the Life of Reginald Pole*, Vol. 1 (London, 1767).

Pierce, Hazel, *The Life, Career and Political Significance of Margaret Pole, Countess of Salisbury, 1473–1541* (unpublished PHD dissertation, University of Wales, 1997).

Pierce, Hazel, *Margaret Pole, Countess of Salisbury 1473–1541, Loyalty, Lineage and Leadership* (Cardiff: University of Wales Press, 2009).

Powell, Sue, *Margaret Pole and Syon Abbey* (Institute of Historical Research, Vol. 78, no. 202, November 2005).

Rous, John, *The Rous Roll* (Alan Sutton Publishing Ltd, 1980).

Russell, Gareth, *Young and Damned and Fair* (London, 2018).

Seward, Desmond, *The Last White Rose, The Secret Wars of the Tudors* (Constable, 2011).

Soberton, Sylvia B, *The Forgotten Tudor Women, Gertrude Courtenay: Wife and Mother of the Last Plantagenets* (2021).

Starkey, David, *Rivals in Power: Lives and Letters of the Great Tudor Dynasties* (Pan Macmillan, 1990).

Steel, Anthony B, *The Receipt of the Exchequer, 1377–1485* (Cambridge University Press, 1954).

Strickland, Agnes, *Lives of the Queens of England,* Vol. 4 (Philadelphia: Lea and Blanchard, 1850).

Weir, Alison, *Britain's Royal Families: A Complete Genealogy* (Vintage Publishing, 2008).

Weir, Alison, *Henry VIII: King and Court* (Penguin Random House, 2001).

Weir, Alison, *The Princes in the Tower* (Pimlico, 1997).

Weir, Alison, *The Six Wives of Henry VIII* (Penguin Random House, 1991).

Whitelock, Anna, *Mary Tudor, Princess, Bastard, Queen* (Bloomsbury, 2009).

Williamson, James A., *The Tudor Age*, (D. McKay Co., 1961).

List of Images

1. Portrait believed to be Margaret Pole, Countess of Salisbury. (Art Collection 3/Alamy Stock Photo.)
2. Farleigh Hungerford Castle. (Photo by nicksarebi.)
3. George, Duke of Clarence. (Copyright: Philip Mould and Company, London.)
4. Edward Plantagenet, Earl of Warwick. (The Rous Roll, Wikimedia Commons, Public Domain.)
5. Edward IV. (Wikimedia Commons, Public Domain.)
6. Tewkesbury Abbey. (Photo by Saffron Blaze.)
7. Elizabeth of York. (Wikimedia Commons, Public Domain.)
8. Henry VIII. (Wikimedia Commons, Public Domain.)
9. Signature of Margaret Pole from a writ she sent to Thomas Wolsey. (Credit: The National Archives, London.)
10. Edward Stafford, Duke of Buckingham. (Wikimedia Commons, Public Domain.)
11. Katherine of Aragon. (Wikimedia Commons, Public Domain.)
12. Sketch believed to be of Anne Boleyn by Hans Holbein. (Wikimedia Commons, Public Domain.)
13. William Fitzwilliam, Earl of Southampton. (Wikimedia Commons, Public Domain.)
14. Thomas Goodrich, Bishop of Ely. (Wikimedia Commons, Public Domain.)
15. The Tower of London. (Photo by Bob Collowan/Commons/CC-BY-SA-4.0.)
16. Reginald Pole. (Wikimedia Commons, Public Domain.)
17. Margaret's Chapel, Priory Church, Christchurch, Hampshire. (Copyright The Friends of Lydiard Park www.thelydiardarchives.org.uk.)
18. Surviving tower of Warblington Castle. (Photo by Geni.)
19. Portrait of Queen Mary I of England. (Wikimedia Commons, Public Domain.)

20. 'Portrait of a Lady', Master A. W., active from 1536. (Photo credit: Courtauld Institute.)
21. Henry Hastings, Earl of Huntingdon. (Copyright Anglesey Abbey, Cambridgeshire, UK/National Trust Photographic Library.)
22. Edward Courtenay, 1st Earl of Devon. (Wikimedia Commons, Public Domain.)
23. Portrait of Queen Elizabeth I of England. (Wikimedia Commons, Public Domain.)
24. Vaughan Porch (Wikimedia Commons: NotFromUtrecht, CC3.0, Courtesy of Leicester Cathedral.)
25. Chapel Royal of St Peter ad Vincula, Tower of London. (Photo by Samuel Taylor Green.)
26. Monument to Lady Dorothy Stafford. (Copyright: Dean and Chapter of Westminster.)

Index

References to plates are given in bold, e.g. **P1**